MUZZLELOADER MAGAZINE'S
THE BOOK OF
BUCKSKINNING VI

Edited by
WILLIAM H. SCURLOCK

REBEL PUBLISHING COMPANY, INC. / TEXARKANA, TEXAS

EDITORIAL STAFF

EDITOR:
William H. Scurlock

ASSOCIATE EDITOR
Linda Cook Scurlock

EDITORIAL ASSISTANT:
Cherry Lloyd

GRAPHIC DESIGN:
William H. Scurlock

COVER PHOTOGRAPHY:
K. Abercrombie (Front)
David Wright (Back)

PUBLISHER:
Oran Scurlock, Jr.

ABOUT THE COVERS

FRONT:
Steven Lalioff, author of the chapter "The Traditional Hunting Pouch" in this book, sews up a pouch in his home north of Indianapolis. Steven is the proprietor of Traditional Leatherwork, 4030 E. 225th Street, Cicero, IN 46034.

BACK:
Tom Hardy of Billings, Montana, shown crossing the Wise River in Montana while on a ride to rendezvous with the Upper Missouri Outfit in 1991.

INSIDE FRONT AND BACK:
"Patton's Run" and "The Long Knife" by David Wright of Nashville, Tennessee. David's artwork has been an inspiration to countless thousands of buckskinners over the last few years. For information on his black-and-white and color prints, write Gray Stone Press, 207 Louise Ave, Nashville, TN 37203. Special thanks to Dick Patton for the use of "Patton's Run."

ISBN #1-880655-01-2

Library of Congress Catalog Card #92-81662

Contents

DEDICATION

To the memory of Madison Grant.
A gentleman of the first order who contributed
much to our knowledge, understanding and interest
in the fine things from America's past.

The Traditional Hunting Pouch

by Steven M. Lalioff

During high school Steven Lalioff worked as an interpreter at Conner Prairie Pioneer Settlement, Noblesville, Indiana, which is an open-air, agricultural, folklore museum aimed at depicting rural life styles during the 1830s. He attended Indiana University for four semesters, studying folklore and history. Steven's interest in Colonial leather work developed during 1979 to 1981, when he worked at Colonial Williamsburg as an interpreter in the harness and saddle shop.

Lalioff returned to Indiana in 1981 to pursue making authentic 18th century leather work reproductions and since 1981 has been enjoyably self-employed, making and marketing a wide variety of historic reproductions. His current endeavors include compiling data and photos of early American hunting pouches in hopes of publication. Steven and his wife, Karen, are active in a number of living history events, including several NMLRA rendezvous, Fair at New Boston, Vincennes, Fort De Chartes. Lalioff's hobbies include log cabin construction, forestry, ceramics and 18th century hot air balloons.

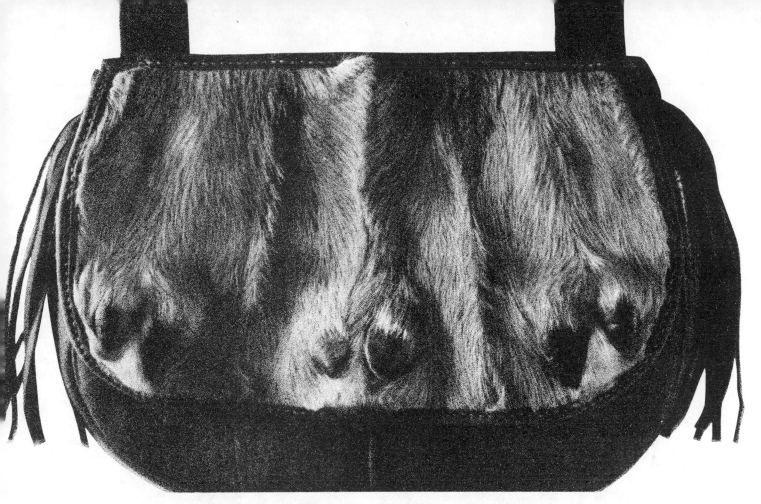

During an all-too-brief conversation with Madison Grant, foremost collector and author of the book *The Kentucky Rifle Hunting Pouch*, Mr. Grant referred to original hunting pouches as "an endangered species." That comment stays with me still. The phrase "an endangered species" lead me to question how many original pouches are still in existence, however I can quote no reliable statistic to even hint at an accurate count.

In the last 12 years of shows and private collections, I have seen fewer than 300 original pouches that I could comfortably date to pre-1850. I include in my count the approximately 100 pre-1850 pouches illustrated in *The Kentucky Rifle Hunting Pouch*, which remains as the best-documented collection of early American hunting pouches. Certainly more research is necessary in tabulating and comparing existing artifacts with the quantities manufactured during the period.

The quantity of period guns that pouches served may help us speculate as to the number of pouches then and now. Tabulating the number of gun makers and their products will be easier because more documentation is available on their trade. Through extrapolation we could learn more about the gun's companion, the pouch.

In pursuing my research, I began with a call to author and gun historian George Shumway. I posed the difficult, if not impossible, question of how many guns were in existence in America during the period between 1750 to 1850 and, in his estimate, how many still exist. In his opinion perhaps fewer than one in ten are presently accounted for. He cited the Kindig collection of approximately 500 and private collections of perhaps 1500, stating that those estimates refer to "high-quality rifles." He believes that perhaps two to three thousand

guns of less refined qualities still exist. Mr. Shumway gave no estimation as to the guns contained in museum or institutional collections.

So, by those estimates, we can be fairly assured of at least 5,000 existing rifles in private hands. If we then apply the one in ten survival rate, we can assume there were at least 50,000 guns (rifles) during the 1750-1850 period. Mr. Shumway admits this figure of 50,000 seems very conservative. The quantity of 5,000 "fine rifles" certainly places their status as rare, and in comparison, I doubt if there are even half that number of "fine" pouches from the same period still in existence. In my opinion these estimates would establish the early hunting pouch as more rare than its companion gun. While exhaustive research would give us a more accurate count, it would not relieve either gun or pouch of the "endangered" classification.

I admit that my opinions are biased, as I have long held the belief that there are considerably fewer original pouches than guns of the same period. I believe this to be logical, because of the fact that a leather pouch is considerably more vulnerable to destruction than an iron and wood gun. I also believe that existing powder horns outnumber pouches by far, for the same reasons.

EXAMPLES OF ORIGINAL & RECREATED POUCHES

WHITACRE POUCH

This original double pouch, which is approximately eight inches long by seven inches wide, is perhaps the most deftly constructed pouch I have ever examined. The hand-stitching is no less than ten to twelve stitches per inch. The gussets are but mere slivers of leather—less than 3/4" at their widest.

The type of leather had me puzzled for a long time. At first inspection I was sure that its main body was of brain-tanned deer-skin because of its light weight (2 ounce), texture and the suede appearance of both sides of the leather. Upon closer scrutiny I discovered that what first appeared to be suede was in fact where the epidermis of the skin had uniformly fallen away from the leather's surface because of decay. Thus, the leather appeared to be brain tanned. Realizing that when it was "new," the pouch's leather did have a slick surface, the leather could not have been brain-tanned. I still believe the type of leather to be deer skin but vegetable tanned. The very back panel of this pouch is a stout four- to five-ounce vegetable-tanned calf or steer hide. At one time the pouch flap had a rawhide skin with the hair on. Almost all of this flap panel has fallen away as well, but there are still a few fragments remaining under the turned edge of the flap's backing. The hair appears to have been a slunk-skin of calf.

All photos in this chapter by K. Abercrombie.

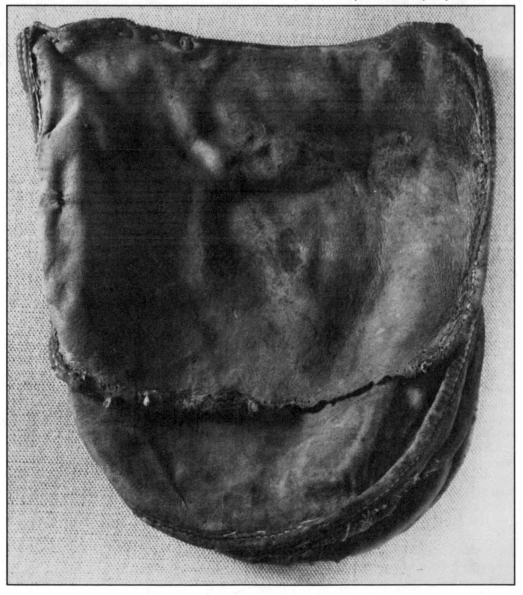

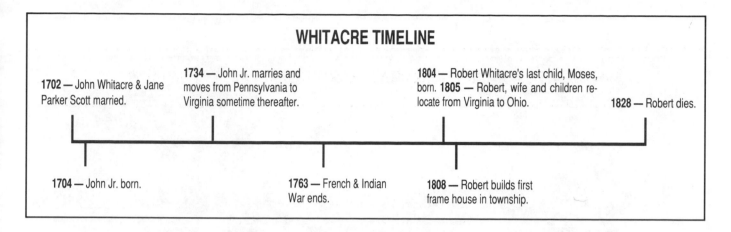

WHITACRE TIMELINE

1702 — John Whitacre & Jane Parker Scott married.

1734 — John Jr. marries and moves from Pennsylvania to Virginia sometime thereafter.

1804 — Robert Whitacre's last child, Moses, born. **1805** — Robert, wife and children relocate from Virginia to Ohio.

1828 — Robert dies.

1704 — John Jr. born.

1763 — French & Indian War ends.

1808 — Robert builds first frame house in township.

I'm tempted to date this pouch very early, but the lack of concrete documentation prohibits me from stating it as 18th century.

The Whitacre pouch was purchased some 10 years ago at an estate auction in Ohio. The family name was Whitacre (English). The surviving relatives identified the flintlock rifle (lock missing), powder horn and pouch as having belonged to their great, great grandfather Robert Whitacre. Unfortunately, the gun and horn were separated at the sale, never to be heard of again. Thankfully, the relatives provided some written family history of Robert Whitacre and his family.

Here is some Whitacre family history I consider pertinent to the pouch: Robert Whitacre was the youngest son of the union of Jane Parker Scott and John Whitacre. They were married in Makefield Township, Buck County, Pennsylvania, in 1702. The family history implies that Jane Parker Scott was a widow of considerable means when she married John Whitacre. Their first son, John Jr., was born in 1704. To my great frustration, no birth date is given for their second son, Robert (our pouch owner). After the marriage of John Jr. to Naomi Hulme in 1734, the family later moved to Virginia. The record states that Robert re-located to the Winchester, Virginia, area and took up farming. The family history continues to say that Robert immigrated to Ohio with his family in 1805 to what is now the town of Morrow. It is recorded that Robert and his wife, Patience, and 7 children spent their first few weeks or months on their Ohio land living in a large, hollow Sycamore tree near the banks of the Todd's Fork River. There they all lived until their log house could be built. The records recount how Robert was an active and prosperous livestock trader, even driving his cattle on foot to the Baltimore markets. (I find it interesting that a "prosperous" man was "on foot." Perhaps this is a liberty taken with the family "myth," sort of like uphill both ways to school.) Robert fathered his last child in 1804 and died in Ohio in 1828.

The reason I recounted this family history is to try to define approximately when this old hunting pouch was made. First, we must make a major assumption, which is that this was Robert Whitacre's hunting pouch. There is always the possibility that this was Robert's son's pouch or perhaps some other relative's or acquaintance's. But for the sake of argument, I'll stand by the family's verbal history that the pouch was Robert's. If so, the only real fact is that the pouch was made prior to 1828, the year Robert died. The question to ask now is how much earlier could this pouch have been made?

If we reason that Robert could have been born between 1704 and 1734, he would have been between the ages of 94 and 124 when he died. It is possible Robert was born a while after 1734, because his brother married in 1734 and did not move until sometime after. Since it is not known how old Robert was when he moved with his brother, we might assume that Robert was still a child or perhaps even an infant. Robert's and John Jr.'s mother, Jane Parker Scott, was a widow prior to her marriage to John Whitacre, Sr. We might ask how old was Jane Whitacre at the time she bore John Jr. and Robert. Having studied some of the marriage ways of early Americans, it is quite possible that she was married to her first husband at age 12, not an unfamiliar practice in the late 17th and early 18th centuries. Considering the high mortality rate in that era, it is possible that she could have become widowed and re-married to John Sr. by age 14 in 1702. Bearing John Jr. in 1704 at age 16, she still could have given birth to Robert in 1734 at age 46, which is not beyond possibility but stretches Jane's childbearing years to the maximum.

If we are then to assume Robert was born in the mid 1730s, that would have made him a man in his prime during the French and Indian War. Could this pouch be the long sought-after example of a pouch of that era? Probably not. It is unfortunate that the rifle is not available for inspection, since deducing its age could be possible. But even if the rifle were of the French and Indian War era, it would be amazing had the rifle's first pouch survived to our day.

The second known period of Robert's life was when he moved his family from Winchester, Virginia, to Morrow, Ohio, in 1805. Certainly Robert was using a rifle and pouch at this time. Probably a necessity when living in a hollow tree. There is a likely chance that this pouch could have seen service during the turn of those centuries. There is nothing about the pouch's design, workmanship or materials that can exclude it from being the product of the mid 18th century or the early 19th century as well. Style and design differences of leather artifacts from the 18th to the early 19th century are often subtle. Defining what those differences are would tend to verge on the sixth sense.

The last period of Robert Whitacre's life, 1805 to 1828, was that of a farmer and cattleman. Through the family history, we are told of how Robert had the stamina to drive cattle 700 miles to the Eastern markets. All this of a man perhaps 70 years old! Was it during this time when the fine pouch was crafted? Or, was the pouch an old tool by then? The multiple repairs attest to its hard wear—the pouch's opening is slick from the thousands of times a hand was thrust within to draw a patch and ball, flint or other. The pouch teases me...I have been given a taste of its history but not enough.

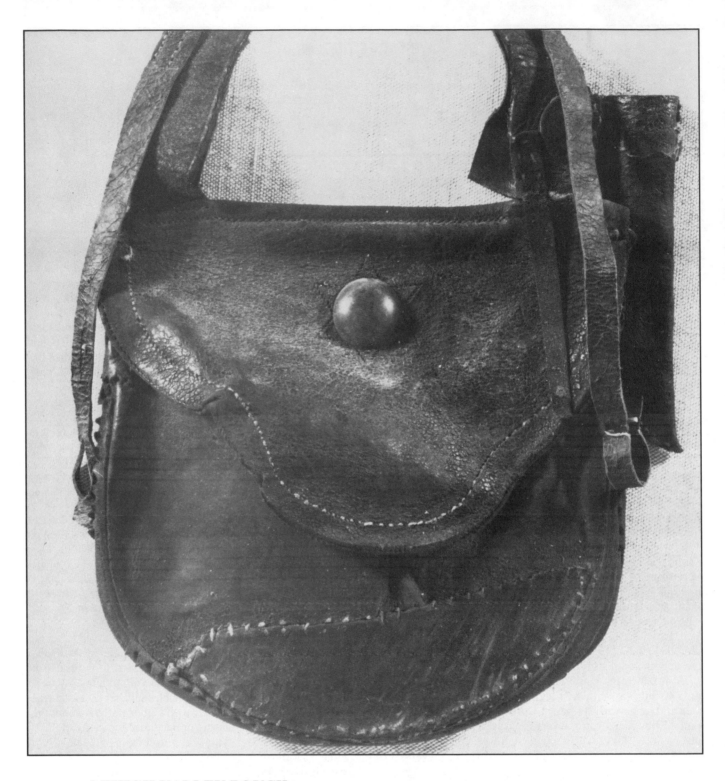

LEHIGH VALLEY POUCH

This hand-stitched, double pouch is dated circa 1820 to 1850 and was collected in Lehigh County, Pennsylvania. The pouch measures eight inches by 7-1/2 inches. Almost every "double" pouch I have found, including this one, has displayed a high degree of craftsmanship, suggesting the work of professionals. Having made several double pouches, I found them to be among the most difficult to reproduce.

The decorative brass spot of this pouch is surrounded by a hand-stitched Star of David, a typical Moravian motif. It still retains the original, hand-forged iron buckle. (See top left buckle in the photo on page 14.) The pouch flap and strap have been tastefully decorated with a simple geometric pattern of round punches of various sizes. The punches do not cut through the thickness of the leather but instead cut only through the leather's surface. When making traditional decorations, it is best to keep to the simple tools.

An interesting detail of this pouch is the belt loop stitched on the back side. This rare addition suggests that it was worn at waist level. Several period illustrations I have seen show pouches worn high and low. I believe strap length was just a matter of preference.

BOOT POUCH

This pouch, circa 1800 to 1850, was collected in eastern Tennessee, measures eight inches across the bottom, seven inches across the top and 6-1/2 inches high. This pouch is the epitome of the homespun pouch—nothing more than a boot top. The maker simply and crudely stitched a line across the opening of the boot. Evidence of the boot pulls are clearly visible front and back. (See the double line of stitching at the bottom of pouch.) The strap is a simple piece of harness leather without buckle.

The closure is unique and just as simple as the pouch. The flap was secured by means of an antler tip or maybe even a twig. This was done by pulling the front of the pouch through the oblong hole in the flap. The pouch front has two 3/4 inch slits in the leather 1/4 inch apart, running horizontally. When pulled through the flap's cutout, it forms a loop whereby an antler tip or such object could be wedged between, securing the flap.

At one time the corner of this pouch was repaired by means of two split-tube rivets. Rivets such as these can be found on Civil War leather work, but I'm not sure how much earlier they can be dated. Military artifacts are a good source for learning about hardware and styles of construction typical to given periods.

BOOT POUCH

I am the proud owner of this extremely ugly pouch, and I include it in this chapter only to give heart to those wishing to make their own pouch. No matter what you do, you probably couldn't make something with less grace or skill than this humble original. But in its defense, I must say that at one time this was a perfectly serviceable hunting pouch.

This is another boot pouch, but this one is from southern Indiana. It is seven inches wide and 6-1/2 inches high and dates c. 1830 to 1870. I give this pouch a later date because of the black glass button wired to the front. Unfortunately, the button didn't make it into the photo. Buttons are one of the best clues for dating some pouches because there are several good reference books pertaining to buttons. Close inspection needs to be made to determine if the pouch retains its original button. It's very possible the pouch lost a dozen buttons before it was retired.

The four slits in the pouch flap are proper to the boot from which the pouch was made. Footware was expensive and it's probable the boot was slit to accommodate a bigger foot than was intended. The slits show no use since the leather was incorporated into a pouch.

HOMESPUN POUCH

Here is another extremely humble pouch. The workmanship is so naive I'm tempted to attribute the work to a child. Nevertheless, it has survived intact. Measuring 8 inches across the bottom, 7 1/4 inches across the top and 6 inches high, this homespun pouch from eastern Tennessee dates from about 1780 to 1820.

However, it's possible that this pouch is even earlier than I have attributed it to be. The button is wiggle-engraved brass and of an 18th century style casting. The buckle is a unique cast brass with lion's heads at either end. The buckle was made to accommodate a 5/8 inch strap. The quality and design suggest that it originally could have been intended to be used in a fancy bridle. The buckle tongue is iron. How this extremely fancy buckle made its way onto this extremely humble pouch I'll always wonder.

It is also interesting to me that the first boot pouch and this one, both from Tennessee, are trapezoid-shaped. The Boot Pouch is a trapezoid because it is the natural shape of the original boot top. This pouch doesn't appear to be boot leather, so is it merely coincidence both are trapezoids and both hail from Tennessee? This is a prime example of why no detail is too insignificant when collecting artifacts. With more data more generalizations can be accurately drawn.

OHIO VALLEY BEAVER TAIL POUCHES *(facing page)*

The original, hand-stitched double pouch on the left is a classic beaver tail, professionally made design. It hails from Indiana, dates circa 1800 to 1850 and measures nine inches high and 6-1/2 inches wide. On the right is a reproduction with an added knife sheath of the back.

Making accurate reproductions of pouches can be difficult, especially with double pouches. Determining the "exact" size can take more than one attempt. Some leathers stretch differently than others, further compounding the problems of exactness. Trial and error are the only lessons needed.

HATFIELD-WASHINGTON
POUCH *(reproduction)*

I made this reproduction directly from the original, which was a circa 1830 pouch collected in Indiana that measured eight inches high by 7-1/2 inches wide. The button was missing from the original, leaving me to speculate for the reproduction. I have named this pouch after the 1834 Hatfield-Washington rifle that was attributed to the set. The long beaver tail and close-cropped fringe is typical of the Ohio Valley region during the "Crockett" era.

REPRODUCTION POUCH
CIRCA 1845 TO 1855

I made this pouch from a photograph in *The Kentucky Rifle Hunting Pouch* by Madison Grant. It is circa 1845 to 1855 and measures seven inches high and eight inches wide.

DEW-CLAW POUCH *(representation)*

I refer to this pouch, also shown on page III of the color section, as a "representation" because I combined elements of two original pouches, as opposed to a "reproduction," which is copied exactly from an original. This dew-claw pouch is representative of mid-18th to early 19th century pouches and measures eight inches high and 9-1/2 inches wide.

The style could be referred to as "Jaeger" and is influenced by pouches of Germanic origin. The use of dew-claws on pouches spans a large time period, having never really gone out of style since the 1500s.

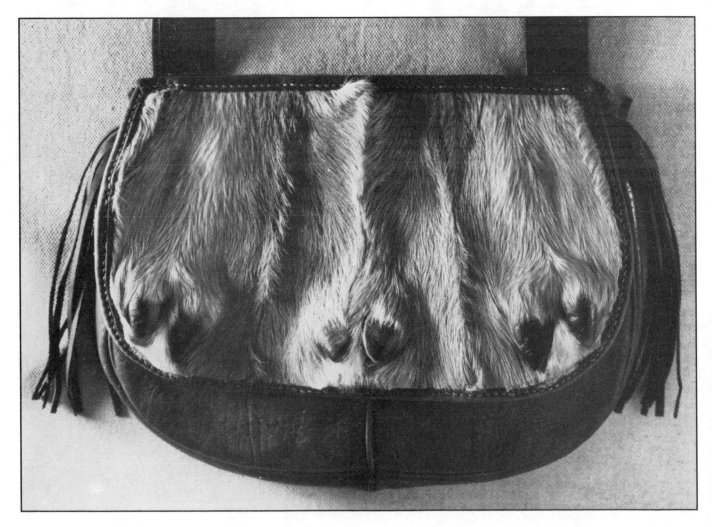

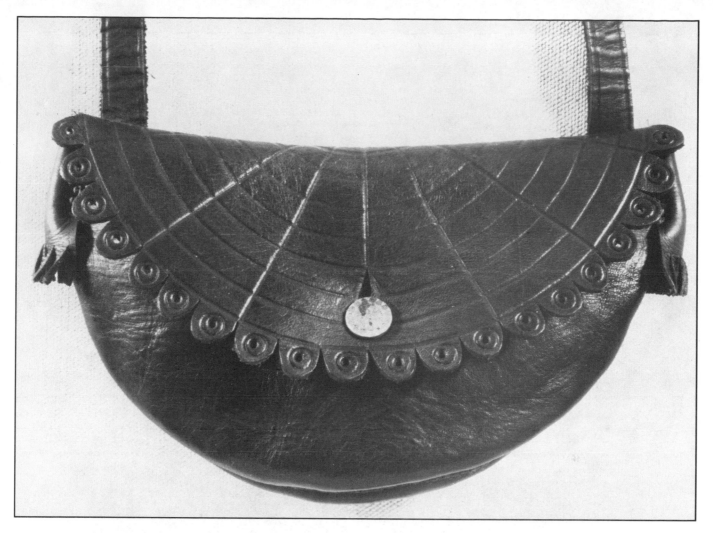

SPIDER WEB POUCH *(representation)*

This small pouch measures only seven inches wide by four inches high, but small size was not uncommon. Only the most basic tools would have been carried—flints or caps, flint knapper, screwdriver, vent pick, priming horn, powder measurer, worm, jag, patching, balls, patch knife. What more would you absolutely need? The "extra" accessories were in a pocket or possibles bag. See photo on page III of color section.

TRIPLE HEART POUCH *(reproduction)*

This pouch is an example of early 19th century "folk art." The heart insets are rawhide deer skin with some hair still intact. The leather has been artificially aged to represent the rich patina that old pouches can acquire if well preserved. Also shown on page II of color section.

11

VIRGINIA GAME BAG *(reproduction)*

The original of this reproduction was collected in Richmond, Virginia, in the 1930s. Even then, the pouch showed a great deal of age. The style and designs incorporated in this pouch exhibit a strong English influence. The original pouch could have been made during the late 18th or early 19th century. The pouch measures 12 inches across and 10 inches high. I can easily imagine a well-healed gentleman with a fine fowler sporting this pouch. Color photo on page VI of center section.

PINWHEEL POUCH *(reproduction)*

The original from which I reproduced this pouch was made between 1840 and 1870. The "hex" designs are strong indications of Germanic influence of the Pennsylvania or Ohio regions.

THE POUCH MAKERS

I have been actively collecting leather artifacts for more than a decade, primarily to gain a working knowledge of their design and construction, but also in reverence to the craftsmen who shared my kindred spirit. Through the study of originals, I have become well-acquainted with traditional craftsmanship. Unfortunately, very little documentation has been uncovered pertaining to the leather workers themselves or how their trade was conducted. By my observations more than half of the original pouches I have seen were of a "homespun" variety, made by the farmer or hunter to suit their basic needs.

The question of who the professional pouch makers were stems from the interesting fact that not even the best-made pouches bear a maker's hallmark. I find this curious indeed, as I have seen many different types of leather work of lesser construction that were emblazoned with a maker's name or hallmark. Surely there are some original pouches in existence that are so hallmarked, but I have yet to see one. (I would greatly appreciate anyone with an original pouch that has a hallmark bringing it to my attention.)

One source of information on who the professional pouch makers were comes from the labels glued inside the lids of early leather-covered trunks and chests. Many of those craftsmen not only gave their name and address, but some also did a little advertising on their labels as well. A typical label might advertise such items as: saddles, harnesses, trunks, portmanteaus, hat boxes, fire buckets, fire hose, saddle bags and pocketbooks (wallets). Many labels further added "military and hunting accouterments of all kinds." Certainly, this phrase was meant to include hunting pouches and game bags.

The saddle maker was perhaps the most versatile and diversified, if not the most talented, of the various leather tradesmen. A saddler would also have the largest assortment of leathers and tools in his shop and a good working knowledge of all types of leathers. He would be experienced working with wood and metal, both materials that were incorporated in a saddle's or trunk's construction.

During the 18th and 19th centuries, the majority of the American public was on foot. Perhaps fewer than half of the population may have known how to ride a horse, let alone have been able to afford one. Therefore, many saddlers must have

Leather trunk label circa 1820-1840.

HORACE GAYLORD,

MANUFACTURER OF

SADDLES, HARNESSES. TRUNKS

AND MILITARY EQUIPMENTS,

ASHFORD, CONN.

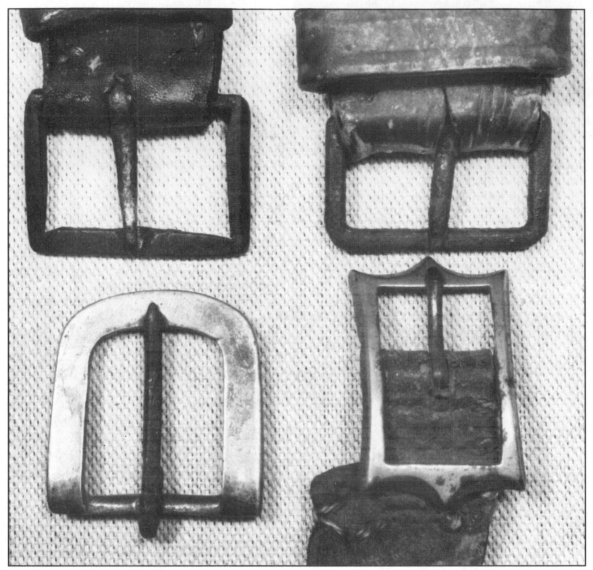

Hand-forged iron pouch buckles (top row), both originally filed bright. Brass buckle with forged iron tongue (bottom left) and decoratively filed iron buckle (bottom right).

found it necessary to diversify their product lines. This can explain the long list of side products frequently found on a saddle maker's label. I believe this is strong evidence that saddle makers crafted hunting pouches.

Certainly harness makers were involved in the production of hunting pouches as well. However, the craftsman who specialized in harness work may not have been as well-suited to the production of large quantities of pouches. Most of the advertisements I have seen published by harness makers rarely list the availability of side products. Perhaps this was because of the greater demand for harness than for saddles during the period. Furthermore, I feel that the style of work I have seen in

fine, old hunting pouches reflects the higher quality of work more commonly associated with saddlery rather than the coarse, heavy work associated with harness making. This observation is not meant to slight the craftsmanship of harness makers, but rather to suggest that these separate but similar trades involve different styles of work.

In addition to saddle and harness making, several other specialized leather trades existed during the 18th and 19th centuries, such as shoemakers, whip-makers and bookbinders. All of these must have made some pouches as a sideline to their main business.

COLLECTING ORIGINALS

Equally important to preserving the physical condition of an original pouch is the effort that should be made insuring a pouch's personal history. So much has already been lost that speculation comprises the majority of knowledge about pouches.

If you are a collector, I implore you to keep the best records possible as to where the pouch was obtained and the family name and, if possible, the name and occupation of the pouch's original owner. No detail is too insignificant to record. The pouch itself makes an excellent receptacle for this gathered data.

Perhaps the saddest injustice suffered by a pouch is the separation from its companions. A lot of clues can be had from the horn, knife and powder measure that are original to a pouch (not to mention the pouch's gun). By being able to see all of these accoutrements in their whole, some knowledge can be ascertained as to the original owner or owners. When separated, these artifacts are only pieces of an intriguing puzzle, diminished from what could have been.

Determining an exact date for an original pouch is impossible. There are too many factors that can upset the best-educated guess. Even if a pouch is accompanied by a signed and dated horn, there is no way of knowing for sure that the original pouch was not worn out and replaced. Even family history cannot be taken as absolute proof of age, since stories handed down are sometimes subject to error.

The most reliable dating methods are period illustrations that can be assigned accurate dates. Unfortunately, period artwork seldom concentrates on the fine details of a pouch, and the artist usually leaves one wanting more.

A machine-sewn pouch can only tell us when the pouch was not made. Sewing machines were not in use prior to 1850. There were experimental models prior to 1850, but they were extremely rare and not designed for sewing leather. Therefore, by no means can we date a machine-sewn pouch before 1850. Furthermore, sewing machines were quite expensive in the mid-19th century, so even after the machine's introduction, it was many years before they were common. With the coming of the Civil War came large contracts to leather shops for military goods. Those large contracts generated the capital enabling many craftsmen to invest in machines for sewing leather. Considering this, I conclude that the majority of machine-sewn pouches were made after 1865.

I have seen several hand-sewn pouches that were mistakenly identified as having been machine sewn. This is a common mistake because the hand stitching of a professional leather worker can be very precise. Distinguishing the difference is often difficult and requires experience. Also do not make the assumption that because a pouch is hand-stitched it must be pre-1865. Hand stitching was employed in leather work throughout the machine period and is still practiced today.

Buttons and buckles can be assigned approximate dates, but again, like dated horns, we cannot be certain that the hardware incorporated in the pouch wasn't borrowed from an earlier piece. I admit that I do take into consideration the age of the hardware and horn. After all, every aspect should be taken into account.

Collecting antique leather work has its demanding responsibilities. Preserving a pouch's documentation is simple compared with the preservation of the artifact itself. There are three primary adversaries to leather. They are insects, bacteria and chemical deterioration. I will give a layman's guide to preservation. However, some leather conditions may require the consultation and aid of a professional conservationist.

Insect infestation is perhaps the simplest problem for the private collector to cure. Hair on leathers is especially prone to attachment by moth larvae. There are several other insects, especially in northern countries, that are common pests to all leathers. If insect infestation is detected, place the artifacts in an air-tight box with a no-pest strip. A garbage can with a plastic liner will do in a pinch; tape the lid for an air-tight seal. There are several brands of these strips made. I have not tried all of them, but I would imagine they are comparable in effectiveness.

Do not allow the artifacts to come into direct contact with the strip as it may stain the leather. Try suspending the strip from the inside of the lid. Keep the artifacts enclosed for three or four weeks. This treatment should kill all of the active adult insects, but insect eggs and pupae are resistant to insecticides. The treated leather should be separated from the rest of your collection for as long as one year. Examine the leather regularly and repeat the fumigation as needed. Good housekeeping and regular inspection should reduce the problem of insect damage significantly.

Bacterial deterioration takes on several forms. It may be visible as fluffy molds or fungi. The application of fungicides to prevent mold growth is useless and at best a temporary cure. The mold growth is caused by excessive humidity and warmth. The solution is good ventilation and a reduction of the humidity level to between fifty and sixty percent, which is easier said than done. Upon first discovering mold growths, use a very soft brush to remove visible contamination. A few minutes in direct sunlight will help kill some bacteria, but prolonged exposure to the sun is not advised. A gentle cleaning may be in order, if the brushing does not remove the growths.

Use a sponge dampened with distilled water and lightly treated with glycerin soap to clean the leather. Take care not to rub the leather's surface too harshly and not to wet the leather too much. Remove any remaining soap with a clean damp sponge. Allow to dry in a cool breeze, away from direct sun. While the pouch is still damp, insert crumpled newspaper into the pouch to encourage the proper shape.

To maintain a low humidity level, the use of silica gel is effective when placed in the display case with the leather. Silica gel, available at good camera stores, absorbs atmospheric moisture. When new, the silica is blue in color, but it becomes light pink when it has absorbed moisture. It can be easily reconditioned by heating it in an oven to 266 degrees Fahrenheit (130 degrees Celsius) until it regains a deep blue color. The reactivation process can be repeated as necessary indefinitely.

Chemical deterioration is the most terminal condition that leather can suffer. The effects of chemical deterioration will eventually reduce all leather to dust. The cause is pollution. Sulphur dioxide from the burning of fossil fuels is absorbed into the fibers of the leather. Leather contains trace elements of iron compounds; these compounds react with the sulphur dioxide to produce sulphur trioxide that combine with water to form sulfuric acid. This sulfuric acid in the presence of oxygen attacks the leather causing it to become brittle, eventually causing the leather to decay completely.

The chemical decay of leather is much more rapid than leather's physical decay. Leather dressings of any kind have little or no effect in protecting leather from chemical decay. Once chemical decay has started, no current treatment can stop its eventual decomposition. Research is still being conducted on halting the effects of chemical decay. The experiments currently under way will only be proven with the test of time. Hopefully, a cure will be found before the entire loss of period leather work has occurred.

The best safeguard against chemical decay is an air-tight and dust-free environment. To my knowledge chemical decay, as opposed to insect or bacterial contamination, is not contagious, thus allowing the safe storage of chemically decaying leathers with those that are yet unaffected.

Leathers that are stiff from excessive dryness can be made more flexible with the application of a good leather dressing. I urge caution, however, in the application of dressings, because they can make leather too greasy. It's very difficult for me to recommend brands of leather dressings. For the most part, all are acceptable provided they have a balanced pH. A dressing that is too acidic can decay the fibers of linen or cotton cord. If in doubt, use nothing and do not handle the leather until a proper dressing can be obtained. I suggest staying away from any kind of neatsfoot oil for old leather as this is a heavy oil that can drastically darken old leather and give it a greasy feel.

Do not be in a hurry to restore original pouches. Too often I have seen poor restoration attempts with disastrous results. It's best to do nothing until the advice of an experienced professional can be had. Failed attempts at restoration can make the expert's work more difficult and possibly do irreversible damage. The exception to this advice would be insect and environmental control. The recommendations I made earlier should be followed to insure that the pouch will survive until expert help can be obtained.

Basic leather-working tools: (top row, left to right) head knife, large harness awl, medium awl, small awl, round awl, edge creasers, edge burnish stick, pricking wheel, (bottom row, left to right) friction dividers, wing-nut dividers, swallow-tail beveler, square-ended knife, pattern knife, needle pliers, beeswax and needles, 4" x 6" square.

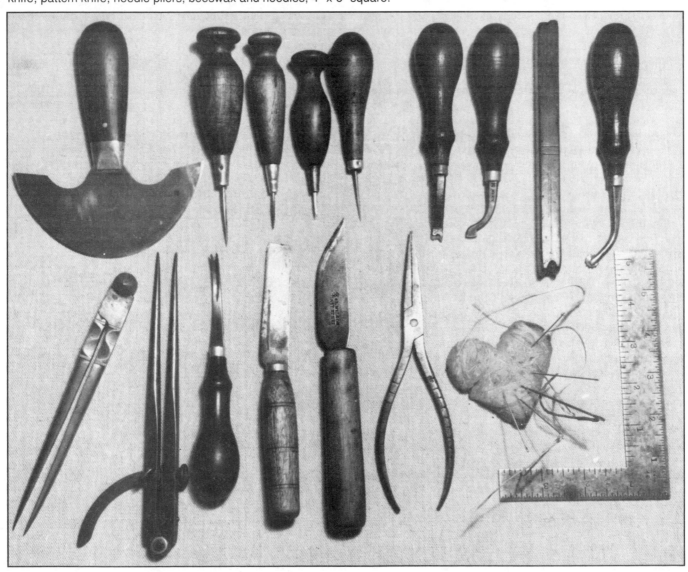

It takes very few tools to construct a homespun pouch. One 1860s pouch I have seen was completely constructed with leather lace; I doubt if more than a pocket knife was needed to make it. All of the tools and materials I recommend should be readily available from the source list provided at the end of this chapter. The following is a brief description of the tools necessary and some particulars to look for:

Stitching Awl and Round Awl — The most important aspect of the stitching awl blade is its sharp point. It may be necessary to hone even new blades to a fine point. Do not sharpen the edges of the blade, because the purpose of its diamond shape is to stretch open the hole you pierce, not to cut the fibers of the leather. The round awl is to be used for tracing the pattern onto leather and for enlarging holes that already have cord in them.

Pliers — You'll occasionally need to use pliers for pulling stubborn needles through the leather. Just about any pair of pliers will do. However, I strongly suggest filing the jaws smooth to avoid destroying your needles.

Knife — A pocket knife with a sheep's foot blade will do. The most important requirement of the knife is that it hold a fine edge. Special knives for pattern cutting are available. The advantage to these is that they are easier to grip and control.

Dividers — These may not be available through the source list, but they are easily obtained at flea markets or hardware stores. The best style has a wing-nut tightener to prevent slippage. You may want to alter the points of the divider, making one side pointed, the other blunt. The sharp edge will serve to scratch a fine line for precise stitch work. The blunt end will work better for applying designs in the leather, as in hex wheels.

Straight Edge — A one-foot square is best and is available at most hardware stores.

Stitching Clamp — There are still good, old stitching clamps available at flea markets and antique shows at reasonable prices. The stitching ponies, a bench with attached vertical clamp, are rather expensive, usually over $100.00. The ponies are fine as long as you're right-handed; the clamps are tilted to the right, making it impossible for south-paws. The older style stitching clamp, known as a "clam," can be used ambidextrously. The clam is about 4 foot long and rests between your legs. They are quite versatile (see photo) and hold your work steady while you're stitching.

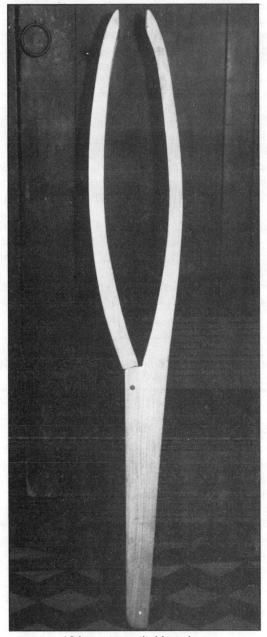

18th century stitching clam.

TOOLS AND MATERIALS FOR A SIMPLE POUCH

Stitching awl	Dividers	Round awl
Harness needles	Straight edge	Pliers
30' 6-ply linen cord	Stitching clamp	Knife
1 pt. 100% neatsfoot oil		Edge creaser
4 sq. ft. 4-6 oz. vegetable-tanned leather		

Edge Creaser — This is a simple hand tool that has a smooth, grooved end. You should be able to buy an adequate one for a few dollars. The concave distance between the groove will give the leather's edge a beaded appearance. The width of this concave area will determine how far in from the leather's edge the crease will be. I suggest an average width of 3/16 inch.

Harness Needles — The attributes of a harness needle are an eye that can accommodate heavy cords and a smooth, blunt point that will not pierce or snag when passing through the leather. They are inexpensive, and I suggest buying the package of 24 to allow for breakage and loss. They come in several sizes. For four- to six-ply cord, I recommend you order #3s.

Linen Cord, Beeswax and Rosin — Linen cord comes in two varieties, waxed or unwaxed, in black or natural white. Unwaxed cord must be pulled through a cake of beeswax or rosin. Cord can come in plies of three, four, five, six or eight. The cord can be doubled up, or the twist of a heavy cord can be separated for a finer cord. Four-, five- or six-ply will serve well for pouch construction. The natural white is more appropriate for historic work.

100% Pure Neatsfoot Oil — Only a small quantity is needed for this project. Again, I stress you use only neatsfoot oil that is labeled "100% pure" and avoid what is called neatsfoot oil compound.

Vegetable-Tanned Leather — The thickness of leather is described in terms of weight per ounce. The leather you want for this project is 4-5 ounce or 5-6 ounce. Ideally, the leather should be close to five ounce for pouches. Don't be distraught if the thickness of the hide you receive varies throughout; after all, this is a natural product. Different grades of leather are available, and the price per square foot will reflect this grade. Don't be afraid to order the "poorer" grades as the quality of tannage will be uniform between the best and worst grade. The difference has to do with how "clean" the hide is. Clean refers to scratches, range scars, brands, butcher's cuts and sometimes even tire treads. The price difference can be significant enough to merit working around the imperfections of a lesser grade hide. Perhaps the best "cut" of leather to buy is a double shoulder. This cut has the least amount of waste and usually is the most uniform in weight and density. Double shoulders range in size from eight square feet to 14 square feet, at prices between $4.00 and $6.00 per square foot. A better-priced and smaller cut of leather that is also suitable is a belly cut. This leather is cheaper because there are more irregular edges and also because this part of the animal can stretch more than any other part. In most bellies there is enough solid hide to construct a good pouch. Prices for bellies should run half that of a shoulder cut.

If you belong to an organization like a gun club or scout group, you may do better to order all your needed tools and materials in bulk. It's possible you could negotiate a better price on leather by ordering ten or more hides at one time.

CREATING THE PATTERN

Realizing how difficult it is to gain access to original pouches, I have included a graphed pattern for a style of pouch that I consider to be timeless in design. There is nothing about this design that would prohibit its use for 18th century reenactments, and by the same token, there is nothing prohibiting this pattern from 19th century events as well.

I suggest making your pattern from poster board or the cardboard from a shirt box. This cardboard is easy to work with and has the body necessary for tracing around its edges. I find myself making notations on these patterns as to how much cord to use and what weight of leather serves best. This information saves time and perhaps prevents mistakes on the next pouch. It's important that your pattern be symmetrical. This is accomplished simply by folding the cardboard in half and trimming away until both halves are identical, just like making hearts in grade school.

I spend some time deciding on the placement of the pattern on the leather, as there are several considerations necessary. First, is there enough leather to cut out all of the pieces of the project? No two hides of leather are exactly alike and some leathers may color differently than others, so it is best to make the project from the same hide of leather. Another matter to consider is how the pattern can be arranged to get the most economy from the leather. Keep the pattern pieces close to each other but do avoid flaws in the leather that you don't desire in the finished work. Carefully check the back side of the leather to see that there are no deep cuts which are invisible from the front. Finally, keep in mind that leather has a grain similar to woven fabric. It will stretch more from belly to belly than from head to tail, so the front and back pieces of the pouch should be laid out in the same direction.

Once you have arranged the pieces of the pattern on the top side of the leather, carefully trace around each one with a round awl, lightly scratching the surface. An alternative to scratching the surface is to trace the pattern on the back side of the leather using a soft grade pencil. I don't recommend using a ballpoint pen, because any ink left on the project will stick out like a 20th century sore thumb. Before lifting your pattern from the leather, make a dot or a hash mark to indicate the center point on all of the parts of the pouch. Keep the hash marks close to the edge of the pieces so they don't show when the pouch is

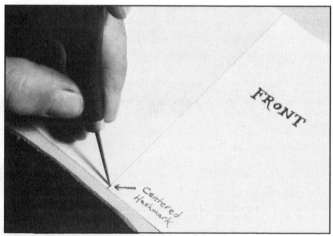

Patterns should be symmetrical. Marking the center on the leather helps to keep the pieces aligned.

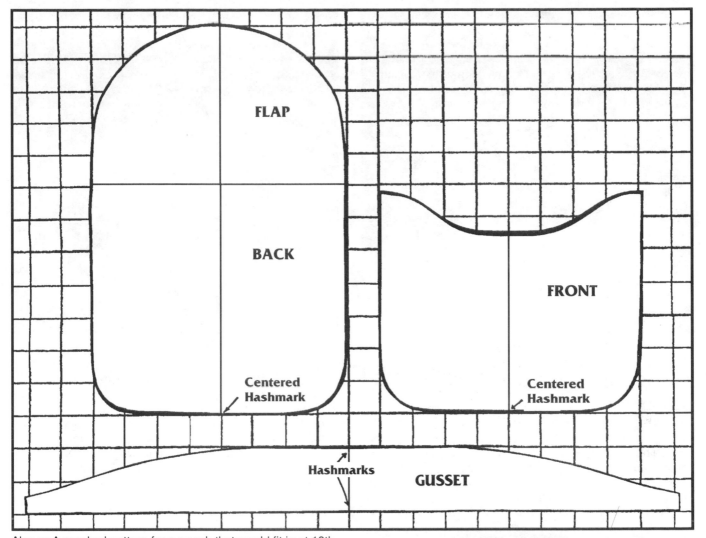

FLAP

BACK

FRONT

Centered
Hashmark

Centered
Hashmark

Hashmarks

GUSSET

Above: A graphed pattern for a pouch that would fit in at 18th
or 19th century gatherings. One square equals one inch.

Right: Avoid putting yourself before the blade. This
photo displays the **wrong** place for your hand to be.

Below: A very sharp knife makes cutting safer and neater.

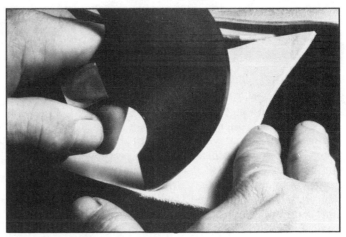

completed. The hash mark will be crucial when lining up the
leather pieces for construction.

Next, cut out the pieces of the pouch. Here is where the
sharpest knife works best. The sharper the blade, the less force
is needed to cut. The less force used, the more control you will
have. The more control you have, the neater job you'll do and
the less chance of cutting yourself. If the blade isn't sharp
enough to shave the hairs off your arm, it's likely the task of
cutting leather won't be as easy as it should be. A hint for
keeping your knife sharp: Do not twist or curve the knife's edge

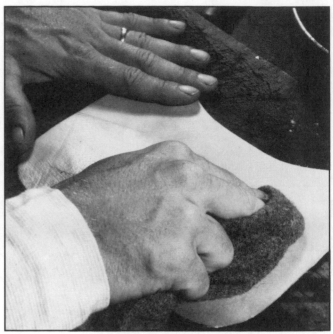

Left: Apply a small amount of water to the leather prior to polishing. Right: Polishing or burnishing with a wool cloth.

into the cutting board; instead, slowly turn the leather when making the curved cuts and keep the blade continuing in a straight direction.

Polishing the leather to give it a shine is the next step. Taking a water-dampened sponge, wipe it lightly over one piece. The goal is to moisten rather than to saturate. When the water from the sponge has soaked into the leather, take a clean wool or cotton cloth, lay the leather flat on a clean work area and begin to buff the leather. You will notice the leather start to take on a glassy shine. You may repeat this process as often

as you like, for with each sponging and buffing, the leather will shine more and more. I refer to this process as "burnishing." If you have difficulty in obtaining a polish, it may be that you are applying too much or too little water. Practice on scrap leather before beginning on the project itself. Also, if you are not using vegetable-tanned leather, you will have little or no success at polishing. Patina is most easily obtained on vegetable tannages. Chrome-tanned or oil-tanned leathers are almost impossible to polish in this manner. Even using vegetable-tanned leather, you will need to expend some elbow grease.

ADDING DECORATION

While the leather is still a little damp, I suggest incorporating any designs you may want to carve, stamp or emboss in the leather. When leather is damp, it has great "memory." The slightest scuff or dent will become part of the finished product. Some of those accidental marks can be rubbed out using a smooth stick or a polished piece of antler, but simply being careful is much easier. Stay away from store-bought stamps, which are easily recognized as modern. You can file and carve simple stamps from scraps of wood or brass. Using iron or steel on damp leather may leave a dark stain when in contact with each other.

Use your small scraps to test designs. Once a design is pounded in, it is there for good! If your design is elaborate, I suggest working the details out on the cardboard pattern to insure that it will fit. Don't worry about being too precise with your designs, however. I've seen very few originals that were perfect. A few goofs can add character.

Perhaps the nicest design you could do would be to use dividers or compass to make "hex" signs or pinwheels. These simple geometrics are very traditional to early leather work and are not terribly difficult to execute. I tend to associate these

pinwheels or hex designs with Germanic influences, common to Pennsylvanian and Ohio Valley pouches. I haven't seen a hex design on what I was certain to be an 18th century pouch, but certainly if I were to state that hex signs didn't exist on 18th century pouches, I'd be shown one. One design I can recommend for being typical of the 18th century is crosshatching. The crosshatching can range from a simple "X" to a busy pattern consisting of hundreds of crossed lines. Crosshatching is seen embossed on many different kinds of 18th century leather work and is perhaps the "safest" design to use, being unquestionably acceptable for accurate reproduction leather work.

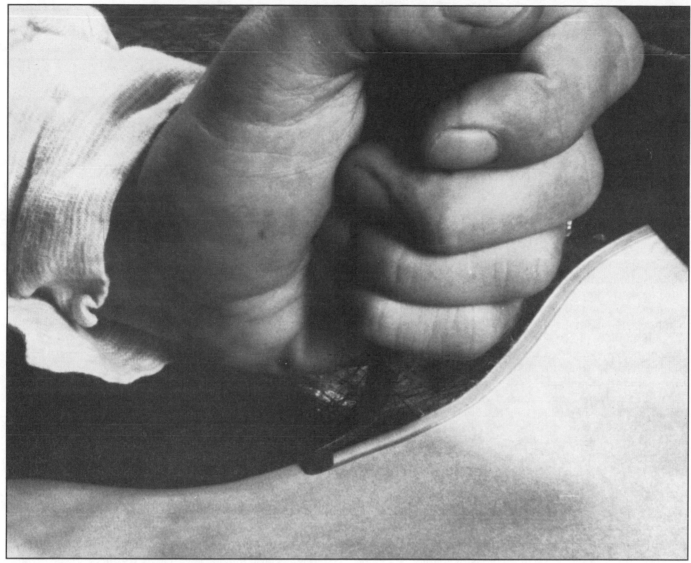

Using the edge creaser to give a finished look. Note how even a right-handed tool can be ambidextrously applied.

When applying your chosen design, you will find it necessary to sponge more water on the leather than you did for simple burnishing. Take care not to apply too much water or the leather will become spongy and the design will lose its sharp detail. After completing your design, burnish the surface of the leather again, following the measures described previously. Take care to allow the leather to dry some after applying the designs, as very wet leather will not polish well and could remove the patina already attained. After completing this stage, set the project aside to dry completely. Attempting construction at this "wet" stage may cause the leather to acquire unwanted dents or scuffs and it may also stretch. I will discuss color later, but consider setting the leather to dry in the sun. By sun drying, the leather will darken according to how long you leave it there. When the final oiling is applied, the leather pouch will have attained a pleasing honey color. Four to six hours would be good for giving the leather a "suntan." Take care not to extend this time for more than a day as excessive sun-drying at this stage may cause the leather to lose too much of its natural oil and moisture, possibly causing it to tear or crack prematurely.

21

After the leather pieces are dry, you can begin the construction process. The sequence for construction begins by attaching the welt and gusset to the front. Once those three pieces are stitched, the back welt and back are attached and stitched to the front pieces. All pieces will be placed right sides (top grain) together. After stitching is complete, the pouch will be turned, thereby putting the raw edges to the inside of the bag. If you are adding a gusset or welt, make sure it is properly positioned with the top grain to the inside.

The traditional method for holding the many pieces of the pattern together until stitched is a series of "tacks," not metal but thread tacks. When I'm doing a lot of stitching, I end up with several needles with three to six inches worth of thread still attached to the needle. I use these already threaded needles to put one loop and knot every inch or so along the area to be eventually joined by final hand stitching. The thread passes through all pieces to be joined and is tied in a knot. Before tacking the pieces together, make certain that they are properly aligned. This is where the hash marks transferred from the paper pattern come into play. Start the tacking procedure from that center hash mark, alternating back and forth up each side. Failure to alternate or not tacking from the center out can tend to stretch one side more than the other, causing the front or back panel to be misaligned. Keep your tacks as close as possible to the edge of your work. You don't want the tack holes to show when the pouch is turned right side out. Remove the tacking threads after stitching.

An easier way to hold the pieces together would be to coat the edges that are to be joined with a rubber contact cement and then stitch the pieces together. Unfortunately, I was taught my construction methods using rubber cement. It was fast and easy but very untraditional. It's hard to break old habits, but I hope I can encourage others to experience more traditional techniques. Aside from being untraditional and expensive, the fumes from those modern glues are quite toxic. It is harmful during the closed window season when the fumes can become concentrated. If you do opt for rubber cement, please follow the safe handling recommendations on the product's label. Be sure to leave no visible glue when finished, as that ruins the authentic effect you are striving for.

Before stitching, you must scribe a seam line into the suede side as a guide for stitching. This guideline should be approximately 1/8-inch to 3/16-inch from the edge of the leather and marks where the line of stitching is to be. (It may be easier to mark this line prior to tacking the pieces together.) You will find the dividers best for scratching the guideline. Lightly dampening the leather's edge first will help the dividers make a deeper and more visible line to follow. Be sure that the welt between the gusset and side panels is wide enough that at least 1/8-inch of the welt is on either side of the stitching. A welt that is too narrow may tear when the pouch is turned.

It is very difficult to explain the stitching technique with the written word. I have worked directly with people and in a matter of minutes had them stitching away. I hope that the illustrations provided will make the learning easier.

The original pouches were stitched using flax cord, also known as linen cord. Real sinew was also employed, but it was

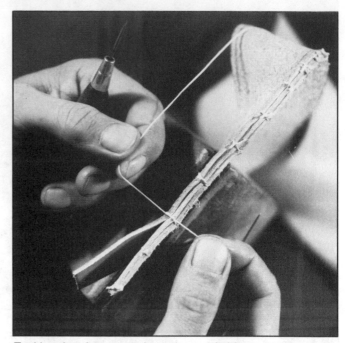

Tacking the pieces together prior to stitching.

more common to rural, homespun pouches. I cannot encourage the use of artificial sinew, as this modern synthetic is so much stronger than the leather's fibers that it can cut through the leather. In time flax can rot and break, but reconstruction is simple because the holes are easily re-stitched. Re-stitching probably won't be necessary for many years, perhaps decades. I could say much more against the use of artificial sinew and synthetic fibers, but suffice it to say that it's not historically correct and definitely not a part of our objective.

For this pouch you will only need a small quantity of cord. Thirty feet should be more than enough. I suggest six-ply unwaxed cord for stitching the body and attaching the straps.

First, pull off seven or eight feet of cord from the spool. Run the cord through a cake of beeswax three or four times. The wax helps give body to the cord, as well as allowing smooth passage through the awl hole and keeping the twist of the cord wound tight. Rosin was also used in place of beeswax. It too gives the cord more manageable qualities as well as keeping the finished stitches tight. Once the cord is waxed or rosined, the ends of the cord should be tapered to allow easier passage through the needle's eye. Taper both ends of the cord because two needles will be attached, one at each end. Tapering is best accomplished by laying the cord flat on a hard, smooth surface, such as a cutting board, provided there is a smooth area on it. A polished granite stone works best but is not something most have around the shop. While holding the cord down with one hand, take a square-end knife and, starting about 1/2" from the end of the cord, push down and tear out about 1/3 to 1/2 of the fibers from the end of the cord. It takes some practice to remove the fibers smoothly and easily but, once mastered, threading

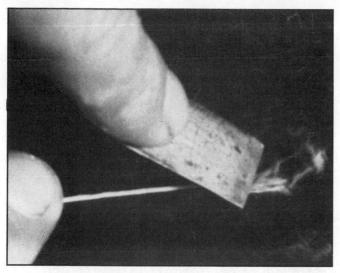

the needles will become a breeze. An old butter knife can be made into a good tool for this task. File the end of the knife square, leaving sharp edges.

Before threading the needles, twist the cord ends into a point. The next step is to lock the needles onto the cord. Explaining how this is done would be much too wordy and confusing, so refer to the accompanying illustrations.

Now that cord and needles are prepared, you are ready to stitch. It is almost impossible for me to explain every motion involved in stitching. I will describe the basics, however I doubt if I can convey every subtle detail. Only practice will

Left: Paring away fibers from cord, making a nice "taper to" for threading the needles.

Locking the needle. Once the eye is threaded (1), the needle's tip divides the ply of the cord (2). Then pull the tapered end through the eye (3), stopping when the divided plies reach the eye (4). Pull the long cord over the eye and the cord will "lock" onto the needle (4 and 5).

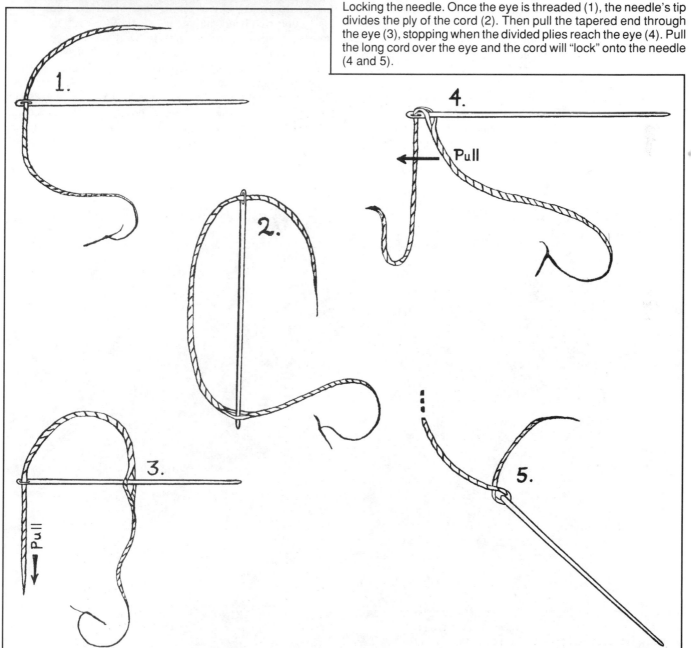

1.

2.

3. Pull

4. Pull

5.

make your hands work with clock-like precision and harmony.

Take the awl in hand. If you're right-handed, hold the awl in the right hand, otherwise hold it in your left. Now, don't set the awl down until you're finished! Don't trade the awl between your hands and don't lay the awl down between stitches. Force yourself to hold the awl at all times. If you lay it down between every stitch, you'll waste a large amount of time retrieving the tool each time, and the stitching process takes long enough as it is. You may argue this, but trust me. At first it will feel awkward, but in time it will become second nature to retain your awl while pulling needles and thread through the leather. With practice you will be able to stitch rings around those who lay their awl down between stitches.

It's best to hold your leather in a clamp. You don't absolutely need a clamp for this first project, but I suggest acquiring one if you intend on making leather work an enjoyable hobby. The clamp makes holding the work so much easier and faster and the time spent making one will be well worth the effort. If no clamp is available, hold the leather firmly with the opposite hand, taking care to avoid placing your fingers where the blade of the awl is going to be.

Place the first awl hole in the guideline about 1/2-inch down from the top edge. You'll be making a couple of stitches up to the edge and then you will come back through the same holes, doubling the cord. Doubling these first couple of stitches is for reinforcement. The beginning and end of a stitch line is the weakest point because that is where the most stress is directed.

When piercing the leather with the awl, make sure the blade enters the leather at a 90-degree angle. This will help appearances and prevent the awl from running too close to the leather's edge and possibly tearing out. The stitch should look the same on the back side of the work as it does on the top. Once you have made that first hole, pass one needle through the hole and pull until there is an equal amount of cord on each side of the project. Now you should have one needle on either side. Moving up toward the top edge, pierce the second hole. Bring the needle on the back side through the back of the second hole. Using your awl hand, pull the needle through the hole toward you. Caution: do not pull the needle directly toward your head. If the needle should jerk free, you could blind yourself. If you're having trouble pulling the needle and cord through the hole, try giving the awl a half twist to stretch the fiber of the leather, thus enlarging the hole. Now that both needles are in the awl hand, send the other needle down through that second hole and pull the needle and cord through using your free hand. At this point your first stitch is in place. You've traded sides

Stitching: The awl blade should be at a 90-degree angle to the work. Keep your fingers out of harm's way but supporting the back.

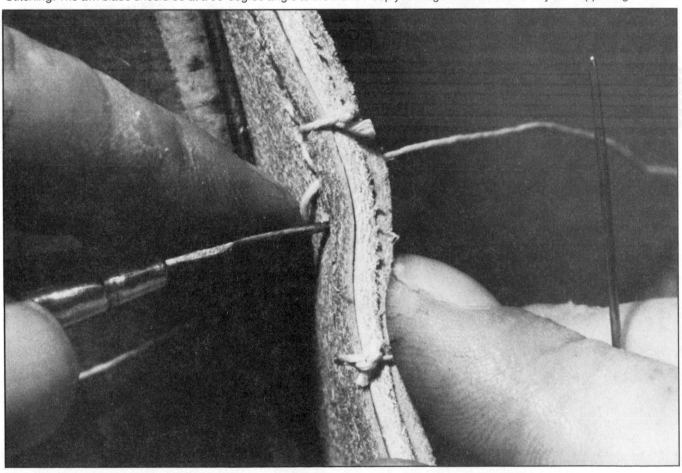

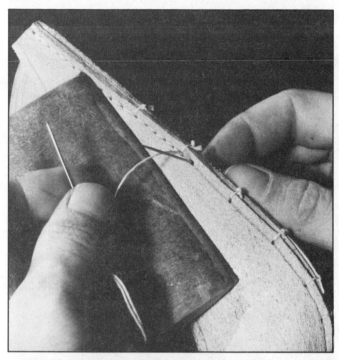

Left: Bring the bottom needle up through the hole first.

Below: Make sure you have not speared the cord in the hole by tugging on the cord at this point.

with the needles, and there should be an equal amount of cord on either side of the leather. Basically, you're making a figure eight down through the edge of the leather. Pull firmly on both ends of the cord to draw the stitch tight and take care not to pull on the needles, because the eye of the needle will eventually cut through the attached cord if you do so. For internal construction it is acceptable to space your holes 1/4-inch apart. Most interior stitching on original pouches tends to run 1/8-inch to 1/4-inch.

You will possibly experience a few problems. The first, and perhaps the most frustrating, is that of spearing the first needle's cord when sending the second needle through the hole. The best way to avoid this is by not pulling the cord of the first needle all the way tight, leaving a small loop. When you push the second needle into that hole, give the first cord a tug to insure that has not been speared, then pull both cords tight. Should you forget to test your cord and you pull the speared

The cord, shown before being pulled tight, forms a figure eight. This is the strongest construction method for leather work.

cord through the leather, the best remedy is to unlock the needle and pull the cord back out. Doing that a few times will help you to remember to tug first.

Another problem you may encounter is crooked stitches. This may be the effect of several different problems. Some tips to help are as follows:

(1) Note that the awl blade is four-sided. When piercing the leather with the awl, be sure to position the awl blade in the same manner each time. This helps the cord to lay more precisely.

(2) Repetition is the key to exact stitching. A mislaid or crooked stitch is often the product of changing methods between stitching. However, for the interior construction of pouches, don't worry that your stitches are not perfectly aligned.

(3) Keep within the stitch guideline and keep the awl reasonably vertical and at right angles to the leather. Once the pouch is turned right side out, most irregularities in your stitching will be hidden.

(4) Do not try to pierce all of the stitching holes at once. Doing that will make pulling the needles through the leather more difficult (the difficulty is caused by the shrinking of the holes). By piercing all of the holes first, you will end up spending more time reopening the holes than you would have by stitching the traditional way, one at a time.

The first two stitches were for reinforcement. Now, you stitch back over them, using the same holes. It will be necessary to enlarge those holes to accommodate the extra cord. Avoid the urge to enlarge those holes with the stitching awl as the cord might tear or be cut by the awl blade. Use the round awl for the hole enlargement to avoid damaging the cord. Now, complete the stitching around the pouch's circumference. When you have reached the end of the stitch line, back up two or more stitches, in the same manner as you did at the beginning. The doubled thickness of cord will hold tight in the holes making it unnecessary to knot. Simply cut the cord flush with the leather.

The type of stitch I have described here is known as a saddle stitch, boot stitch or double running stitch. There is no stronger method of construction for leather. Having seen double running stitches on almost all homespun pouches, I believe this stitching technique was basic knowledge to many rural families.

Now that the front of the pouch is attached to the welt and gusset, you will need to attach the back of the pouch to the gusset using the same tacking method described before. Don't forget the second welt strip that goes between the back and gusset. At this point you will experience some difficulty turning the edge of the gusset to lay against the back. To make this easier, take a dauber of water and wet 1/2-inch of the gusset's edge, relaxing the leather. Again, line up the center hash marks of the back and gusset. Tack the back onto the gusset and welt and mark the stitch guideline. Attach the back with the same stitching as the front. Now, you're ready to turn the pouch right side out.

TURNING THE POUCH

Submerge the entire pouch in tepid water. Ten to fifteen minutes should be sufficient to saturate the leather completely. Once saturated, begin turning the mouth and flap of the pouch back over the main body. Push the bottom of the body through the pouch's mouth. If it fights back, keep at it. I have wrestled some heavy leather pouches that I thought would never turn. Eventually they yield. When the pouch is turned, the seams may require some extra stretching. A baseball bat or smooth stick will help force the pouch into the desired shape. Hold the bat between your knees and push the bat along the seam while holding the lip of the pouch. Take care not to stretch the front, back or flap while pushing the seams out. A little stretch will probably return to shape when dry. When the leather is almost half dry, you may want to stuff a rag or newspaper inside for shape.

When the leather is completely dry, you will notice the nice polish you applied earlier is now gone. Fear not; a damp sponge and a little more burnishing will bring the patina back quickly.

Soak the leather before turning the pouch right side out.

Turning the pouch. Push the bottom of the body through the pouch's mouth. If it fights back, keep at it.

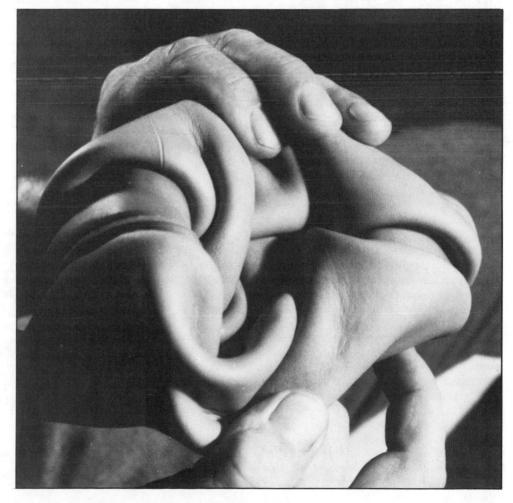

Attachment of the strap is the last step of construction. The width of the strap is usually determined by the size of buckle you are going to use. Some research is necessary for choosing the proper style of buckle. Most of the earliest pouches I have seen were fitted with hand-forged iron buckles. Most of the "reproduction" iron buckles I've seen don't resemble these early buckles very closely. Early pouch strap buckles were seldom much heavier stock than 3/16-inch. I believe most of the original buckles were also filed bright, leaving few if any hammer marks. Brass buckles were also available during the 18th century. A primary difference in early brass buckles is that the tongue was always of iron. The style of buckle is important for 18th century authenticity. Luckily, there are hundreds of surviving examples of 18th century buckles. Researching archaeological reports of 18th century digs, such as Fort Ticonderoga and others, will acquaint you with typical buckles of the period. If access to a proper buckle is too difficult, consider using no buckle at all. Many period pouches were strapped without buckles. It is better to omit the buckle than to stick on a buckle that is "sort of right."

Cut a "V" to accommodate the buckle's tongue.

The length of your strap will be determined by your size and where you wish the pouch to hang on your body. Many original pouch straps are rather short, thus making the pouch ride above the waist. A high-riding pouch is good for running, since you can clamp your arm down over the pouch and keep it from flopping about. However, there is nothing inappropriate about a long strap. I have seen many period illustrations of men wearing pouches where the top of the pouch comes to the waist. A low hanging pouch is certainly easier to load from. An adjustable buckled strap is the best of both worlds. The buckle is proper worn in front or back. Personally, I have my strap buckle in front.

Constructing the strap is fairly simple. The weight of the leather for straps should be between five and seven ounces in thickness. If you are cutting the strap from the same leather as the pouch, remember to reserve the long straight areas of the hide just for straps, welts and gussets. Most original straps I have seen are absent of decoration. Decoration on some merely consists of a creased line running the length of both sides. Edge creasing (the edge creasing tool is described in the tool list) should be done while the leather is still damp after the first, surface burnishing. This same creased edge is appropriate around the edge of the flap as well as the pouch's opening. Again, as with most of these techniques, I suggest testing newfound skills on scraps.

Stitching the buckle onto the strap. This sequence of shots shows how to change the needles from one side to the other.

Below: Pulling the needles through the fold.

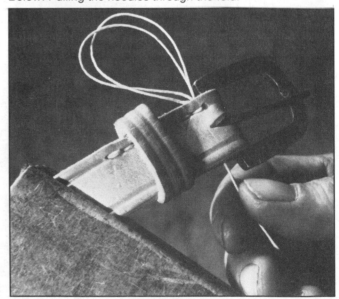

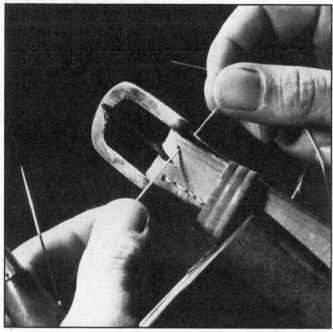

Beginning the new row of stitching down the other side.

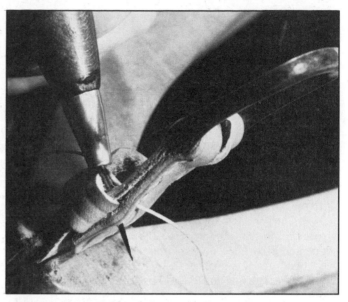

Stitching under the keeper requires angling the awl blade.

Securely stitching the strap to the back of the pouch.

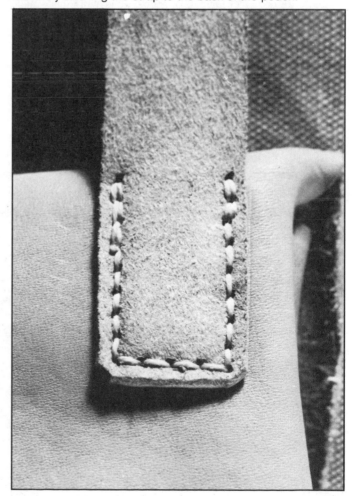

The strap's rough edge should also be burnished. For this type of burnishing, you need to dampen the edge with a dauber and rub the groove of the burnishing stick back and forth across the edge of the strap. The heat caused by the rubbing condenses the fibers, making a very smooth edge. The flap and pouch opening should also be edge-burnished for a more finished look. After you have completed the pouch, you can go back over these edges with beeswax and rub the beeswax in with a canvas cloth. Doing this will make a very smooth edge that will last indefinitely.

It is easier to attach the buckle to the strap before attaching the strap to the pouch. To do this fold the strap back two inches, then with your knife cut the hole for the buckle's tongue by making a "V" notch in the center of the fold. Next, cut a small strip of leather about 1/2-inch wide and as long as it needs to be to wrap around two thicknesses of the strap. This piece becomes the "keeper" and will be stitched between the fold and below the buckle about one inch, just like a belt. When stitching the keeper and buckle into place, be sure to allow enough loop in the keeper to accept the strap. The keeper, too, may be creased to match the strap.

Once the edges are burnished and creased and the buckle is attached, the last thing is to stitch the straps into place. Place the end of the strap at least 1-1/2 to two inches down from the top edge of the pouch. Stitch three sides around the strap's end but not across the top. Stitching across the top can weaken the strap, so confine your stitches to the sides and bottom.

DYEING THE POUCH

Adding color to the leather can be simply achieved by a few applications of 100% pure neatsfoot oil. The neatsfoot oil will not only darken the leather to a honey color, but it also will be the best preservative you can apply to a new piece. A little neatsfoot oil is good, but a lot is *not* better. Too much oil will make the pouch greasy to the touch as well as bleeding oil onto whatever it rests against. I've heard a lot of negative talk about neatsfoot oil. Some say it will rot linen cord. This is true of neatsfoot oil *compound* but not of 100% pure neatsfoot oil. The term "compound" means that the oil has been cut with other agents. I believe these compound agents are responsible for the cord rot. I have never had a problem when using 100% neatsfoot oil, nor do I know of others experiencing problems with the pure oil. Read the product label. If the oil you choose lists silicons or compounds, stay away from it. Neatsfoot oil is an organic product rendered from the hooves of cattle. It's been made and used for centuries. I doubt if a bad product would have been manufactured for so long. If pure neatsfoot oil is not obtainable, try using cod liver or castor oil. Either will perform well.

Most of the original pouches I have seen are of such a dark brown color they appear almost black. I believe most of these pouches were originally the honey brown color when new. Time, grime and sunlight will darken vegetable-tanned leather to that dark brown color. I have seen leather work that I made ten years ago that has almost turned that brownish-black color. It's easy to imagine that with twenty more years of use, it will be the same dark color of the original pouches.

If you don't wish to wait thirty years for a dark color, I have had rather good success darkening vegetable-tanned leather with walnut hull dye. The recipe I use is as follows:

Signing your work is important and ethical when reproducing items from the past.

Walnut Dye

1 bushel walnuts with hull (soft hulls)
2 cups isopropyl alcohol
5 gallon iron kettle and firewood

Fill the kettle with the hulls and water. Simmer hulls in water until hulls are completely broken down. This may take several hours. Add more water to replace evaporation during rendering. Two gallons of rendered walnut dye is what this quantity of hulls should produce. Once rendered to two gallons, allow it to cool. Draw dye from pot, straining solids. Store in canning jars. Add 2 shots of alcohol to each jar. This prevents dye from molding during storage. This dye is good for making writing ink, too.

Walnut dye works differently from leather to leather. I have found that open-pore leathers, such as pigskin, soak up lots of the walnut pigment and can turn very dark. Tight-grained calf skins may not take up as much pigment, but I have always been pleased with the colors I have obtained. It gives a very "natural" look.

The easiest way to dye a pouch is to completely submerge the leather in the dye. Once saturated, wipe off the excess dye and hang to dry. Also, before dyeing, make sure the leather is absolutely dry. Any water present in the pouch will prevent the dye from soaking in and may prevent the pouch from dyeing evenly. Do not attempt to dye the leather if neatsfoot or other oils have already been applied as the dye will not penetrate. To save a step, you may use the dye to soak the leather for turning the pouch right side out. (Be prepared to experience dark hands, but a "true" leather worker won't mind this.) If you are using dye water to turn the pouch, don't forget to dye the strap at the same time for uniform coloration.

30

There are several commercial dyes available on the market, enabling you to dye leather any color of the rainbow, but as far as traditional hunting pouches are concerned, colors from honey brown to brownish black are the most realistic. Using commercial dyes successfully takes practice. However, commercial dye is the only practical way I have found to achieve very dark colors. But, do *not* submerge the pouch in commercial dye! These dyes should be applied with a brush or dauber. As with commercial leather glues, follow label directions and precautions.

If you wish to dye your pouch brownish black with commercial dye, I suggest mixing one part black dye to six parts dark brown. I don't recommend using straight black dye. Black dye, even when dry and buffed well, still tends to rub off on your clothes. Also, if you take a close look at the color of the originals, you'll see that they are not a true black. Setting a true black color next to the old pouch will make this obvious.

After dyeing, either with walnut dye or store-bought dye, buff with a soft cotton or wool cloth to bring back the shine and, finally, oil as described before. One of the nicest qualities of vegetable-tanned leather is the mellow patina it will acquire with age and use. Once a year or so, a light application of oil may be needed.

I've presented to you the basics of pouch construction. I encourage you to study the design and construction techniques of original pouches. After you've made one pouch, you'll then be able to examine originals with a new perspective and appreciation.

The author at work on a hunting pouch.

FINAL THOUGHTS ON LEATHER

One of the most crucial aspects to the authenticity of reproduction leather work is the choice of appropriate leather. The primary tannage of leather in historic Anglo pouches was vegetable tan. Vegetable-tanned leather is one of the oldest tanning methods, dating back at least to ancient Egypt's pre-seventeenth dynasty. The ancient Celtic people also made vegetable-tanned leather. In fact, the word "tan" is the Celtic word for oak. Oak bark was, and still is, the principle organic source for tannic acid in Europe and North America. Tannic acid is the chemical agent responsible for keeping the protein from breaking down and decaying, thus making raw skins useful. The attributes of vegetable-tanned leather are many. The feel, smell, durability, color and manageability of bark-tanned leather is unsurpassed.

Another type of tannage that is even older than vegetable tan is brain tan. Brain tannages were primarily applied to undomesticated animal skins. Supposedly, all animals possess enough brains to tan their own skin. I will not discuss the process of brain tanning, as the subject has been thoroughly described by others more capable than myself. I will mention that brain-tanned skins of deer, elk and other wild animals were readily available not only to Indians and frontiersmen, but also could be obtained in the most urban cities. I have read many advertisements in 18th century American newspapers offering large quantities of brain-tanned or "Indian tanned" deer skins for sale. Considering the quantity of deer skins offered for sale, compared to cowhides offered in advertisements, it leads me to believe that during most of the 18th century, brain tan was more plentiful than vegetable tan. However, I do not find as many brain-tanned wares as vegetable-tanned wares when I inventory historic artifacts. I refer to Anglo-made wares only. Certainly the majority of leather work in Indian culture was of brain-tanned leather. Perhaps I find more 18th century ads for brain-tanned leather because its demand was such that more advertising was needed to sell a surplus to a society that favored vegetable tannages.

Brain-tanned skins are perfectly acceptable for making accurate pouch reproductions. However, most of the deer skins I have seen used in old pouches was of a vegetable tannage. I am currently doing research concerning how to make my own vegetable-tanned deer skin. Perhaps it will make for a good future chapter.

Today the majority of leather is made using a mineral tanning process commonly referred to as chrome tan. Salt of chromium is the agent used in chrome tanning. It also prevents the protein of raw skins from breaking down and in terms of longevity may be superior to vegetable tan. However, many traditional leather working techniques cannot be employed upon chrome-tanned leather, since chrome tan is highly resistant to water and, therefore, to forming and shaping. Chrome-tanned leather also lacks the unique character and patina we appreciate and value in vegetable-tanned leathers.

Examine your raw materials carefully!

DEDICATION

Madison Grant 1905-1990

Madison Grant was the forerunner who first recognized, cataloged and presented to us what still remains as the best documented collection of early American hunting pouches in his book *The Kentucky Rifle Hunting Pouch*. I doubt if I have ever shared in a serious conversation about hunting pouches without referring to some standard of knowledge presented originally by Madison's work. He began his collecting and documenting at a time when few appreciated the significance of this subject. Madison Grant truly had an eye for Americana.

APPENDIX A: WORKS CONSULTED

Baker, Oliver. *Blackjacks and Leather Bottles*. London: W.J. Fieldhouse, Esq., 1921.

Curtis, John Obed. *New England Militia Uniforms and Accoutrements*. Meriden, CT: Old Sturbridge, 1971.

Grant, Madison. *The Kentucky Rifle Hunting Pouch*. York, PA: Madison Grant, 1977.

Neumann, George C., and Frank J. Kravic. *The Collector's Illustrated Encyclopedia of the American Revolution*. Secaucus, NJ: Castle Books, 1977.

Plenderleith, H.J. *The Conservation of Antiquities and Works of Art*. London: Oxford University Press, year?

Waterer, John W. *A Guide to the Conservation and Restoration of Objects Made Wholly or in Part of Leather*. London: G. Bell & Sons, 1973.

APPENDIX B: RESOURCES

Leather, tools and supplies:
S & T Leather Company
2135 S. James Rd.
Columbus, OH 43232
(614) 235-1900
Hours are: 9:00—5:00 (Central), Monday—Friday. Ask for Dennis. Free catalog available upon request.

Hand-forged, 18th century-style buckle reproductions:
Aubrey Williams
RR 16 Box 465
Brazil, IN 47834

Leather and some supplies:
Leatherhead, Inc.
1601 Bardstown Rd.
Louisville, KY 40205
(502) 451-4477
Hours are: 11:00—6:00 (Central), Tuesday—Saturday. Ask for Nick. No catalog.

Handmade, 18th century-style stitching clamps ($50.00—$80.00):
Dale Hulsey
R.R. 2
Kinmundy, IL 62854
(618) 547-3168

Horse Gear East & West

by Bob Schmidt and Tom Bryant

Bob Schmidt (mounted) is descended from great grandparents who journeyed to California in 1865 in a covered wagon via the Oregon Trail. He was born in San Antonio, Texas, and grew up in Oklahoma. After a two-year stint in the Navy, he returned to Oklahoma City and went to work in a saddle and boot shop where he learned the leather-working trade.

In 1952, Bob married Nita Holcomb, and they have three sons and four grandchildren. Bob and Nita now live in Corvallis, Montana, in the Bitterroot Valley. They own and operate Historical ReEnterprises and specialize in making fur trade saddles and tack. He has been a member of the NMLRA since 1974 and a member of AMM since 1983.

Tom Bryant was born and raised in south Georgia and grew up working with horses and mules. In 1969, he moved to Montana and graduated from the University of Montana in 1970. For the next ten years, he was recreation director for the city of Missoula, Montana. In that capacity he wrote a weekly column for the Missoulian newspaper on outdoor recreation plus feature stories on hunting, fishing and adventures on horseback.

Tom lives and works in the beautiful Bitterroot Valley in southwestern Montana where he writes, cowboys, trains horses and mules and packs into the backcountry every chance he gets.

The evolution of horse gear, riding and packing equipment began when man first domesticated horses and/or mules thousands of years ago. The Bible makes many references to the use of the wild ass that freely roamed the plains of northern Africa before man began recording history. In the *Wyoming Wrangler*, Rhonda Sedwick quotes Jonathan Periam and A.W. Baker from the *Encyclopedia of Livestock and Complete Stock Doctor* in discussing the wild ass that was indigenous to the Arabia Desert and the countries that formed the Babylonian Empire:

Those found in the northern region of India are said to be so fleet, in the hill country, that no horse can overtake them.... Job is quoted as saying, "Wild tenant of the wasted I see him there; Amongst the schrubs to breathe Freedom's air. Swift as an arrow in his speed he flies; sees from afar the smokey city rise." (Sedwick 7)

We know that the Romans were among the first society of people to domesticate and use horses and mules on a large scale. Initially, the Romans used horses and mules as work animals. The Romans employed them in races and were among the first people to see the military value of horses and mules, using these animals to pull chariots in their Olympiad races hundreds of years before the birth of Christ. The Romans also built up large mounted units of men, and while all soldiers are known for their grumbling, one of the Roman soldier's primary complaints was that their buttocks became galded from riding sweaty horses. This problem was solved by placing a blanket between the horse and the rider, providing some comfort for both.

The mounted soldiers also complained that their feet and legs grew numb from dangling down on each side of the horse. Many times when the early Roman soldier would dismount a horse, his legs were so numb that it was some time before he could function properly—a disaster in battle. Then some sage whose name is lost in history came up with the idea to slightly support the soldier's feet while he was mounted, thereby taking some pressure off the thighs and legs. And voila, the stirrup was born. After a halter and bridle, the stirrup was one of the first pieces of horse gear developed. Although this small piece of equipment has undergone many changes in design in different countries and cultures, the function remains the same, to offer support to the rider's feet and legs.

The original stirrup was probably no more than two pieces of wood with foot holes carved in them, connected with a leather strap that was draped across the horse's back. The Roman soldier still had to be assisted in mounting a horse, but once seated he was ready for the long ride (Vernman 63).

While the Romans were tinkering with bridles, bits, stirrups and the like, the Celts, Moors, Chinese and Spanish were also working with horses and mules developing and improving horse gear of their own. The goad or spur is thought to have been invented in Spain about the year 900 B.C. The Moors and the Spanish generated tremendous influence in the development of horse gear in the old world. Richard Ahlborn in *Man Made Mobile* states, "Archaeological evidence of riding in Spain occurs in Rock Art dating before 2,000 B.C. About the same time, bent-knee riders in saddles of concave silhouette appear in Iberian Stone carvings, bronze castings and vase paintings" (5).

Ahlborn also states that some authorities place the origin of the saddle in China, no earlier than 200 B.C. and that its use reached the Roman Empire no earlier than 400 A.D. (4). The saddle was probably not invented in one fell swoop but rather evolved through trial and error and was greatly affected by customs and countries. As more and more countries adopted the horse as a method of transportation and warring, customs and cultures spread across Europe and Asia and types of horses and horse gear were invented, adapted and improved. In *The Heavenly Horses*, Virginia Johnson states that in 376 A.D.:

Attila the Hun rode out of the East to ravage what was left of the Roman Empire, his hordes galloping over what became Hungary, Italy and France, and after the Huns came the Avars and then the Mongols led by Genghis Khan....The Mongols practically lived on their horses and treated them well. The men would not tie bundles behind their saddle nor waste the horses' energy by chasing game. (11-12)

The first horses and gear to arrive in America were brought into what is now Florida by the Spanish Conquistadors in the early 1500s:

By the 1520s, the conquistadors had already set up two colonies that would carry Spain's flag into the land that eventually became the American West. The first of these colonies was Cuba, established in 1511. The second was Mexico, then called New Spain....
The governments of both Cuba and Mexico were authorized by the king to explore the vast unknown land mass between Florida and Baja (lower) California, whose shores had already been touched by Spanish captains....The first important expedition was launched from Cuba in 1528. Some 300 men under Panfilo de Narvaez landed on the west coast of Florida, struck out northward—and apparently vanished from the face of the earth. (Daniels 25)

Four men actually survived that ordeal and wandered about America for eight years. They were finally found along the Sinaloa River in western Mexico by another Spanish explorer, Nunez de Guzman. The survivors told tales of golden cites and unlimited wealth waiting to be plucked, all lies as it turned out, but the race for America was on.

So the powers in Spain sent 27-year-old Francis Vasquez de Coronado to check out the survivors' stories, and he led an expedition from Mexico into what is now Arizona and New Mexico (Daniels 27). Documents of the Coronado expedition specify the types of *brida* (bridles) and *junta arms* (saddles), which Ahlborn said were probably an Arabic-Spanish (lightweight) type.

According to Ahlborn the Spanish also introduced the

Sillas jinetas, a light cavalry saddle, and the *silla de armas*, a war saddle with heavier leathers and a high front pommel (8). It is well-documented now that horses and equipment from Coronado's expedition strayed or were stolen by Indians and the re-establishment of horses in America began.

The Indians adopted the horse as their own, and many western tribes quickly rebuilt their culture around the horse, as had the Moors, the Celts, the Spanish and the Mongolians. The American Indian of the Western plains used the horse for transportation, hunting and making war. They also developed much of their own riding and packing gear using equipment and patterns from the Spanish.

The Spanish also established missions in the Southwest and in California with one major purpose being the raising of cattle and the exportation of hides and tallow. The local Mexicans and Indians were originally converted not only to Christianity and field hands, but also later into Spanish-American cowboys called *vaqueros*. They developed their own horse gear adapted for roping and holding animals. The *vaqueros* became excellent horsemen and further developed the Spanish saddle with a specially designed horn. They became experts in the making and use of the *laretia*, a rawhide lariat, and many other pieces of horse gear.

It is from this background that the Western saddle was developed. The Mexicans and the Indians adapted horse gear from the Spanish. The American settlers in the West adapted horse gear from the Mexicans and the Spanish settlers, adding to the English, French and German influences they had brought with them and those adaptations made in the Eastern Colonies and in the exploration of the West.

Randy Steffen's series, *The Horse Soldier 1776 - 1943*, is probably the best source documenting the evolution of horse gear in America, especially in the Eastern United States. In four volumes Steffen covers military saddles and horse gear from 1776 to 1943. A better depiction and description of American horse gear is hard, nay impossible, to find. These are the books used as reference by the U.S. Quartermaster Museum at Fort Lee, Virginia.

Steffen points out that the first army put together by this country was the Continental Army, conscripts who brought with them the clothing and equipment that they had on hand. "Officers were required to furnish their own horse, saddles and other horse equipment as well as their arms and accoutrements" (Steffen 5). And in his drawing of a private of the light dragoons, Steffen writes:

His horse is equipped with a civilian-type saddle that has had rings and staples added to it for fastening holsters, blanket, saddlebags and breast harness. The bridle and halter are semimilitary type in wide use during this period. Four thicknesses of folded blanket pad the horse from the saddle's bars and skirts. A crupper aids the breast harness in keeping the saddle in place on the horse's back, no matter how rough the going. (11)

So it is well established that our first Army was made up of conscripted civilians, and they used horses and horse gear they had on hand. This gear came to America mostly from Europe, and most saddles, bridles and halters showed strong English, French or German design. An excellent reference on pre-America horse gear is *Horses and Saddlery* by Major G. Tylden, published in association with the Army Museum Ogilby Trust. There is also a fine book titled *British Sporting*

Paintings by Judy Egerton that shows paintings of American and English horses, riders and horse gear from the Colonial period. These pictures show very large, very good-looking, thoroughbred-type horses sporting the small, flat-seated, English saddle. Some of the horses are shown wearing a snaffle bit and some are wearing a Pelham-type bit, which is actually two bits in one (Egerton 10).

Some of the saddles have a surcingle that encircles both saddle and horse, and most saddles show short skirts, which were lengthened in Colonial and military models. Steffen states:

Civilian saddles of this period were not too unlike some European military saddles. Converting them for use by mounted soldiers meant attaching rings and staples at necessary points on cantle, pommel and skirts for the securing of necessary equipment—holsters, saddlebags, valises or portmanteaus, carbine, buckets and so on.

...the common riding saddle that was found throughout the colonies during the period of the Revolutionary War...was the model for later military saddles adopted by the young United States government.

Built on a wooden tree with slab sidebars, it has a moderately high cantle and a peaked pommel set over padded underskirts. The outer skirts are squared at the bottom and long enough to prevent interference of the bottom edge of the skirt with the top of the rider's boots—a characteristic subsequent military saddles retained. (22-23)

American horse gear is like American people, a conglomeration of parts and pieces of other peoples from other lands. It has been said that America is the great melting pot of society. Nowhere is this more true than in the development of American horse gear. People from many countries settled America and each brought with them a little of their past—their own traditions and customs, their own horse gear and in some cases their own horses. When you talk or write about horse gear in America, you are talking about horse gear from around the world and how it has been changed to fit the needs in a new country.

The great Hollywood movie producer John Huston, who gave us so many great westerns, reportedly said that the American West was like no other place on earth. The people who trekked west seemed to develop a life and a culture to match the rawness and openness of the land. And that's the way American horse gear evolved; it took on a life of its own so as to meet the demands of long, hard use in a tough and often hostile country. The horse gear we use today in America continues to change as the country, the people and horses continue to change.

HORSE GEAR OF THE FUR TRADE ERA

When most people talk about the fur trade era, they're speaking of the period in American history from 1820 to 1840. But as Charles Hanson, Jr. wrote in *The Book of Buckskinning V*, it actually started in the 16th century along the East Coast shortly after settlers from Europe started moving there (66). When the development of the West began, after the Lewis and Clark expedition (1804-1806) fur trading had been going on steadily in the East and constantly moving West. The development of American horse gear moved right along with this westward rush.

Most of the information we have gained has been through reading and researching journals, books, magazine articles and, in the case of Bob, from his travels and experiences as a saddle maker. Books such as *Man Made Mobile*, *The Horse Soldier 1776-1943, Vol. I,* and *Riders Across the Centuries* are valuable sources, and the nation's museums can also add greatly to your understanding of both Eastern and Western horse gear. In this chapter every effort has been made to illustrate only pictures of saddles and equipment used from 1790 to 1840. Museums at some historic sites such as Mount Vernon and Colonial Williamsburg, Virginia, own restored original saddles, some of which were the models used by Randy Steffen in his illustrations for *The Horse Soldier 1776-1943, Vol I.*

Volume 1 of Steffen's series of books has some excellent illustrations on the Continental Light Dragoons, 1776-1783. Saddle bags shown in Steffen's drawing of a light dragoon soldier have a strap over the seat and another behind the cantle with the crupper strap going over the top of that strap. A bearskin-covered pair of pommel holsters is attached to the front of the pommel of the saddle (Steffen 10). Steffen also depicts American horse gear from 1812 to 1821 (Steffen 1: 22-23). This description accompanies four photographs of civilian saddles used in the Colonies:

...an English-type saddle built on a wood tree reinforced with metal plates. It had a moderate-height cantle and solidly stuffed knee and thigh rolls sewed to the skirts for steadying the rider over walls and fences. This type of saddle was popular for riding to the hounds.

Fitted with double skirts, the inner one to protect the horse from chafing by girth buckles, this saddle was probably equipped with iron stirrups and a linen girth; neither found with the restored model at Mount Vernon. (Steffen 23)

The seat of riders of that time was one with long stirrups to steady the rider when he rose in the irons (stirrups). Cruppers were attached to the rear of saddles and ran under the horse's tail to prevent the saddle from moving forward. A martingale (a type of breast collar) was used in front and this, with the crupper, held the saddle in place regardless of how rough or steep the ride.

Halters used during the period were made of leather with a lead strap tied to a ring on the right side of the saddle when the rider was mounted. At the time, there appeared to be no established military halter, called head collars by the British, but rather were the civilian type used by everyone. Some of the bridles used were with single cheek pieces; another, the Pelham type, used double reins to accommodate the double bit (a snaffle or bar and a bar or port with short shanks to provide more "whoa" power).

The English saddle was built with four pieces of wood but with a flat seat and no horn. They were covered with cloth, padded and covered with leather. The English, German and French saddles were extremely well built but very complicated when compared to the Spanish and, later, the fur trade saddle.

The early Spanish saddle started like the English saddle, but the Spanish saddle was built to stand the strain and stress of roping and holding large animals. The Spanish saddle had two side boards that lay along the back of the animal and a pommel that was usually cut from the fork of a tree. The pommel, the side boards and the cantle, which is the back of the saddle and supports the rump of the rider, were covered with wet rawhide attached with hide glue and sewn together with strips of rawhide, making a very strong, almost indestructible unit called the "tree." This is the same basis upon which most American and especially fur trade era saddles were built.

It has not been established when the Americans first saw the Spanish saddle. In 1805, while in what is now Montana, Lewis and Clark noted in their journals that they saw Shoshone Indians with a Spanish saddle. Captain Zebulon Pike, while in present-day Colorado, saw the Spanish saddle in 1807.

An English-style civilian rig built by Bob Schmidt includes the bridle and reins, a martingale (breast collar), a pistol bucket, saddlebags portmanteau and crupper.

Right: Close-up of the crupper and portmanteau made by Schmidt.

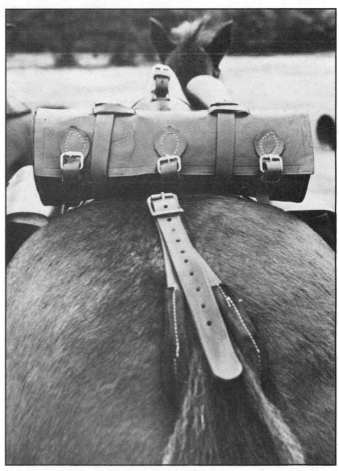

To cover the vast open spaces of the great American plains, the Americans had to resort to the use of animals as transportation, i.e. horses and mules. And that meant some modification and adaptation of horse gear that was available when the West opened up to fur trade. Records show that the Americans were using the Spanish saddle in the 1800s. The Spanish saddle was a great improvement over the flat seat of the English saddle. The Spanish saddle was simpler, was ruggedly constructed and required less maintenance; just about perfect for the harsh conditions encountered in fur trading and trapping trips. The records of the Western Department of the Western Fur Trade Company show that trappers and traders were using the Spanish-type saddle in the 1820s. American trappers wintering in Taos, New Mexico, and some as far away as California, were exposed to the Spanish saddle and no doubt preferred them to the crude, Indian-made saddles they were used to seeing (Ahlborn 43).

There is no record of any trappers, traders or settlers adapting Indian-made horse gear, although the reverse was true. During the 1830s, when the fur trade was at its peak and probably at its best, many saddles were purchased in Saint Louis for those the trappers and traders were dealing with, as well as for the personnel of the fur trade companies. Saddles bought and traded were of both English and Spanish type, with the Spanish being the most favored.

Eastern-style saddles and gear can be used in 18th and early 19th century reenactments. The English saddle was still in use when the fur trade was opening up in the Rockies.

The importance of the Santa Fe trail contributed to the prevalence of the Spanish saddle during this same time period. While surveying the Santa Fe trail, United States Commissioner George C. Sibley bought Spanish saddles in Taos, New Mexico, for his returning survey party (Ahlborn 43). Spanish saddles were also, no doubt, brought up the Santa Fe trail by Mexican traders and quickly purchased by Americans going west.

Americans, especially early Americans, know a good thing when they see it, and it wasn't too long before American saddle makers began producing their own "Spanish saddle." Thornton Grimsley of Saint Louis, Missouri, began building Spanish-type saddles and selling them to the American Fur Company in 1822. About the same time, Jesse Prichett, Saint John Township, Missouri, was building saddle trees for the American Fur Company. William H. Ashley was the first man to take a caravan of mounted men and supplies on pack animal overland from Missouri to the Rockies for the purpose of trading. In a letter to Maj. Joshua B. Brant, Army Quartermaster at St. Louis, dated 24 April 1833, Grimsley states that Ashley was the first person to use the Spanish-type saddle that he (Grimsley) had built. When Lucian Fontenelle was leaving St. Louis in 1831 with supplies for the trappers' brigades, he received 30 Spanish saddles for his mounted men. In 1834, Nathaniel J. Wyeth requested that his outfit procure Spanish

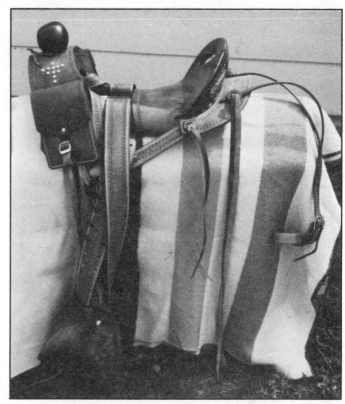

Figure 1: Gourd horn saddle.

saddles for him and his men (Ahlborn 43-44).

In 1834, the inventory from Fort Union, North Dakota, shows iron stirrups, hemp and woolen girths, horse shoes, six American saddles, plated spurs and leathers and saddle bags. In 1854, it includes: "one super Spanish riding saddle, one American fair saddle, two American black seat saddles, 19 common Spanish saddles, 38 American pack saddles and two Indian saddle cushions..." (*Things* 143).

Today, the term "Santa Fe saddle" is often used for modern mountain-man saddles. The term probably came from names that saddle tree companies used to identify a certain type of tree they were building. The so-called Santa Fe saddle is like the Spanish saddle, having a large, flat horn and hand holes in the cantle. Some of the early drawings show some saddles with hand holes in the cantle and some without. A quote from the Army Quartermaster in Philadelphia in 1846 reads, "We obtained a fairly good idea of the Spanish tree, its tall and slender horn and high, steep-pitch cantle. The tree was to be covered with leather partly tanned [rawhide]" (*Things* 143).

If you found one of these old saddles and planned to use it today, you would find that they won't fit the backs of our modern horses. Most horses available to trappers during the fur trade period in the West were small, wiry, Indian-type ponies weighing about seven to eight hundred pounds and standing from thirteen to fourteen hands tall. Those who want one of the Spanish-style saddles should have it built to fit today's horse, which averages over one thousand pounds and stands about fifteen to sixteen hands. Bob rides an American quarter-type horse, which is constantly overweight, so the gullet on his saddle is spread to fit the back of this 20th century mutant without pinching the horse's withers and back.

There are usually four different gullet widths available today to fit the backs of different sizes and breeds of horses: the regular, 5-3/4 inch; the semi-quarter horse, six to 6-1/4 inch; quarter horse, 6-1/2 inch; and full quarter horse, 6-3/4 to seven inch. However, any size gullet can be custom built to accommodate any size horse.

Accompanying the text are illustrations of gourd horn saddles. Figure 1 shows a gourd-horn saddle with hand holes in the cantle. This saddle is skeleton-rigged with a ground seat built in. A different type of gourd horn is pictured in Figure 2. I refer to this horn as a Chihuahua horn. The face is cut off at about a 90-degree angle. This saddle is also skeleton-rigged with ground seat and has bulldog nose *tapaderas*. The word *tapaderas*, also spelled *tapaderos*, comes from the Spanish, meaning a thing that covers, in this case toes.

Figure 3 is of two saddles. The one on the left is what I call a St. Louis horn or Ashley contract saddle. This one has a buffalo hide *mochila*. And here we go back to the Spanish

Figure 2: Chihuahua horn saddle.

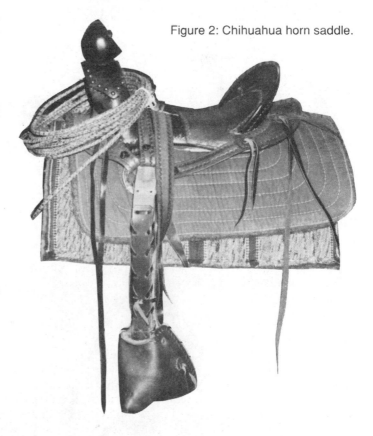

41

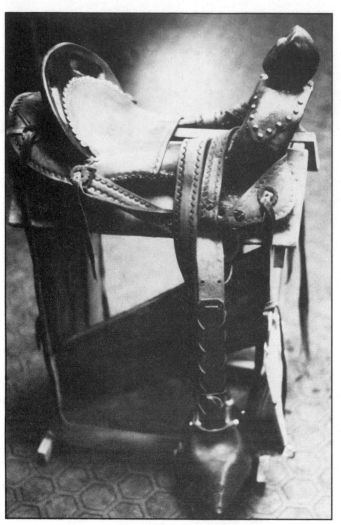

again; *mochila*, also spelled *mochilla*, is a loose skin that covers the saddle. Pony Express riders used a stiff *mochila* with pouches sewn on to carry the mail, and the whole outfit, cover and pouches, could easily be removed when the rider changed horses. Many of those riders called this leather covering a *macheer*. The saddle next to the one with the *mochila* has a tree I picked up in old Mexico and is patterned from trees available after the fur trade era, about 1865. An Ashley contract saddle with a plain leather *mochila*, gun strap around the horn and bulldog nose *tapaderas*, all ready to start that long horseback trip, is shown in Figure 4.

A Rio Grande or early California-style saddle is pictured in Figure 5. The saddle was copied from a drawing done by Jose Cisneros for the book *Riders Across the Centuries*. Cisneros says that this style of saddle was being used in the Baja Rio Grande in about 1770 (62). This saddle has an apple horn, gun strap, pommel bags and extended leather tail piece, called an *anquera*, which covered the rump and sometimes the flank of the horse. The *anquera* served as a handy seat for the ladies of Spanish nobles to ride behind them, a popular custom in their country. This custom also led to the development of hand holes in the cantle. The Spanish were, and many still are, great horse people and had a good thing going with the rumble seat for their lady friends. The *anquera* also served to protect the extra rider's clothing from the sweaty flanks of the horse and many

Left: Another view of the Chihuahua horn saddle.

Figure 3: On the left is a St. Louis horn or Ashley contract saddle with a buffalo hide *mochila*. The saddle on the right has a tree that came from old Mexico and is patterned after trees available about 1865.

anqueras were elaborately decorated simply for looks.

The *tapaderas* on this saddle are an early Spanish style and the saddle is laced with 1/4-inch strips of silver, adding to the decoration and value of the saddle. It should be pointed out that to the early Spanish and Mexicans saddles were prized possessions and many were decorated heavily according to the desire of the owner.

Several different styles of head stalls, the leather part of the bridle without the bit and reins, are shown in Figure 6. Some have buckles on top of the bridle and some have buckles on both cheek pieces for adjustment. One bridle shows a buckle on the near (left) side of the cheek piece. Early bridles were also made of braided rawhide, braided horse and/or buffalo hair. The same materials are used in making these pieces of horse gear today, even though buffalo hair is hard to find and horse hair is getting more expensive all the time.

The Spanish, the Mexicans and the early American settlers all used rawhide or grass to make ropes. The Spanish were particularly adept at making and using rawhide ropes that they called *reatas*, also spelled *rita*, which means "to bring together," as in braiding. The *vaquero* referred to his *la reata*, and of course the Americans mispronounced this as "lariat" and bastardized that into "lasso," "lass rope" and "lazo."

Hobbles were used to keep the animals close by camp

Figure 4: Ashley contract saddle with leather mochila.

Figure 5: Rio Grande/early California saddle.

43

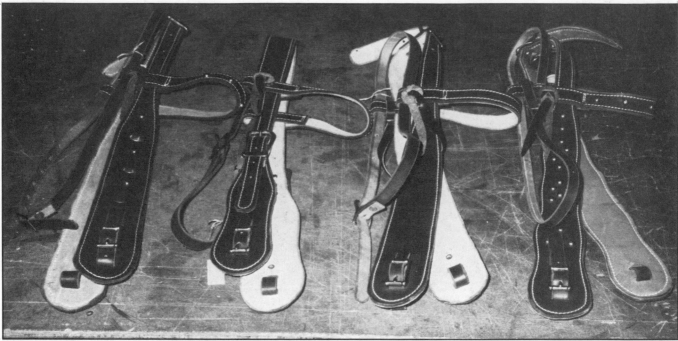

Figure 6: Head stalls.

when grazing. Most hobbles were made of leather with buckles on one end or of braided and twisted rawhide or horse hair. They can be made out of harness leather, saddle skirting, rawhide or rope. Latigo hobbles tend to stretch when wet and will lose their shape, tear or both. Most hobbles are made of harness leather and are traditionally used on the front legs. The Spanish used side hobbles connecting a front foot to a back foot when transporting animals aboard ship. These were called sidelines and were later used by the U.S. Army. Many cavalry soldiers carried a set of sidelines on their saddles along with feed bag and grooming equipment.

Figure 7 shows four types of hobbles. The figure-eight hobble has a center ring and the Utah hobble has two rings. They are used to tie the front feet together by placing them around the horse's front legs, normally below the knees, but

some riders place the hobbles above the knees. The single foot cuff or hobble is used on either front leg. A long cotton rope, normally about 30 feet long, attaches the single hobble to a picket pin that is driven into the ground. The rope may also be tied to a small tree or log. Animals must be trained to be picketed.

Some modern cinches, which are not too different from cinches that have been used down through the centuries, are shown in Figure 8. The cinch on the far left is a pack cinch. It is 26 inches long by four inches wide and made of canvas webbing. It has a 3-1/2–inch ring on one end and a hook on the other and is used for lashing top packs onto pack animals. The cinch in the middle is a common type used on riding saddles. It is made of 17 twisted cotton strands and is 34 inches long and has no tongues in the rings. Some modern cinches have tongues

Figure 7: Hobbles.

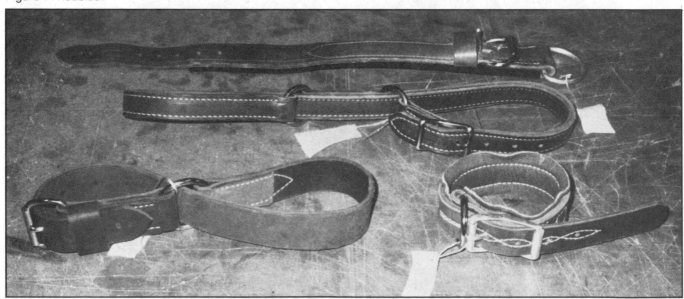

to facilitate the fastening of the *latigo* to the cinch. The large, double wide cinch is a pack saddle cinch used primarily on sawbuck pack saddles. The side with the double ring in it goes to the front of the pack animal and can be used to lash down loads, thereby eliminating the need for the lash cinch.

Next to the double cinch is a mohair hackamore rope that can be used to make up a *mecate*. A *mecate* is a rope normally 32 to 38 feet in length that was originally made of the mane or tail hair of horses. Today, *mecates* are not only made of mohair or horsehair, but also of cotton and nylon and are used to make a combination lead rope and one-piece reins. The *mecate* is usually attached to a *bozal*, which is a strap of leather, usually braided rawhide, that encircles the lower face of the horse immediately above the nostrils. A *bozal* is oftime used in place of a bit, but in training a young horse may also be used in conjunction with a bit. The Spanish and the Mexicans, and later the early Californians, were very big on starting their horses in *bozals*. The *bozal* put pressure on the horse's nose and saved the mouth. Most Spanish, Mexican and Southwestern riders used a *bozal* on a horse until the animal was four or five years old. At about age four they would have the animal start packing a spade bit along with the *bozal*. Between the ages of five and six, when the animal was completely broke and responding well to the bit, the *bozal* would be removed.

The round, fuzzy-looking pieces of equipment shown at the bottom of the cinches in Figure 8 are wool skin-covered cinch ring covers. On a very fat horse or mule or one that is soft and hasn't been used much the cinch ring may sore the

animal. For more information on saddling and packing, see our chapter, "Pack Saddles and Panniers," in *The Book Of Buckskinning V* (249).

The purpose of the cinch is to anchor the saddle on the animal as comfortably as possible in the position in which the rider or packer wishes the saddle to stay. Cinches, also spelled *cincha* and *cinchas*, are made of cords of cotton, mohair and horse hair. They are also made of leather, webbing and canvas. Many of the old cavalry cinches were made of horse hair and are still in use today. But some of the horse hair cinches coming out of Mexico today are made strictly of tail hair of the horse, and they're not as good as the ones we used to see that were mostly mane hair. Mane hair is preferable because it is the safest; it is softer and will bend and flex more, whereas tail hair is stiff and more likely to break.

The most common cinch you see today is the cord cinch. It is usually built with fifteen to seventeen cords per inch, with a fifteen-cord cinch being narrow and a seventeen-cord being wider. Cinches are measured from the end of a ring on one end to the end of the ring in the other end. It is important to note that cinches come in different sizes for different animals just like there are different size belts for different size humans. Again, we refer you to *The Book of Buckskinning V* for placement and adjustment of cinches on animals and other pertinent points of packing and riding and using horse gear.

The interesting thing about horse gear is that it has evolved through the centuries according to the needs and means of the horse people. The English developed small, flat saddles used

Figure 8: Cinches.

45

mostly for pleasure riding. The Spanish developed saddles not only for roping and holding large animals but to accommodate an extra rider. The Americans borrowed the best of both worlds and have developed saddles that are comfortable to ride and can still be used in ranch work. However, the modern world of horse and mule showing still necessitates the use of the English saddle, and some people just seem to like that small, flat seat.

Even as we approach the 21st century, horse gear is still being invented, altered and improved. Today there are saddles made of a modern cloth called Cordura which is weatherproof and wear resistant. Man has invented artificial wool skin that looks like the real thing even if doesn't work quite as well.

People still raise and use horses in an era where we can drive a vehicle in thirty minutes the distance it took our ancestors a full day of hard riding to travel. We use horses and horse gear today primarily because we love the animals and the riding and packing. The kinds of horse gear used during the formation of America was as varied as the people who came to settle the country. Horse gear, like horse people, came from all over the world and developed a new life in America.

THE ULTIMATE TEST OF HORSE GEAR: A RIDE TO A RENDEZVOUS FROM THE 1989 JOURNALS OF SILVERTIP SCHMIDT

Many people sit and read and dream of things they would like to do, and I have found that most buckskinners do like to dream—dream about how it would have been to be a mountain man during the heyday of the fur trade era. Many times I think about those mountain men out a'horseback in the early 1800s, riding into unmapped territory, not knowing what was over the next ridge or knowing what kind of excitement the day would bring. To me that would have been living at its finest. I would have loved it.

So it is that in the latter part of the 20th century, I like to take rides as did my kindred and forefathers a hundred years ago and experience just what it was like to be a mountain man on the edge of life in a new country. Every year, for many years now, I have ridden to a rendezvous somewhere in the West. For the past seven years, my friend Bud Ice from Odessa, Texas, has ridden with me to the Western national rendezvous. Traditionally, these rides have lasted from four to seven days. On our ride in 1988, we talked about doing a 30-day ride into the 1989 Western national at Craig, Colorado.

We invited seven more 'skinners to join us on this trip. Our plans were to ride from Emigrant Springs, just north of Kemmerer, Wyoming, on the old Oregon Trail, and ride in a round-about way to Craig, a distance of some 250 miles. We planned to stop at the 1825 rendezvous site on Henry's Fork north of McKinnon and at the 1834 rendezvous site at Old Fort Bridger, which is on the old Oregon Trail, then to Fort Davey Crockett at Brown's Hole and on into Craig. I contacted the Chamber of Commerce at Kemmerer to find out where we might meet and have a place for our animals to stay for a few days. We were able to use the local roping arena, which worked out well for us. Most everywhere we were met with interest and hospitality.

Each person on the trip was required to wear "period" clothing and use only period horse gear. Each person was to have a riding animal and one to pack and carry enough supplies to last for 30 days. This proved to be quite involved, since it is not easy in this day and time to gather up fur trade era riding and pack gear. Like most other 'skinners, we either made or had made our riding and packing gear.

Bud Ice rode a Santa Fe-style saddle that I had built for him back in 1983. It has a 4-1/2" flat horn cap and is built on a semi-quarter horse tree. The gullet is six inches wide with Arizona bars. The cantle is three inches high and Bud rides with a

Buffalo hide *mochila*, wooden stirrups with round Spanish style *tapaderas*, a crupper and a pair of pommel bags. On this trip Bud switched from riding a horse to riding a mule and was packing two animals using sawbuck pack saddles with panniers. He tied his top packs on with single diamond hitches, just like in the old days.

Dave Fowler was also riding one of my Santa Fe-style saddles, this one built in 1982. It has a 4-1/2" flat horn cap and is built on a semi-quarter horse tree with Arizona bars. The gullet is six inches wide and the cantle is three inches high. He has a leather *mochila* with a piece of home-tanned sheepskin he lays over the *mochila*. Dave's saddle packs pommel bags, has a gun strap, crupper and steam-bent wooden stirrups. Dave rode a mule, when he rode, and packed a mule with a homemade sawbuck that he has used since 1983. Dave's ride was like a shooting star—spectacular but short.

Frank Costanza is also a boot and saddle maker and was riding a saddle of his own design: California-styled, built on a regular tree, with a 5-1/2" gullet, same horn and a three-inch cantle. Frank's *mochila* is two pieces and laced up the middle. He rides large wooden stirrups with round, Spanish style *tapaderas*. Frank rode a thoroughbred-type horse and packed another horse with a sawbuck saddle using rawhide panniers. Being the versatile guy that he is, saddle maker, movie actor, model and the like, Frank could ride or pack either animal, a handy feat on a rendezvous ride. Frank's biggest problem on the trip came not from his animals but from insects in the sagebrush, namely ticks that feasted on his knees.

Jay Van Orden was also riding a California-style saddle of his own making with a low cantle and small horn built on a regular tree. It had a five-inch-wide gullet and a three-inch cantle. Jay sat on a two-piece, leather *mochila* and had long *tapaderas* covering his bent-wood stirrups. He rode a horse and packed a horse with a sawbuck saddle using canvas panniers.

I rode an Ashley contract-style saddle with a small domed horn and quarter horse tree with Arizona bars. It has a 6-1/2" gullet and 4-1/2" cantle with hand holes. I sat on a buffalo hide *mochila* and had a leather *anquera* which covers old Henry's ample rump. The saddle is held in place by a crupper and breast collar, which I find necessary for mountain riding. The saddle has cut-down, rawhide-covered stirrups with round, Spanish style *tapaderas*. I packed a pair of pommel bags that contained

Our brigade of mountain men at Ft. Bridger.

a small camera and first aid kit. I rode Henry, my quarter horse, and packed Hanna, a cantankerous but loving molly mule, using a sawbuck pack saddle, canvas panniers and top pack that I lashed in place with a double diamond hitch. I made all the horse gear used by myself and several of the other riders, and I'm happy to say we had no trouble with the equipment. But the riders and the animals? Well, that's the rest of the story.

May 31, 1989, Emigrant Springs, Wyoming. Was cloudy and about 38 degrees this morning at 7:30. We fixed breakfast and started the greenhorns, Frank Costanza and Jay Van Orden, on their packing lessons. They both packed their horses

off and on until about 3:00. I believe they will do okay as they are a lot better now than this morning.

We have been laying out all our foodstuff and pots and pans so we can see what we need to take. It has been raining off and on most all day. Dave Fowler shot a cottontail, so we will have rabbit stew with wild rice for supper.

It's now 7:00 p.m. and raining pretty hard. I'm glad I brought a small tent. We have been camping here for three days waiting for the others to get here. We'll start in the morning for Slade Creek.

June 1, Thursday. Frost is on everything this morning. We're waiting for the canvas to dry out before we pack up the animals. We had oatmeal and coffee for breakfast. Have all the

Bob Schmidt, Henry and Hanna at Ft. Bridger.

animals saddled and packed and are ready to ride.

It's 11:00 a.m. and Dave Fowler was mounting his mule when the critter started bucking. Dave lasted about three seconds—not a very long ride—and wouldn't have gotten many points in a rodeo. He was bucked off and landed on his tail bone, which ain't too good. I think he hurt himself, and his mule ran away.

We caught the mule, Dave got on again, and we started for Slade Creek where we would make our first camp. We made about five miles when Dave had to get off and walk because his back was hurting so bad. We went on about four more miles and camped in some aspen trees.

We had to pitch Dave's tent for him, and then we fixed some soup for supper and went to bed early. It looks like we will have to take Dave back to Kemmerer in the morning and maybe to the hospital. He ain't looking too good. We picketed all the animals out to graze for a while before we put them on the high-line (rope tied between two trees) for the night. Was a real pretty sunset. We'll try to get an early start tomorrow.

June 2, Friday. Clear sky but frost on everything again this morning. Another real nice day. Picketed out the animals while we fixed breakfast. Dave didn't feel any better so we decided to take him to a hospital.

He was hurting too bad to ride and walked most of the way. I walked with him some of the way as I did yesterday. We rode into Willow Springs where there is a bar and cafe. I went inside to see if we could get someone to haul Dave the rest of the way to Kemmerer. One guy was fixing to leave and said he could

haul Dave with him. So we left Dave in Willow Springs, and we headed back to the rodeo grounds where we departed from yesterday.

I tied Dave's two mules behind my pack mule and rode back to the camp. About 2:00, Dave came in and said the doctors told him not to try to ride anymore. We now had to find some way to get Dave to Craig, Colorado, where our trucks and trailers were parked. As we were discussing our plight, some people with a camper stopped by to see what we were doing. A bunch of buckskinners never fails to draw a crowd.

Frank and Dave got a ride back to Kemmerer with the people. They stopped by the sheriff's office to see where they could get a bus out of town. They were told that there were no buses running out of Kemmerer. The Highway Patrol hauled Dave to the county line where a sheriff's deputy met him and took him to Rock Springs. From there Dave was able to catch a bus to Denver, then into Craig.

I thought it would be better if we stayed around the rodeo grounds until we heard something from Dave. We still had his mule and all his gear and didn't want to take that with us on the ride.

The Brigade travels along Cottonwood Creek, south of Ft. Bridger.

June 3, Saturday. Got up around 6:30. It was a cold, clear but windy morning. Looked like rain clouds to the south. Got breakfast over and turned the animals out to graze. Lay around camp all day, and this evening it started to rain and rained most all night.

June 4, Sunday. It's cleared up and nice this morning. Fed the animals and had breakfast, and a man from Kansas City stopped by. Said he's out here for the summer as a volunteer for the Forest Service clearing trails. Said he's a lawyer and taking the summer off from his practice. I got him to take me to Kemmerer so I could call Craig to see if Dave was there. Talked to Dave and he's leaving in the morning to drive back to Kemmerer to pick up his outfit and return home to Montana. We thought it would be better to wait until morning to ride out, so we had a good supper of steak, baked potatoes and tomatoes. Put the horses in the corrals for the night and called it a day.

June 5, Monday. Clear morning again. Up at 6:30. Left the roping arena about 8:00 and rode through town with the whole outfit. Met Dave at the edge of town and he was headed back to old Montana. We stopped at a Taco Bell for coffee, and some lady from the newspaper took our picture and said she'll send Frank some copies. We have named Frank "Road Kill Costanza," because it appears he'll eat anything.

We did about 15 miles today. Stopped at an indoor roping arena to fill up canteens and water the animals. Water to drink is hard to find. The owner invited us to stay the night. It rained hard all night and was real nice to be bedded down under cover.

June 6, Tuesday. Got up about 6:00, fed the animals and ate a cold breakfast. Stopped later and fixed something else to eat. We rode 19 miles today over some pretty country. Rode through a small place called Carter that is on the railroad tracks. It was named for a trader at Fort Bridger who hauled supplies for the Army when they were stationed there.

We followed part of the Oregon Trail. It is the same trail that the Army used into Fort Bridger. We camped on the trail by some bluffs, and I found some iron that went in the tailgate of a wagon. Probably from some poor immigrant over a hundred years ago.

Sitting next to a bluff, out of the wind, I think of the diary of my great grandmother, Mary Shackleford, who emigrated from Missouri and traveled by wagon train to California in 1865. She probably passed this very spot.

Her journal entry for Thursday, August 17, 1865, reads:

The roads have been tolerable good, wth some rock. It rained very hard this evening. We are camped on Black Fork, 12 miles from Fort Bridger. Dr. Howard came up and gave Mary and me some medicine. Mary is no better. He charged Frank [her husband and my great grandfather] *five dollars for the little quinine and morphine.*

And from Friday, August 18, 1865:

We came over very rough roads with mountains on each side. We crossed several creeks but I never heard the names of them. We came through Bridger, a pretty place with a great many nice houses.

Frank met with Mr. Carter here, the man he built a house for in Boone [Boone County, Missouri]. *All the town, nearly, belongs to him. Frank got more medicine here. They charged ten dollars for what little he got. He got a letter from Dettie and put one in the office. We came on and crossed the creek two or three times. We camped tonight five mile from Bridger, where there is no wood, water or grass.*

Sitting here watching the animals graze while Bud and Road Kill try to get a fire started, I ponder what thoughts my great grandmother must have had going through here. The wagon ruts are pretty deep going up the bluff, so you know that those people and their animals had it rough going along about here. We fed our animals and put up tents, as it looks like it might rain tonight. We got a bite to eat and went to bed. It's been a long, hard day

June 7, Wednesday. Got up at 5:30. Real nice morning. No rain. Made coffee and fed the animals. Tried to get a good start for Fort Bridger. Got off at 8:00 and stayed on the Oregon Trail and rode into Fort Bridger about 11:30 and were met by the curator, Mrs. Linda Byrnes, a real nice lady. We made camp at the old Bridger Stockade and planned to stay for the next three days.

June 8, Thursday. Lay around Ft. Bridger all day just resting and taking it easy. The animals seem to be enjoying the break. We talked to many visitors who came down to the Stockade, an interesting place that was rebuilt just as Jim Bridger originally put it up.

June 9, Friday. Nice day. We ate with Linda and her husband, Terry, tonight. We spent most all day getting our gear ready to leave tomorrow. I called home. Things are okay there. My kitchen pass is still good. Got permission to be gone a few

June 11, Sunday. Beautiful morning. Clear Sky. Up at 6:30, hobbled horses and turned them out to graze. Fixed oatmeal and coffee for breakfast. Had animals saddled and ready to leave by 10:00.

One of the city boys, who shall remain nameless, hung his bridle in a tree last night and this morning couldn't remember where he put it. It took us awhile, but we finally got him and his horse dressed and ready to ride.

We followed Cottonwood Creek south a mile or so and then headed for the mountains to the west. The going was pretty rough, and we kept turning into washouts, bluffs and dead ends that caused us to have to backtrack and look for other routes. It took us about four hours to work our way out of this badland country. Finally we came to a hilltop and saw where the highway cut through the unbroken country and offered us a

more days. We're rested and feeling good. The animals are in good shape, and we're all ready to get back on the trail.

June 10, Saturday. Finally got going about 8:30 and had a nice ride until around 5:00 p.m. We rode through some country that looked like the Badlands, really rough looking stuff, and camped on Cottonwood Creek. I fed my animals and put up my tent. Looks like it might rain tonight. Jay must have felt rain was coming, as he moved his bed in with me for the night.

way out of the mess we were in. We decided to head toward the road and follow it to Henry's Fork (In modern aviation pilots call this IFR—I Follow Road.) We made good time along the road. Got to Henry's Fork about 6:00 p.m. and stopped at a ranch to fill our canteens; it had been a long, hot, dry ride.

The rancher told us we could camp in one of his pastures and there we could turn our tired horses out to graze. We got supper going and Frank and Jay found ticks on their legs and knees and they (the 'skinners) got more than a little upset. It was the first time either guy had had ticks on them, and them boys were pretty unhappy about it.

June 12, Monday. Clear morning. Up about 6:30. Slept good last night. Bud's pack mules, Speck and Wampum, got into the food last night. We had everything covered with manties but they pulled the covers off and helped themselves to whatever they could get.

The people at the ranch, the Robinsons, told us their great, great grandfather had come to this valley from Taos with Kit Carson in the 1830s and taken a Shoshone wife and settled here.

According to D.A. Kouris, writing in *Brown's Park*, the trappers and mountain men made Brown's Hole an important fur trading center between 1826 and the early 1840s. "Included in this special breed were: former teamster on the Santa Fe Trail and employer of the American Fur Co., Uncle Jack Robinson (or Robertson), Joseph "Joe" La Fayette Meek, Robert "Doc" Newell and Kit Carson arrived in Brown's Hole in 1829 while trapping with Uncle Jack Robinson" (Kouris 7). I wondered if this man could be the same Robinson that settled here with his Indian wife.

We got away about 11:30 and rode down the west side of Henry's Fork. We rode about four hours and made camp on Henry's Fork across from where the 1825 rendezvous was held. This is real nice country. Lots of grass and water. We made camp, fixed supper and went to bed.

June 13, Tuesday. Clear morning. Up about 7:00. Fixed breakfast and put animals out to graze. Frank didn't feel so good last night—him and Jay are worried about them tick bites. But he got up and ate a good breakfast—that *we* fixed—and we got going about 11:00.

We had to cross and re-cross the river several times as there are bluffs on both sides and it was hard to find flat ground. The land across the river is all privately owned and we didn't have permission to trespass, so we picked our way along the west side.

We rode into McKinnon, Wyoming, around 4:00 and tied up at the only business there, a post office/grocery store. The Wilds, who own the store and a ranch nearby, are A.M.M. members and invited us to camp on the ranch down by Birch Creek, which runs by the ranch house.

June 14, Wednesday. Left early, about 7:00 this morning. Didn't fix breakfast as we wanted to get to Manila, Utah, today. We had to ride along the highway all day and got into Manila about 1:00 and ate lunch there.

Jay had been wanting to quit for quite a while—I think the ticks got to him—so he decided to leave us here. We rode on

Re-packing after a wreck on the trail.

down the road toward town until we came to the county rodeo arena. I went to the sheriff's office to see about us staying there tonight.

The sheriff got permission from the county commissioners for us to stay. We were told to turn our animals loose for the night in a five acre pasture with water.

I believe that I have lost about 15 pounds as I now need my suspenders to keep my pants up. Bud and I did our laundry and re-packed our panniers so we could get a good start in the morning. We turned in early tonight.

June 15, Thursday. Woke up at 5:00. A real nice morning. Saddled the animals and got going down the road by 7:00. About four miles out-of-town, a lady and four children rode out to meet us on a four-wheeler. The children brought us popsicles and gave some to the mules which was a real nice treat for all of us.

We had a real hard climb over the mountains today. We made it to a nice draw where there is a lot of aspen trees and beaver dams and plenty of grass for the animals—a perfect place to camp and rest a while.

I fixed a supper of rice and soup and it rained off and on; nothing serious, just summer showers in the mountains. We're going to stay here tomorrow, so we are soaking pinto beans for the crock.

June 16, Friday. Up around 7:00. Staked out the animals to graze all day. Had bacon and hotcakes for breakfast. Started cooking those beans and hominy with dry tomatoes for dinner. Turned out to be a real good meal.

The animals grazed and rested all day just like we did. The wind is blowing real hard and has broken down two aspen trees close by. We packed everything up tonight except tents and bedrolls and will leave early in the morning.

Wrecks are always a hazard on horseback treks, but Bruce Ashley and his animals came out of this one (on our 1990 ride) in good shape.

June 17, Saturday. Up around 6:00. Wind blew most of the night. We had breakfast of oatmeal and coffee and saddled the animals. Had to ride along the highway as all trails from here lead to Flaming Gorge Reservoir. We found a good spring to fill canteens and rode until 1:00 before stopping for lunch. We had some soup and rested the animals. Started out again about 4:00. We rode until 6:00 when we found some good grazing and made camp. We are now about nine miles from Dutch John, Utah.

June 18, Sunday. Father's day. Clear night; nice morning. Up at 7:00. Got animals ready to saddle and got going about 8:30. We crossed over the dam at Flaming Gorge and the horses didn't like it one bit. They did a lot of prancing and dancing and otherwise acting foolish, but we made it into Dutch John around 4:00. We found an agreeable place to camp by a real nice little spring with some good grazing. We talked to a game warden about a cut-off route, and he said it'd save us about 20 miles of hard traveling.

June 19, Wednesday. Left Dutch John at 9:00 to find the trail over Goslin Mountain. We followed Green River to the last camping spot. On the way there, we passed two old log cabins with caved-in roofs. There was a nice spring and a little meadow there. Later we found out that this was an old hideout of Butch Cassidy and the Sundance Kid.

We followed a trail up the side of the mountain and then up a creek bed. The trail gave out, but we followed some trail flags on up the mountain, picking our way as we went. It was pretty rough going so we turned the animals loose and hazed them up so they could pick their own way.

I held onto Henry's tail and let him help me make the climb. Two of Bud's mules got enough of the hill and turned around and started down. My critters, Henry and Hanna, turned around and joined them. I caught Bud's mules and tied them to a tree.

Then I took off after my two. Frank was the last man coming up the hill and I hollered down to him to stop my animals but he didn't and they didn't and Frank's pack horse joined in the rout. When I got down to him, I inquired as to why he let 'em get by, and he said he was too tired to move.

I took off running down the hill as I knew we had to stop them critters before they went all the way back to the river. I caught up with them about halfway down. Tying the two pack animals together, I got on Henry and started back up. Before I got back up to Bud and Frank, I found another trail marker so I followed it to the top of the mountain.

I thought the other guys had gone on over the top and we'd meet at the bottom, so I stopped and took a breather. Then I noticed that Henry had thrown a shoe going through all that shale rock. So now I had to get off and walk. Working my way down slowly, it took me three hard hours.

Frank's pack horse pulled back and broke away from Hanna and headed back up the hill. I was about ready to shoot a horse, but I turned around and went after him and it was dark when I got to the bottom. The bottom was covered in cedar trees and it was very hard to track in. The place was crawling with crickets—the biggest I've ever seen and most in one place. They were about three inches long, and as I rode through the cedars, they'd fly up all around me. I was real lucky to find that horse.

I tried to find a place to camp that had a little grass and water. My canteen was empty, and I was needing a drink real bad. I finally found some springs running into a dry creek bed and filled my canteen and watered the critters. I decided to camp here for the night. I had no idea where the other two guys were. I feel for old Frank; I've got all his food and gear with me. Maybe next time he'll be a little more active when his pack animal takes off.

June 20, Tuesday. Didn't get much sleep last night. Had bad cramps in my left leg most all night. Must have been caused from all that walking up and down that mountain.

Was clear and cool this morning. Full moon last night. Got up at 6:00. Picketed the horses out and fixed a little breakfast. Found some powdered milk and cookies in Frank's plunder. All our food had been put in Bud's panniers yesterday so we would know where all the grub was. It was now with Bud somewhere, and all I had to eat was trail mix and jerky.

The cramps left my leg so I walked up the creek bed to try to find any sign of my friends. All I found was a big, old mountain lion track in the sand. I walked back to camp and saddled the animals and started toward the east. I was walking on a bum leg, and old Henry was about lame with that shoe missing so we had slow going.

I walked about nine miles and came to an old cabin on a ranch run by the Bureau of Land Management (BLM). This is the old Jarvie homestead. It is an old dugout that Jarvie and his wife lived in, and there is a log building where he kept his store and blacksmith shop. In 1880, John Jarvie, with his new wife, moved to Brown's Hole on the north bank of the Green River

near the old military road. They lived in a dugout while building the log home and store.

The dugout and store are still there and as I rested there, a lady working at the ranch came and gave me two sandwiches and a can of pop. Then I went on down the river a couple of miles and made camp under a big cottonwood tree right by Green River. I figured I had about nine more miles to go to meet up with the other guys and I figured since I would have to walk, I'd better wait until tomorrow.

But my luck was about to take a turn for the better. About 7:00 p.m. Bud and Road Kill rode into camp, and I was sure glad to see them and see that they were all right. They had gone back down the mountain and camped last night at Butch Cassidy's old cabin. This morning they crossed the Green River and followed a cattle trail over the mountain and re-crossed the river just above me this evening.

June 21, Wednesday. Wind blew hard all night. We slept in until 10:00 and fixed oatmeal for breakfast. We grazed the animals until about 2:00 then started for the Utah/Colorado state line where we met up with the rest of the party.

About 6:00 p.m. we rode up on a set of old corrals about one mile into Colorado. This looked like a good place to rest up for a few days, so we camped here. I had had to walk much of the day and lead old Henry as he is pretty footsore. There is good grazing for the animals along the creek. We found some asparagus along the creek bank, cut it up and put it in some soup for supper. Looks like there are lots of beaver working the creek. A good place to camp.

June 22, Thursday. Rangers from the U.S. Department of Fish and Wildlife, across the road from the corrals, came over to visit with us this morning. They brought us some pop and beer and goodies to eat. Frank ate all the popcorn in one sitting.

The rangers are real nice folks. They said we could come over to their shop and take showers. That's a real good deal for us. Our animals are doing real good from two days of resting and all the grass they can eat. Now we have to attend to our own personal needs, and I have the need for a shower, real bad.

Bob Cat and John Johnson from Texas drove in this afternoon. We showed them how to pack while we waited for Ernest Cook from Louisiana to get here. As it's getting pretty late, he'll probably come in tomorrow. Anyhow, hope he's okay and traveling well. We're all still pretty tired, all except the new guys, so we ate an early supper and went to bed.

June 23, Friday. Got up around 6:00 and fixed coffee and oatmeal. I hauled old Henry into Craig to get him re-shod today. It's 100 miles one way, but I'm too old and too tired to learn to shoe horses now. As we were driving out the gate, we met Ernest driving in. We visited with him a minute, then Bud and I headed for Craig.

The Old Timer's Rodeo was under way when we got there and a friend, Judy McDowell, helped us find a shoer at the fairgrounds. After we got Henry re-shod, we drove back to the corrals. Pulled in about 10:00 p.m. and went directly to bed. It's been a long day.

June 24, Saturday. We figured it would take us another five days to ride to Craig, and the Western rendezvous was about to start. So some of us left camp in trucks and trailers and drove to the Gates of Lodore on the Green River, while others decided to ride. The Gates are said to be named for a poem

written by a surveyor of Powell's when his party was mapping the Green River. This is a real pretty place; I can easily see how it inspired a poem.

On May 24, 1869, John Wesly Powell's party of the Major (Powell) and nine men with four wooden boats and enough gear and supplies to last ten months, pushed away from the bank of what is now called Expedition Island, just below the town of Green River, Wyoming.

One of the boaters, Andrew Hall, remembered the last line of a poem by Robert Southey....'and this way the water comes down at Lodore.' As Andrew Hall wished, this canyon was named Lodore. The giant walls of the Gates of Lodore became a threatening place of hidden secrets. (Kouris 21)

We had a nice visit with Glade Ross, the superintendent of the Gates, which is also called Dinosaur National Park. Glade was the person who discovered the location of Fort Davey Crockett.

According to the book *Brown's Park*, Ft. Davey Crockett, located on the left bank of Green River and Vermillion Creek, was built by William Craig, Phillip Thompson and St. Clair sometime in the 1820s. They named the structure after the famed frontiersman who had been killed at the Alamo. "In August 1839, a tired and hungry Thomas J. Farnham arrived at the fort with his group called Oregon Dragoons. They were traveling from Peoria, Ill. to Oregon with hopes of ending the British Fur monopoly and establishing a settlement there" (Kouris 6). Kouris describes the fort as "a hollow square

of one-story log cabins with roofs and floors of mud. Around these we found the conical skin lodges of the squaws of the white trappers who were away on the fall hunt" (6).

It is believed that Brown's Hole got its name from a French Canadian trapper, Baptiste Brown. It is possible that he built a cabin and lived in the valley with his Blackfoot squaw and was one of Henry Fraeb's men who battled the Indians east of there on the Little Snake River.

Bud and I rode out to meet the other guys that were riding from the corrals. About 4:00 we met the rest of the riders near the site of Fort Davey Crockett. We looked around and found where there had been an old ferry crossing on the Green River. There were two old log cabins nearby. We could see the spot where the explorer Fremont had come down through George Canyon to see the old cabins that had once been Fort Davey Crockett. I read in *Brown's Park* that there had been a rendezvous at Fort Davey Crockett in 1842.

According to the book *Kit Carson*, on Fremont's second expedition with Kit Carson guiding him, "They marched rapidly northeast to Ft. Uintah, which they reached on June 6, thence to Green River and Brown's Hole" (Estergreen 121).

We rode on down the river a couple of miles and made camp under some cottonwood trees. This may sound peculiar to some people, but as I was riding along the bluffs by the Green River, and it must have been about 90 degrees, I felt a chill at the base of my neck and my hair seemed to stand on end. It was as if someone or something from the past was watching me. I looked around to see if I could spot something, but of course nothing was there. When we got to camp that evening, I mentioned the incident to Bud and he said that he had had the same feeling. Perhaps there really was something out there. Perhaps the ghosts of some long-gone mountain men were watching us.

The conversation that evening around the glow of the campfire brought to mind the memories of the day just past and made us glad that we had had the chance to travel this country with good friends and, of course, with good horses, mules and horse gear.

June 25, Sunday. Nice morning. Fixed breakfast and grazed animals for a couple of hours, then packed up and headed for the Gates of Lodore where we left the vehicles. We loaded our gear and animals in the trucks and trailers and drove to Judy and Kendall McDowell's place near Craig. Pulled in there about 4:00. We had planned to ride from here to the rendezvous site southeast of Craig but learned that we'd have to travel along the highway. There was no water available for the horses, so we decided to just drive on in as it would be much easier on the animals.

We got all the animals moved to our new camp at the rendezvous and later did some riding in the national forest nearby. But while camped at the rendezvous, I had more time to think about the trip and how the men and animals fared. As for the men, we lost weight for sure. Road Kill and I lost about 30 pounds each and Bud lost a noticeable amount also.

All the animals looked good and were in fine shape after losing their hay bellies. My fat old Henry looked trim and fit, but I'm not so sure how he feels about all this. All the horse gear made the trip without any need of repair.

As we sat around the campfire the last evening, talking and laughing about some of the happenings on our ride, I felt a unique bond with this group of buckskinner friends, a close friendship that comes with good fellowship among men with common goals and interest.

If you are thinking about taking a horse trip, be sure to have sound animals, good friends and good horse gear. And don't forget to plan your trip well. Study the maps, talk with people along the route and select your friends, your animals and your horse gear with care. If you have any troubles preparing such a trip, give me a call at 406-961-4243. Have a good trip and, who knows, maybe our trails will cross somewhere. Wagh!

APPENDIX A: WORKS CITED

Ahlborn, Richard E. *Man Made Mobile*. Washington, D.C.: Smithsonian Institution Press, 1980.

Daniels, George C. *The Spanish West*. Alexandria, VA: Time-Life Books, 1976.

Egerton, Judy. *British Sporting Paintings*. Seattle: University of Washington Press, 1985.

Estergreen, M. Morgan. *Kit Carson*. Norman: University Oklahoma Press, 1962

The Things of Life; Transportation, River, Stock, Horse Furniture." Inventory list. Fort Union Trading Post National Historic Site, Williston, ND.

Hanson, Charles E. Jr. "Trade Goods for Rendezvous." *The Book of Buckskinning V*. Ed. William H. Scurlock. Texarkana, TX: Rebel Publishing, 1989.

Kouris, D.A. *Brown's Park*. Greybull, Wy: Wolverine Gallery, 1988.

Johnson, Virginia W. *The Heavenly Horses*. Missoula, MT: Mountain Press Publishing, 1986.

Sedwick, Rhonda. "Ancient History of the Mule." *Wyoming Wrangler* May (1987): 14, 16.

Shackleford, Mary. Personal Diary. 1865.

Steffen, Randy. *The Horse Soldier 1776-1943*. Vol. I. Norman: University Oklahoma Press, 1977.

Vernman, Glenn R. *Man on Horseback*. New York: Harper and Row, 1964.

APPENDIX B: WORKS CONSULTED

Bryant, Thomas, and Bob Schmidt. "Pack Saddles and Panniers." *The Book Of Buckskinning V*. Ed. William H. Scurlock. Texarkana, TX : Rebel Publishing, 1989.

Cisneros, Jose. *Riders Across the Centuries*. El Paso: University of Texas Press, 1984.

Tylden, Major G. *Horses and Saddlery*. London, England: J.A. Allen, 1965.

Watts, Peter A. *Dictionary of the Old West*. New York: Promontory Press, 1987.

Making A Wooden Bow

by Jim Hamm

Jim Hamm was born in Ft. Worth, Texas, in 1952, and practically grew up with a bow in his hands, graduating from small game to deer hunting when only twelve. His interest in archery never faded, and about the time he married, he discovered traditional bows, or bows made entirely from wood, a discovery that was to consume his adult life. Though Jim spent his early years operating heavy equipment, working freight docks and "becoming a promising young executive," he finally went into archery full-time. He has been, as he puts it, "self-unemployed" for the last 12 years, making bows, researching, writing about bows and, recently, teaching others the age-old skill of wooden bow making through intensive, hands-on seminars conducted at his home. Jim also owns and operates Bois d'Arc Press, publishing archery-related books both old and new.

During the Revolutionary War, when the Colonists were desperate for muskets, powder and ball, Benjamin Franklin wrote to General Lee, "I still wish, with you, that pikes could be introduced and I would add bows and arrows: these were good weapons not wisely laid aside" (Elmer 108). An astute man, Franklin recognized that bows were nearly as accurate as the muskets of his day, as well as being relatively easy to procure. And as a student of history, he knew that arrows had slaughtered tens of thousands of men in Europe at Hastings, Crecy and Agincourt.

The bow had been a lethal weapon for warfare with a range of 200 yards and a much higher rate of fire than a muzzleloader. But its main drawback, compared to a firearm, is the strength and skill required to use it effectively. A man requires little strength to shoot a rifle and relatively little practice to shoot it accurately, which is one of the primary reasons that firearms supplanted bows after the advent of gunpowder; the armies and militias of the day did not have to practice constantly to maintain a high level of proficiency.

But in the western part of North America, in the mountains and on the prairies, the Indians were slower to give up the use of a bow. According to Lt. Col. Richard Dodge, "When I first came upon the plains only a very few of the Indians were possessed of firearms.... Even the Indians who owned guns still held on to the bow as the more reliable weapon in a close fight" (348).

The whites who travelled into the Western wilderness were often surprised by the skill with which a bow was used by the Indians. Of his travels in the 1830s, George Catlin wrote:

[The bow], *in the hands of an Indian, on a fleet and well-trained horse, with a quiver of arrows slung on his back, is a most effective and powerful weapon of the plains. No one can easily credit the force with which these missiles are thrown...until he has rode by the side of a party of Indians in a chase of a herd of buffaloes, and witnessed the apparent ease and grace with which their supple arms have drawn the bow, and seen these huge animals tumbling down....* (33)

The early explorers gave no thought to wooden bows being "primitive," they simply came to understand how effective they were when used for hunting or warfare. The muzzleloading rifles of the time were superior to bows but not by a great deal. They were much more accurate and had greater range but were slow to load. Col. Dodge wrote about the problem of single-shot firearms when facing mobile Indians as follows:

The Indian and the old hunter or trapper of the plains rarely come into collision. The later is too cool and dangerous a customer to be attacked without due and careful preparation.... [With a muzzleloader] the man who fired a shot without sure death to his enemy was very likely to 'go under' himself. The Indian has great respect for a loaded, but none for an empty, rifle. One unaccustomed to Indian warfare would naturally

59

About the time the fur trade played out in the late 1830s, repeating firearms came into being and began to render both the bow and muzzleloader obsolete. But for those of us who have our feet planted in an earlier time and who like the idea of a challenge, the age-old lure of the wooden bow remains a strong one: the beauty of a drawn bow, the soft hiss of an arrow streaking through the air, the remarkable killing power of so lovely a missile.

It is easy to succumb to the lure of a bow made from wood. Especially since there is probably a tree growing within a quarter-mile of you that will make a fine weapon. But wait, you say, Osage orange doesn't grow within a thousand miles of me, and I wouldn't recognize a yew tree if it fell on the house. And those are the only real bow woods, aren't they? I'm glad you asked, since it's a valid question.

Yew is the traditional wood of the longbow, and when archery as sport—among Anglos anyway—gained a foothold in this country during the middle of the last century, their bows naturally became a carry-over from a familiar form, the narrow, thick, English yew longbow. There were experiments with other woods such as Osage orange, which the Indians often used, but the results were always the same: other woods were inferior to yew. Osage orange made into a longbow configuration was, and still is, an unqualified failure. The much greater mass of Osage built into long limbs caused the bows to kick and vibrate in the hand when an arrow was released. Although a beautiful yellow wood, it tended to follow the string and shoot slower than the familiar yew.

It was only later, in this century, when men such as Young, Nagler, Hickman and Klopsteg began experimenting with different configurations (configurations that Native Americans had been using for generations, by the way) that Osage came to be regarded so highly in the literature as a bow wood. They discovered that Osage makes a superior bow when made with a rectangular cross-section about 1-1/2" wide and limbs shorter than the longbow's.

Other woods were tried with the new "flatbow design," as it was called. It was found that while Osage will shoot as well as yew with this design, other woods, such as ash and hickory, which tend to follow the string and be flabby in cast, will not. So they wrote that while yew and Osage are excellent bow woods, others are inferior and not suited to bows. They were making the same mistake that others had committed almost a century earlier.

In recent times men such as Paul Comstock, Tim Baker and others have begun questioning some of the old dogmas about bow woods and their design. They have helped pioneer new ideas that allow superb bows to be made from "inferior" woods, such as hickory, elm, ash and oak.

Their design is innovative and incredibly simple. Since the "white woods" are weaker in compressive strength than the hard-as-nails Osage, they make their bows wider to stand up to the strain. It is an elementary principle, but long overlooked, allowing white wood bows to shoot as fast and as far as the more traditional woods. I have even seen an excellent bow made from hackberry. The old-timers must be spinning in their graves.

But Paul and Tim are modest men, insisting that they are

John Muench, a park ranger from California, takes the first draw on the bow he just completed in one of the author's classes. Note the otter fur string silencers.

suppose that cover, rocks, thickets, &c., would be the safest place...no more fatal mistake can be made. The safest position for a small party is on a perfectly level plain without timber, rocks, holes, or other cover. A good plainsman, when travelling with a small party on unknown ground, is always on the lookout for such favorable positions, and if 'jumped' by Indians in bad ground he gets back to the last good place without loss of time. These tactics are always adopted by the old trappers and hunters of the plains, and by all plainsmen, old or new, who know Indians; and so well have the Indians come to understand

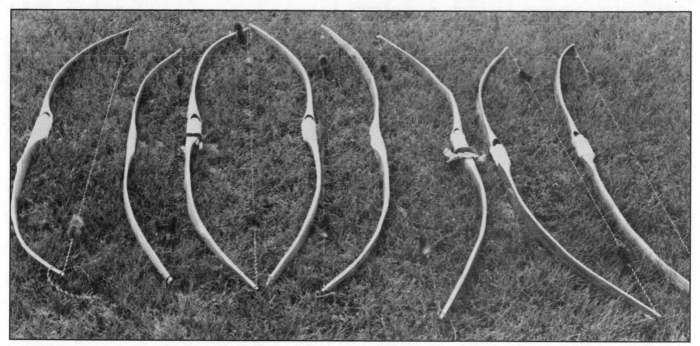

Bows made by students in one of the author's traditional archery classes. Several of these bows have since taken game.

only re-inventing the wheel. And in a sense it's true, as their bow design can be traced back thousands of years, through people who probably never discussed or much cared which wood was supposedly superior. They simply made bows that worked well from the materials at hand, with wide, flat, thin limbs.

This all adds up to good news if you are interested in using traditional wooden bows for hunting or plinking, because the white woods are far easier to make a fine bow from than the notoriously contrary Osage orange and yew.

Osage and yew are normally twisted and full of knots. It is difficult to find a straight piece, and when you do it often splits in a spiral, yielding a bow that looks more like a biplane propeller than a deadly weapon. With Osage, an even greater problem is taking off the layer of sapwood down to a single growth ring of heartwood. By the time you draw-knife, rasp, scrape, sand and dynamite down to a single growth ring, deer season may well be over. And so will your bow-making interest.

It is far easier to begin with ash, elm or hickory and avoid all of the problems. One or more of these woods are found throughout almost the entire country. They grow straight and they usually split straight. With these trees the bow can be made from all sapwood, which makes up the bulk of a log anyway, and they will perform as well as a bow made from Osage or yew. Once you've perfected the techniques of tillering and finishing and have arrived at a weight and design, you can always make a bow from the romantic yew and Osage. But it is best to start with wood that is cooperative, which brings us to the actual making of a bow.

The trees for white wood bows are cut in the summer as opposed to the winter, when yew and Osage are normally cut. There is a very practical reason for this. In the summer the bark is damp and can easily be peeled off with no residue left on the wood. More about this in a moment.

The most important trait of potential bow wood is its straightness. The white woods normally grow this way, but if you have trouble finding a straight one, keep looking. Far better to spend an hour searching for a better tree than to spend a day wrestling with twisted, crooked wood. The tree should be at least eight inches in diameter or bigger. How much bigger depends on how far you have to drag it and how much you like swinging a sledgehammer. I once spent four hours splitting a snarly 28-inch Osage log into two halves. It was backbreaking work, but the bigger logs yield many more staves.

Anyway, once you locate a tree, examine it carefully, walking all the way around it looking for knots, cavities, insect damage or bark that seems to spiral around the tree, which indicates twisted wood. The tree should also be living; a dead standing tree may be shot through with decay.

The standard draw length is 28 inches for a man, so that's how we'll base our measurements. A white wood bow should be at least 68 inches long to accommodate a 28 inch arrow, and when laying out a bow, it's always helpful to have extra wood to avoid cracks, wood borer damage or other defects. So cut the tree a minimum of six feet long. Of course, if you want a shorter bow for horseback use, or if you plan to sinew-back it or if you have a shorter draw length, then it can be made proportionately shorter. But for a standard-length hunting bow start with six feet.

Once the tree is cut, either with chain saw, axe or handsaw, immediately coat the ends of the log with a waterproof compound to prevent evaporation. Some use latex paint. The old timers used tar or wax. I've come to prefer carpenter's glue applied to the ends of the log with an old paint brush. This coating prevents cracks or endchecks from splitting the ends of the log as the wood dries.

Next, split the wood lengthways using wedges, sledgehammers and an axe. You can do this immediately after cutting or you may store the log out of the weather for months, but I recommend splitting it right away. Reduce the log to fourths or eighths or maybe even sixteenths, depending on the

A hammer, wooden and steel wedges, an ax and a hatchet are the tools the author uses for splitting out bow staves.

however. The grain will have dips, twists and ridges in it that were not visible until the bark was removed. Don't be tempted to scrape or smooth out the back. The single grain is untouched at this stage and anything you do to disrupt the layer will only give the bow a potential place to begin breaking. After all, the slight imperfections only give the bow character.

Seasoning the wood is simply a matter of drying it. Paul Comstock dries his wood artificially by placing it in an attic during the summer or in a box heated with light bulbs. He has good results, but without a moisture meter to check the water content of the wood, there is the real danger of drying the wood too much and making it brittle. Brittle as in break. I've ruined some good staves by getting them too dry in an attic. A week or two won't hurt the wood, but if you live in a hot climate or leave the wood too long, you may be in for a heart "breaking" experience.

Before drying the wood, draw the outline of the bow on the back of the stave and cut it out, either with band saw, hatchet, rasp or a combination of these. I recommend cutting the stave 2 to 2-1/4 inches wide at the widest part of the bow and 3/4 inch at the tips. The narrowed handle section should not be cut down to final shape at this stage, only narrowed slightly if you wish. This is so that, if the string doesn't exactly line up once the bow is strung, the handle can be placed to accommodate its true alignment. There are many options for shaping the bow, but two good ones are shown in the adjacent drawing of the Sudbury and Holmegaard bows. The Sudbury bow is an Indian bow made of hickory found in Massachusetts during the 1660s. The other is known as the Holmegaard bow, from a peat bog in Denmark. It is made of elm, and radio-carbon tests date it to about 6000 B.C. You can see that we are indeed re-inventing the wheel.

In laying out the bow, the easiest way to line up the tips and handle is to use a straight shadow from the edge of a building. Jay Massey showed me this trick, and it is far superior to using a ruler or chalk line. The shadow will lie straight across valleys, humps or twists in the wood, allowing you to visualize how the

size of the tree. The staves should be split into pieces approximately three inches wide.

Pull the bark off as soon as the wood is split. Work the bark loose at one end and peel off the entire strip from summer-cut wood. If you've ever worked Osage, this is the stage when you will fall in love with the white woods, because when the bark is removed, you are staring at the back of your bow. No draw-knifing down to an interior growth ring. No scraping. No dynamiting. Almost half of the bow-making battle is already won, because the interior growth ring along the back of the bow, which keeps the bow from breaking, is perfectly intact. You never even broke a sweat working on it.

The back of the bow will probably not be flat and smooth,

Two traditional bow designs that make excellent weapons.

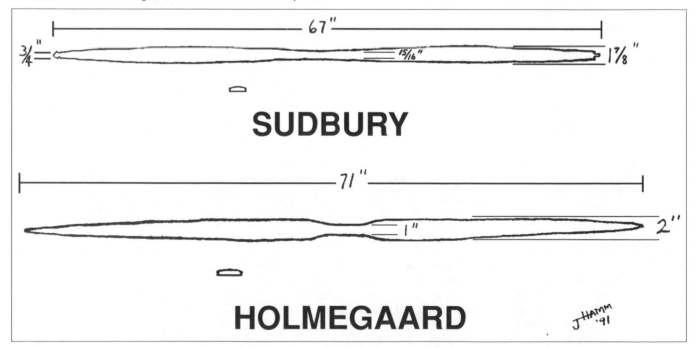

67"

3/4"   15/16"   1 7/8"

SUDBURY

71"

1"   2"

HOLMEGAARD

J HAMM '91

bow should be situated. Mark the center of each tip and the center of the handle, and your bow should be in perfect alignment when it is strung.

I like to place the handle in the exact center of the bow. Some bowyers prefer to put the handle an inch or more below center, so that the arrow, instead of the bow hand, will be at the middle of the bow. The traditional English longbow is made in this way. But there is no difference in the way the two types of bows shoot, and by placing the handle in the center, the limbs are of equal length, allowing you to choose which will be the upper and which the lower limb after stringing the bow. More on this point when we talk about tillering, but I've discovered over the years that it's best to give yourself all of the leeway you can for as long as you can.

After shaping the bow, lay out the depth of the handle and limbs. You should leave plenty of wood for your bow at this stage, but the idea is to work it close to the finished shape so that there won't be such a massive amount of wood to dry. The thickness should be about two inches at the handle and 5/8-inch along the limbs.

Don't attempt to bend the bow at this point. Put it aside where it is off of the ground and protected from the weather for a couple of months. At the end of that time, the wood will be dry and ready to finish. Naturally, this process is fine if you are only making one or two bows, but if you have 20 pie-shaped wedges from a log, it is time-consuming to take them all down to this stage. Rather, store the staves like the semi-finished bow but be aware that it can take up to a year for them to dry completely.

We'll assume at this point that your wood is well-seasoned (6-10% moisture content, depending on the area of the country and time of year) and the silhouette of the bow is cut to shape, though the handle is still wide. Tillering the bow is the next step. This involves removing wood from the belly side of the bow, which is the side facing you when holding it, until the bow limbs bend in an even arc, with both limbs bending equally, and the bow is the draw weight that you want.

Tillering is the most demanding stage of bow making, but the process is really quite simple. Take wood from the areas that are stiff and don't bend and leave alone the areas that bend too much. Repeat the preceding sentence like a mantra until it is firmly imbedded in your subconscious as you start tillering your first bow.

The initial step is to lean into the bow, with one tip on the ground, to check the bend of one limb at a time. This is called floor tillering. It is helpful if you have a finished bow, either of wood or fiberglass, that is about the same configuration and weight as the bow you are making. Floor tiller the finished bow, watching the bend along the limbs and feeling the amount of pressure you have to put on the bow to make it bend. Now it is much easier to judge how much wood must be taken from the bow-in-progress until it begins to bend.

At this stage the limbs will undoubtedly be too stiff. Place the bow in a vise, taking care not to mar the back, and use a woodworking rasp to take wood from the belly of the limbs. Do not take off wood in just one spot, but rather make long, sweeping strokes with the rasp. Work the limb from both edges, so that they remain equal. The thickness of the limb should gradually taper down from the widest part to the tip, and both edges of the limb should be the same thickness.

Take the bow from the vise and floor tiller it again. It probably still won't bend. Repeat the process. Depending on the thickness of the limbs, you may have to repeat it 10 times

Floor tillering a bow. Note that the tip of the bow rests on a piece of scrap wood to protect it from damage.

before the limbs start to bend. If the limbs were 5/8- inch thick when you began, then they should begin to bend soon. If you find yourself saying, "I'm gonna take off a lotta wood this time since nothing's happening—I'll make this sucker bend," then you should gently lay down your rasp, go in the house and take a cold shower. You are well on the way to making a bow with a 30-pound pull from the one you intended to be 60 pounds. There is not a great deal of difference between a limb not bending at all and one bending too much. When you gain experience you can go faster. For now the idea is to make a bow

Close up of the string nocks on ash (left) and Osage orange bows.

not win a race, so proceed slowly while floor tillering often.

When the bow at long last bends evenly while floor tillering, it should still be considerably stronger than what the finished bow will be. At this time cut nocks in the tips so the bow can be pulled on a tillering board with a long string. The nocks can be cut with a chain-saw file, Dremel tool or even a pocketknife, but be careful not to cut across the back of the bow. The nocks should also be smooth and slightly rounded on the edges so they don't cut the string. The tillering board is simply a board with a cut-out at one end to accept the handle of the bow and notches along its length so that the bowstring can be pulled and held at various lengths, allowing you to see the bend of the bow from a distance.

Once you have pulled the bow on the tillering board 12 to

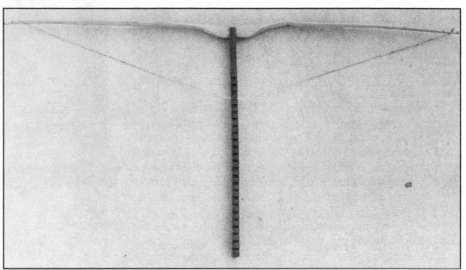

Left: A tillering stick. Top: The bow handle is placed in the notch at the end of the tillering stick. Note the extra long string used at this stage. Bottom: Testing the shape of the bow by pulling the string on the tillering stick.

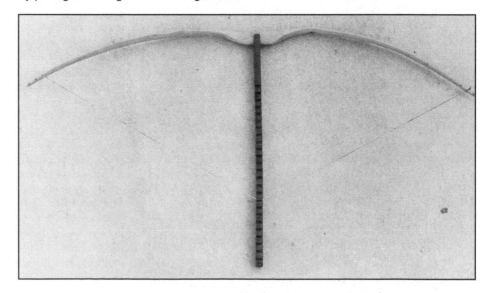

15 inches to begin with, the relative bend of the limbs will be apparent. Remember: take wood from the areas that are too stiff and don't bend and leave alone the areas that bend too much. It is helpful to mark the stiff areas with a pencil to see where to remove wood.

At this stage progress should slow to a crawl, as the rasp is exchanged for a scraper. A knife held at right angles to the wood works well. More precise than a rasp, this scraper takes off very little wood at a time, lessening the chance of removing too much. Look at it this way: another hour or two during the construction process really doesn't matter if you'll be shooting the bow ten years from now. So take it slowly.

Use long, sweeping strokes with the scraper across the area marked for wood removal. If the blade starts to chatter or make ridges, change the angle of the blade or scrape from a

Knots for the bow string. Left: A simple overhand loop is used for the top limb. Right: An adjustable timber hitch is used for the lower.

Be careful to control the bow while stringing it. A twist or slip can result in damage.

different direction. Take off 20 or 30 strokes from each area, then check the bow on the tillering stick again.

The first objective of tillering is to get an even bend in the limbs. The bow should bend gracefully from the widest part, next to the handle, to within five or six inches of the tips. The bow will have to be scraped and adjusted to accommodate the weakest place in the bow—the place that bends the most. It is similar to the weakest link in a chain. The area that bends the most should be left alone and the rest of the bow adjusted to it. You may have a 65-pound weak place and the rest of the bow still pulls 75 pounds. When the bow is tillered and evened up, it will pull about 65 pounds. Or it could be that you got in a hurry, in which case you may have a 35-pound weak place in a 60-pound bow. That is why bowyers are so popular among kids. The kids wind up with the lighter-than-intended bows.

But I hope that you proceeded slowly and your bow now has a graceful arc and both limbs have approximately equal stiffness. If the limbs bend throughout their length, but one limb is still much stiffer than the other, then slight amounts of wood should be removed from the length of the stiffer limb.

When the limbs are even, the bow is ready to be strung for the first time. You can use a commercial string, but it is much easier and cheaper to make your own. Traditionally, wooden bows were usually strung with linen, silk or sinew, which takes some practice because the fibers require splicing to make a string long enough. A much simpler alternative is to use Dacron, available on spools from most archery stores, or even artificial sinew, though this material stretches, requiring frequent adjustments. For the beginner Dacron is probably the best choice. A good rule of thumb is to use one strand for each four pounds of bow weight, though you want the string to have an

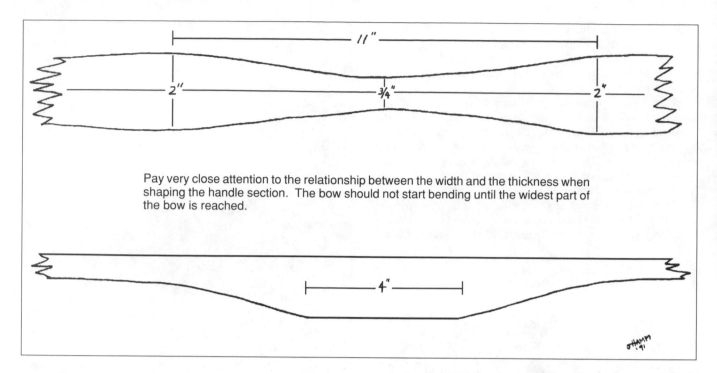

Pay very close attention to the relationship between the width and the thickness when shaping the handle section. The bow should not start bending until the widest part of the bow is reached.

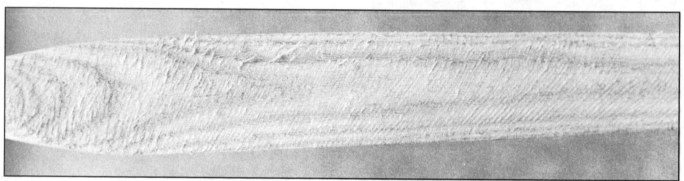

This view shows the growth rings on the belly of the bow as it is being worked.

even number of strands. Divide them into two equal bunches; seven and seven for a 14-strand string, for example. The string is made using a two-ply, reverse-wrap method, the same way cordage from any fiber is made, each half twisted clockwise and the two halves twisted around each other counter-clockwise. Sounds difficult, but after making a couple of strings, you'll be able to do it in your sleep.

Modern strings and the traditional Flemish strings used on English longbows have a loop at each end. I've come to prefer a loop on only one end, the upper one, with the string attached to the bottom limb with half hitches or a timber hitch. This method allows for quick adjustment, as well as keeping the string in place on the bow when it is unstrung. The loop for the upper limb can be plaited in when beginning the string, but a simpler and equally effective loop can be made by tying a simple overhand knot.

Once the string is complete, the bow is ready to be strung. The fistmele, or distance from the string to the bow when the bow is strung, should be about five to six inches, so that when an arrow is nocked, the feathers do not touch the bow. If you find the bow impossible to string, it is still too strong and needs to have wood removed from both limbs.

Once you have adjusted the string length and strung the

bow, check the string alignment. With your eye near one tip, look down the bow and determine where the string lies across the handle. With a straight piece of wood and careful layout of the design, the string should lie down the center of the bow, just as the design is drawn on the back. If this is the case, the handle can now be cut to final shape.

If, however, the string should lie slightly off center, then that side can become the one across which you release the arrow, the left side for right-handed shooters and the right side for left-handers. This is the advantage of making both limbs the same length. The bow can be flipped over and either limb can be on the top or the bottom.

If the string lies badly out of center, the handle may be adjusted since we left the handle section wide for just such a problem. Draw a new handle section reflecting the true position of the string, then cut it to shape.

Once you have shaped the handle, check the bow on the tillering board again. If it is still even, or in tiller, then you can

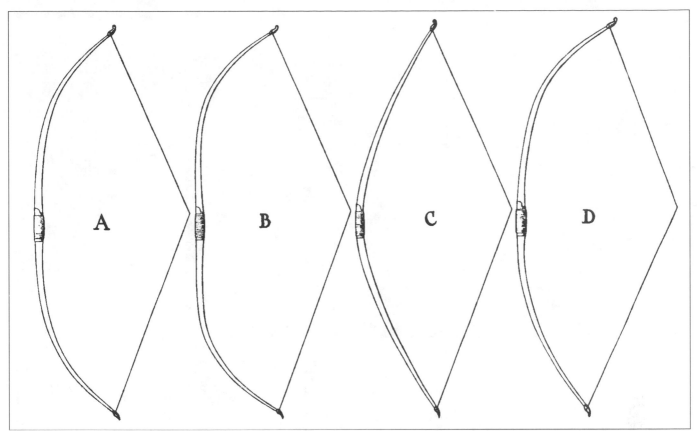

Views of a bow during tillering: (A) correct, (B) bends too much toward the tips, (C) bends too much at the handle, (D) uneven bend. Drawing based on illustration in *Archery Tackle* by Adolph Shane.

Checking the weight of the bow using a bathroom scale. The string is placed in the notch on top of the stick and the bow is pulled to draw length as marked in advance. The bottom of the stick rests on the scale.

begin to pull it. Pull gently and smoothly to about half the draw length 20 or 30 times. Check the tiller again. It may well have changed as the limbs react to the stress placed upon them. If so, mark the stiffer area or limb and make 10 to 20 strokes with the scraper. The bow can be placed in the vise while it is still strung, which saves time, but be careful not to cut the string with the back of the scraper. Take the bow from the vise and pull it again at half or two-thirds draw length. At this stage the bow must be drawn and worked every time wood is removed, even very small amounts. Remember: the first objective is to make the limbs bend evenly. From there we adjust the weight. The bow can be placed in the tillering stick and the string pulled to about half-draw and locked into one of the notches. From ten feet away it will be relatively easy to see if the limbs bend evenly and where to remove wood if they don't.

A word here about the weight of the finished bow. The amount of weight you can pull and the amount you can shoot are two different things entirely. I can pull a 90-pound bow, but I can't shoot a 90-pound bow but maybe a few shots and only with a prayer of hitting the target. You should be able to shoot your bow comfortably a hundred times or more. If you find yourself tiring and shooting erratically after two dozen shots, then the bow is too strong, no matter what its weight. Don't get caught up in the testosterone-induced fantasy that your bow

When the bow is at full draw, its weight will register on the scale. The scale must be zeroed before the draw begins to assure accurate measurement.

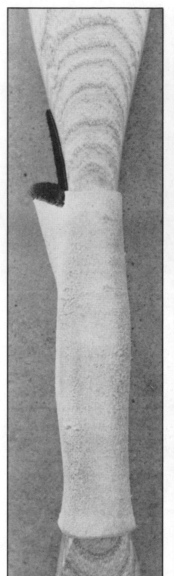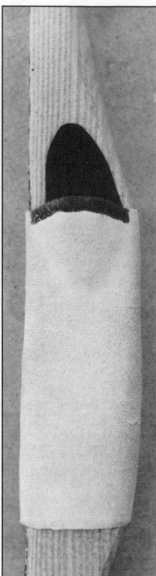

The grip and the arrow rest as seen from the belly (side facing shooter) and the side.

has to pull 80 pounds before it can kill anything. Speed is a vastly over-rated commodity when it comes to archery. It is far more important to shoot well than to shoot fast, and if a bow is too strong, you can't shoot it well. A half century ago hunters took elk, moose and bear with bows that drew 50 pounds and less, and the animals haven't gotten any tougher since then.

When the limbs are even after testing at shorter draw lengths, then the pull can be increased, feeling the strength of the bow as you go, until the bow is brought to full draw. If the bow is still clearly far too strong, do not pull it to full draw until you have reduced the weight. This unnecessarily stresses the limbs and causes them to follow the string, keeping a permanent bend when unstrung. The bow should be five to eight pounds stronger than the desired weight at this stage because it will "settle in" and lose some strength during the first few hundred shots. But again, do not pull a bow to full draw that is much stronger than the finished bow will be.

After pulling the bow to full draw with the tiller remaining even, check the weight on a scale as shown in the photo. The bow may still be too strong, in which case you should again remove wood throughout the length of both limbs. It may be that the bow is too light, which is a common occurrence with first bows. You can either give the bow to a son, niece or neighborhood child (making their day) or else cut one inch from each tip and fashion new nocks. Normally, the tiller won't change and the weight will go up. Cutting one inch from each end of a 68-inch bow will increase its weight from 50 pounds to about 58 pounds, for instance. Of course, this stresses the wood more, but with a well-tillered 66-inch bow, there should still be little danger of breakage.

Once the bow reaches the proper weight and is perfectly tillered, you should shoot it for several days. You may want to add a temporary arrow rest to prevent the arrows from cutting your hand. But the bow should be shot several hundred times to insure that the tiller doesn't change and the weight settles in

where you want it.

When you are satisfied with the bow, it is ready to finish. Round and taper the handle with a fine rasp. The edges of the limbs can be slightly rounded with a pocketknife held at right angles. Gently scrape out any telltale rasp marks, then sand the belly and sides of the bow with 220 grit sandpaper, then 320. Next switch to 400 grit, and go over the entire bow, back included. Finishing with 600 grit will leave a smooth, polished appearance.

If you plan to hunt with a white wood bow, it may be a good idea to stain or paint the back to reduce the glare. Or you may want to glue a snake skin to the back with wood glue, giving perfect camouflage and a nice finishing touch.

The bow can also be treated to help waterproof it. Animal fat or grease, applied regularly, will work, as will the modern finishes such as urethane. But I've come to prefer liquid tung oil in the form of furniture finishes, thoroughly dried and lightly steel-wooled between coats, until five or six layers have been built up. This not only waterproofs the wood but yields a

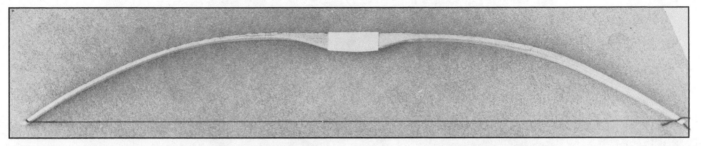

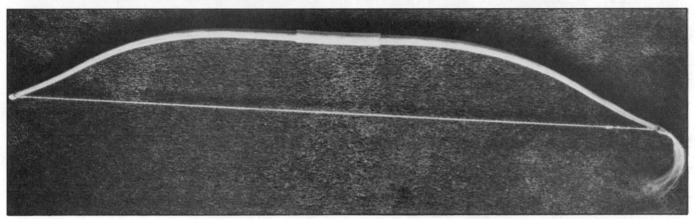

Two completed bows with proper tiller: ash (above) and hickory.

Two designs of leather-back quivers with carrying pouches for extra bowstrings and sharpening files for broadheads.

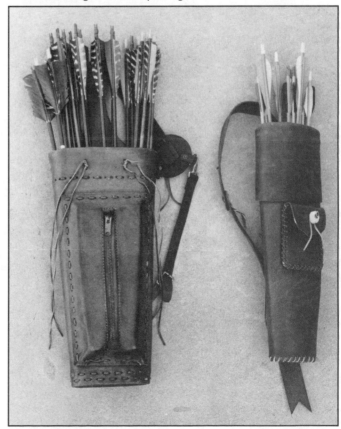

beautiful, glossy coat.

An arrow rest fashioned from harness leather and glued to the side of the bow with contact cement adds consistency to shooting and protects your hand from being nicked by feathers. A buckskin or cloth handle cemented where the hand will go completes the weapon.

Once a bow is complete, some feel compelled to make arrows to match, cutting dogwood and switch cane, stripping out sinew and flaking arrowheads from glass or flint. It is an enviable goal, using bows and arrows crafted entirely with your own hands. But since arrow-making is so tedious and a newly finished bow screams to be shot immediately, many choose to buy them ready-made, and for a beginner this is probably a realistic approach. Some of the better archery stores carry wooden arrows, and there are many custom makers listed in magazines such as *Traditional Bowhunter*. Be sure to order arrows with the correct spine, or stiffness. Arrows are spined in five-pound increments and should be matched to the weight of your bow so they will fly properly. I strongly recommend wooden arrows, as they fly straight, are effective and are beautiful in their own right. Aluminum arrows will work, technically, but shot from a hand-made wooden bow they are an affront to anyone who loves traditional archery, Mom and apple pie. It would be like mounting a variable, range-finding scope on a flintlock.

The only other gear you need is an arm guard to protect the bow hand against the slap of the string, some type of glove or tab for the fingers that draw the arrow and a quiver. Any buckskinner can make all of these accessories himself in a few

Henry Chidgey shoots his new bow for the first time. He later took a large black bear in Canada with this bow.

evenings or over a weekend.

So, these are the basics for old-time archery, and they fit the bill for those of us interested in an earlier, rustic way of life. The weapons are simple, lovely, fairly easy and inexpensive to make and, most of all, incredibly effective. Just how effective are these "primitive" bows? Every bit as effective as a laminated fiberglass bow in the same configuration and weight, as extensive chronograph tests performed by Tim Baker and myself have proven. A good rule of thumb is to add the weight of your bow plus 100 to yield the feet per second the arrow is traveling. For example, a 60-pound wooden bow (without recurves, sinew-backing or other tricks) will shoot at about 160 feet per second—more than adequate speed, with a 500-600 grain arrow, to take any game in North America. In the last five years, men have taken bear, caribou, elk, moose, deer and antelope with wooden bows, many of them shooting flint-

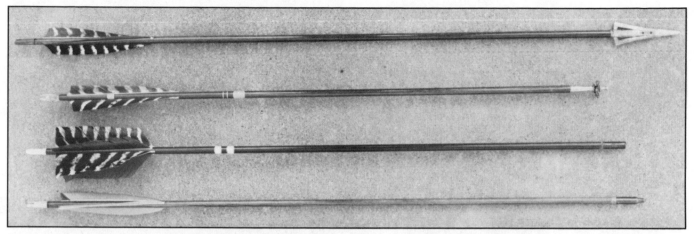

A variety of tips are used on modern wooden arrows (above). Shown from top to bottom are a steel broadhead, a Judo tip for moving and small game, a flu-flu with blunt tip for birds and squirrels and a field point for practice. Handmade wooden arrows are shown below. From the top are a dogwood-shaft arrow with a flint point, a plains style arrow with a steel point and a cane arrow with an obsidian point.

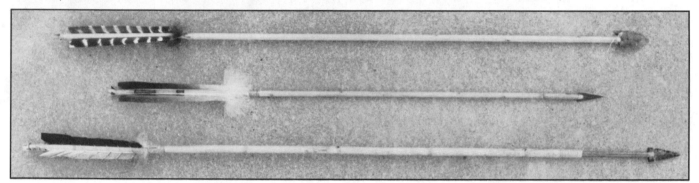

tipped arrows.

Of course, there are ways to get more speed from a handmade bow, but as mentioned earlier, speed is vastly overrated when dealing with archery. It's a question of give and take. For everything you do to increase speed, you give up something: accuracy, stability, or durability. For example, the Turkish composite bows, which pulled well over 100 pounds, were only about three feet long and reflexed to a remarkable degree. They were fast, incredibly fast, and they would shoot

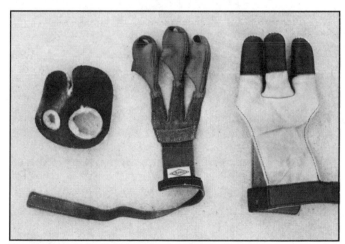

Finger guards for the shooting hand: tab, fingertip glove and full glove.

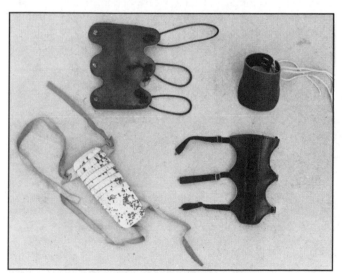

Arm guards protect against the slap of the bowstring.

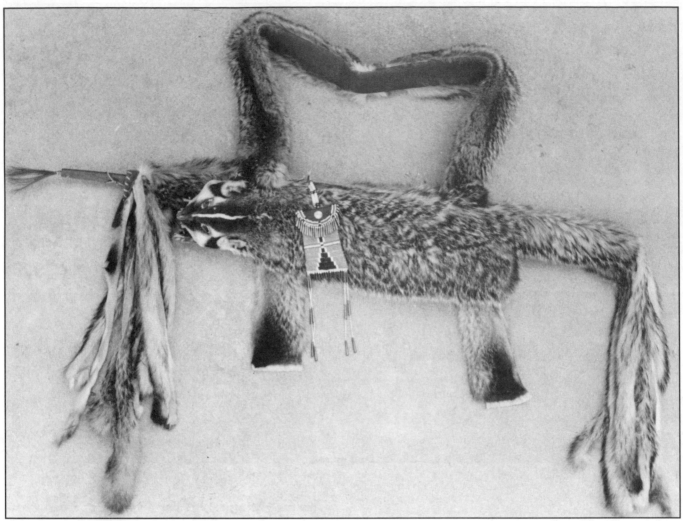

Buckskinners can create their own accessories such as this plains-style quiver and bowcase. Note as well the attached beaded pouch for flint and steel.

an arrow out of sight. But try hitting a target with a 100-pound bow that's only three feet long. To gain speed, the Turk's forfeited stability and accuracy. Conversely, a bow ten feet long would be silky smooth to shoot, with no finger pinch, but you could *throw* an arrow nearly as fast as such a bow would shoot it.

When all things are considered, a bow between 64 and 70 inches makes a good all-around weapon. It is no accident that such bows have been around for thousands of years. It is simply a bonus that they are among the easiest to make.

CONCLUSION

A final word of warning: wooden bows are like potato chips. You can't make just one. You'll know you are hooked when you gaze at a bow you just finished and think, "Next time, I want it to be a little stronger" (or longer, shorter, narrower at the handle, recurved, ad infinitum).

Experimenting with different designs is part of the great fun of traditional archery, but the secret to shooting well is making a bow that is the weight you want and sticking with it. Shoot it daily at different targets, at small game, standing, kneeling, bending, sitting and you'll soon be deadly with it

at hunting ranges. Those who practice regularly can expect to place their arrows into the kill zone of a deer every shot at 25 yards.

There are few things more rewarding than taking game with a weapon that has been fashioned purely from materials gathered from nature. The diligence and skill you develop in making such a weapon gives a tangible connection to the countless archers who stand in the shadows of our past, perhaps nodding sagely with knowing smiles on their faces.

APPENDIX A: WORKS CONSULTED

Clark, J.G.D. *Neolithic Bows From Somerset, England, and the Prehistory of Archery in North-western Europe.* England: The Prehistoric Society, 1963.

Catlin, George. *Letters and Notes on the Manners, Customs, and Conditions of the North American Indians.* Vol. 1. London: 1844.

Comstock, Paul. *The Bent Stick.* Delaware, OH: Private Printing, 1988.

Dodge, Lt. Col. Richard. *The Plains of the Great West.* New York: 1877.

Duff, James. *Bows and Arrows.* New York: MacMillan, 1944.

Elmer, Robert P. *Archery.* Philadelphia: Penn Publishing, 1926.

Hardy, Robert. *Longbow.* Portsmouth, England: Mary Rose Trust, 1976.

Heath, E. G. *The Grey Goose Wing.* Berkshire, England: Osprey Publishing, 1971.

Hickman, C. N., et. al. *Archery: The Technical Side.* Milwaukee, WI: National Field Archery Association, 1947.

Massey, Jay. *The Bowyer's Craft.* Girdwood, AK: Bear Paw Publications, 1987.

Pope, Saxton T. *A Study of Bow and Arrows.* Berkeley: University of California, 1923.

Shane, Adolph. *Archery Tackle.* Peoria, IL: Manual Arts Press, 1936.

Thompson, Maurice. *The Witchery of Archery.* New York: Charles Scribner's Sons, 1878.

If you would like to learn more about wooden bows, Jim Hamm's book, Bows and Arrows of the Native Americans, *is available for $16.95 postpaid. Jim is also the co-author and editor of* The Traditional Bowyer's Bible, *a comprehensive guide to making fine weapons from natural materials, available for $22.95 postpaid. To order books or inquire about Jim's bow-making seminars, write: Bois D'arc Press 4, PO Box 233, Azle TX 76020. Traditional Bowhunter Magazine is a good source to find suppliers of arrows and other goods: P.O. box 155831, Boise, ID 83715.*

American Powder Horns

by Mark Odle

A craftsman in every sense of the word, Mark Odle has been making powder horns since 1976. At age 21 Mark fashioned a rudimentary powder horn from an old cow's horn he found in the street in Wilmington, Delaware. That experience spawned an early interest that has continued to this day.

The son of a DuPont executive, Mark moved around the country as a youth, never getting the opportunity to sink his roots in any one location. Summers were often spent on his grandparent's farm in West Virginia where Mark learned the value of self-sufficient farm labor.

A drive toward self expression through art has carried him into combining art with his pioneer heritage. Beyond understanding the honest simplicity in stylistic folk art patterns, Mark also understands the value of mechanics. In addition he feels that the quality of the material used in his work is of utmost importance. Much of what is used is gathered and prepared by Mark himself, whether it be wood from trees cut on his property or the fine brain-tanned deerskin from the deer hunted there also.

A hunter and a woodsman, Mark knows the demands that will be placed upon his work in the field. He has studied and mastered many facets of the independent pioneer life style and tries to live accordingly on his farm near Reedy, West Virginia. He shares his interests with his wife, Anna and their daughter, Mairin.

"He who wanders far from home
With rifled gun in arms alone,
Will strap me to his breast with pride
and there shall find his powder dried!"
Thomas E. Ames, c. 1978

To the longhunter, the settler and the frontiersman who carried it and whose very lives daily depended upon it, the powder horn became a very personal part of existence. A powder horn often mirrored thoughts, feelings, philosophies, even political views in a new and often violent land. Horns reflect the times in which they were made and the personalities of those who made and carried them. They came to be valued as more than just powder containers and were displayed proudly by sentimental men long after their careers had ended. If the horns could talk, the tales they would tell; they had been there and they had seen it all.

Horns had been used for centuries but probably reached the height of artistic craftsmanship in 18th century America. Horns were certainly used elsewhere in the world, but as a powder carrier they were the first choice for many early Americans, rich and poor alike. Many males owned at least one horn for hunting or military service. It is safe to say that by the early 19th century, many rural homes had at least one gun, usually more than one. Each of these guns was attended by a horn and a pouch. Considering all these facts, one may surmise the vast number of horns made and used in North America.

For today's living history enthusiast, the powder horn presents an avenue where one may apply creative energies. Making and decorating a horn provides the opportunity to add a personal touch to an essential part of one's accoutrements and keeping the horn historically correct to one's persona should be of prime importance.

It should be noted that we are now rediscovering what was once considered common knowledge. Many pertinent facts have been lost to time. Therefore, it is sometimes necessary to make educated guesses as to what might have been. Obviously, information can be gained by studying written records of the time, paintings of the era and other contemporary sources. However, there are gaps in that knowledge and the picture is like a puzzle with pieces missing. For those who desire historical accuracy in their accoutrements, who wish to evaluate original pieces or who simply wish to know what characterizes horns from different time periods and sets styles apart, this chapter hopefully will serve to answer your questions and to further an interest in our unique heritage.

The American powder horn as we have come to know it did not just happen. It evolved along with the development of guns and gunpowder. Flasks and horns were used throughout the world to carry and store powder as the need arose. However, in America, they developed into a unique folk art.

ORIGINS OF THE POWDER CONTAINER

It is generally felt that the flask for carrying powder started its development in the 14th or early 15th century (Riling 1). It is impossible to state exactly when or where these first flasks developed or what they looked like. It is believed that the first designs included bags, pouches or pockets that carried loose powder. Woodcuts seem to indicate that around the year 1500 horns and flasks were in use. By the mid-16th century, flasks had developed patterns that would last nearly another 200 years (Riling 3). These early flasks were of two sizes: a small primer generally no more than three inches tall and a larger flask for loading the weapon (Houze XI).

Bandoleers, basically sashes or leather straps worn over the shoulder from which hung a number of pre-charged cylinders, were used in the 1400s. These pre-charged cylinders were a predecessor of paper cartridges, and by the end of the 16th century, paper cartridges had become the standard for the military (Riling 8). It was standard drill procedure both in America and Europe to prime from the cartridge, shut the pan and load the charge. Even though pre-made charges were common for the military, troops still carred horns or flasks as a secondary means of loading the weapon once the cartridges had been spent.

The military, as always, had the most standardization when it came to equipment, but standardization certainly was not the norm with the developing sporting arms and their attendant flasks and horns. Richly decorated flasks were a means of social identification, and it became fashionable to carry ornate and lavish arms and accoutrements. Flasks of every conceivable material were made including: stag antlers; ivory tusks and teeth; exotic horns; carved rare woods; turtle and tortoise shell; embossed and hardened leather, sometimes called cuir-boulli; ostrich eggs; bones; and various metals, both precious and base. They were carved, inlaid and otherwise decorated to the limit (Riling 13). Craftsmanship was unrivaled but was reserved for the wealthy client.

The powder horn was what the average man in both Colonial America and Europe carried, although it should by noted that in Europe the ownership of firearms was generally restricted to the upper classes and the military. In the new world, people found it necessary to be armed. In fact it was a must, not only for protection, but also as a means of putting food on the table. Some horns were simple affairs with the base plugged and the small end drilled and made into a spout. Some were rough, others carved. Some had mechanical closures, a holdover from the days of flasks, and others were heated and flattened. Whether it be rough and crude or refined and elegant, Colonial America witnessed the birth of the powder horn as a unique art form.

The history of the growing colonies—French, English, Spanish and others—had a direct bearing on the use and decoration of horns. Each group settling in America brought their own traditions and styles. For example one such style, as it pertains to horns, was the English Queen Anne. This style followed the European tradition in the use of flasks. Some of these flasks were brought to America, however, many were of Colonial manufacture. The Queen Annes were small, the caps easily lost, and they soon proved to be unpopular (Grant 117).

An 18th century horn flask. Sheets of horn were heated and pressed in a mold. The sides are not flat but are shaped.

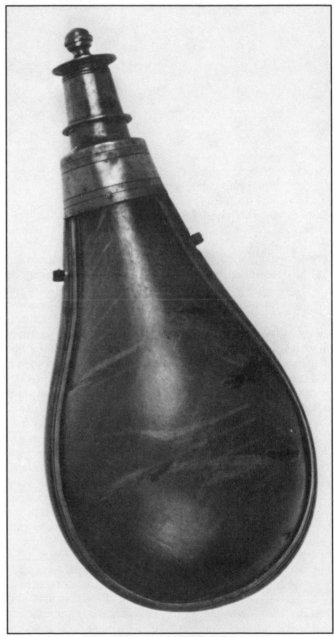

All original horns except those so noted are from the collection of Thomas Ames.

Queen Anne style, screw-tip flasks. These flasks were made in America and are considered a later style. The larger of the two has an acorn-turned top and a chestnut base. The smaller has a base of walnut.

All photos by Chuck Connors, Tantra Photographic, unless otherwise noted.

To demonstrate the distribution of the various peoples, it may be necessary to review a bit of history. By the early 18th century, French settlements had grown up around their fur trading posts from the mouth of the St. Lawrence River to the Great Lakes. They extended south to Lake Champlain in New York, then west along the Great Lakes. From there the posts went south along the Mississippi to St. Louis and New Orleans. The French were mainly interested in the fur trade while the English wanted the fur trade as well as the land. The English were boxed in between the Appalachian Mountains and the Atlantic. Land speculators hoped to reap vast profits from yet-to-be-settled areas (Grancsay 4).

In 1745, Scottish Highlanders fighting for Prince Charles were defeated at Culloden. Proscriptions sent many of these people to North America. They were soon followed by Highland regiments who were sent to fight the French and Indians (Ritchie 25). All this set the stage for the struggle known as the French and Indian War. For the better part of the next three decades, culminating with the end of the American Revolution, conflict ruled. This era was to be known as the "Golden Age of Horns," and it produced some of the finest horns with regard to their engraving and architecture.

THE GOLDEN AGE OF HORNS

The Golden Age of Horns had its beginnings early in the 18th century and came to full flower in the French and Indian War, 1755 to 1763. Although many fine horns continued to be made during the Revolutionary War, it is considered the decline of the Golden Age.

Colonial and early America was a largely rural and agrarian society. The frontier population as a whole was generally illiterate or poorly educated. Commercially made horns were not available and many horns were made by the men who carried them. These horns were mostly simple affairs, either entirely unembellished or possibly marked with just initials or a date.

As a container for powder, horn was perfect. It was not affected by water or extremes in temperature. It would neither break easily nor would it rot, and metal does not cause horn to spark. In addition, it does not readily ignite and if the horn itself was properly constructed, it was fairly airtight and watertight. Horn was the plastic of that time. There was no suitable

The British royal coat of arms engraved on a contemporary horn.

alternative that could take the place of horn. It could be used as a natural container, or it could be easily cut, shaped and molded into a multitude of other useful articles.

At this time Colonial troops and militia supplied their own equipment, but powder was provided by the army and transported in barrels or kegs on wagons. Individuals would have their horns filled from these kegs, and if they wanted their own horn back, they needed an identifying mark (duMont 4). Soldiers manning forts and outposts had plenty of time on their hands and perhaps to fill that time they would turn to personalizing their equipment. This would of course include engraving powder horns. Some of the more skilled or artistically inclined could have traded their talents as engravers or horn makers for other goods or services (Swayze 16).

The elaborate or professionally done horns were for the most part out of reach to the common man unless he had the ability to craft one himself. Thus, the elaborately engraved horns are more the exception than the rule. Many professionally engraved map horns have been found in England, leading one to assume they were made there (duMont 5). Many of these horns show little or no wear, indicating that they were not used and possibly were made as mementos or souvenirs for English officers serving in North America. However, the original idea of the map horn is thought to be Colonial (duMont 5).

The maps of the day were not particularly accurate and the ones found on horns were even worse (Grancsay 11). However, these map horns did serve an important purpose as they showed the main routes and places of note. Most of these areas were basically uncharted. No one travelled without weapons and

their attendant horns, therefore, it was natural to engrave a map on a horn. Besides, there were few printed maps and these were easily damaged or destroyed (Grancsay 4). Some map horns may have been done by army cartographers or engineers (duMont 6).

Map horns show mainly the Hudson Valley and Mohawk Valley river routes in New York which led to Canada and the Great Lakes. This was the principal region of conflict during the French and Indian War. New York map horns generally did not show much territory below Albany, as this area was fairly settled and Albany was considered the starting point for journeys to the north or west.

Map horns are not limited to New York even though these horns appear to be the most numerous. There are also maps of New England and of the Cumberland Valley route to Fort Duquesne in Pennsylvania. Fort Duquesne, later known as Fort Pitt, was situated on the confluence of the Monongahela and the Allegheny Rivers and was of vital importance as a gateway west. Horns with maps of the Carolinas, Cuba, Canada, Florida and the East Coast are also known to exist.

Besides maps, another frequent subject on French and Indian War-era horns, especially those engraved in England or those carried by English officers, was the royal coat of arms with the British crown at the top. This consisted of a shield flanked on the left by the guardant British lion facing the viewer. To the right is the chained Scottish unicorn. Around the shield is a garter with the motto "HONI SOIT QUI MAL Y PENSE," which translates to, "Shamed be he who thinks evil of it." The shield itself is composed of quadrants, the upper left of which usually has the Red Lion of Scotland and three Passant leopards walking with one paw raised. In the lower left is the Irish harp. The lower right contains the White Horse of Hanover and more leopards and the upper right quadrant has three fleurs-de-lis. Under all is the supporting banner proclaiming "DIEU ET MON DROIT," or "God and my right" (Swayze 230). It should be noted that not all the coats of arms found on horns were the same. Later, during the American Revolution, some horns carried bastardized and satirized versions of the royal coat of arms, obviously showing the American lack of sympathy to the crown.

Another subject often found on what are thought to be professionally engraved horns is Cuba. Most Cuban horns have the appearance of being engraved by one person (Swayze 18). These horns commemorate the departure of British troops from Havana on July 7, 1763, at the end of the French and Indian War (Swayze 18). These horns show Havana from the water and depict forts and other strategic locations. In the Paris agreements ending the war, France ceded control of Canada to England, and Spain, who was allied with France, exchanged control of Florida for that of Cuba, hence what came to be known as the Cuba embarkation horns (Grancsay 14).

Blank cartouches were also found on professionally engraved horns, leaving a space in which the owner's name could be added. Professional horns tend to be more thoroughly planned and display even quality throughout. Some even appear to have been varnished or shellacked, thus preserving some of the original color (Grancsay 3). From some of the styles on these horns, it is felt that the pieces originated in England and influenced Colonial craftsmen, Europe being the trend-setter.

Professionally engraved horns show much similarity, but those made by individuals for their own use or for trade to others are completely unique. The powder horn served as a sort of canvas on which a man could express himself in words or pictures, fact or fancy. As a medium, horn was perfectly suited to the folk artist. Regardless of talent, education or mechanical skill, anyone with the desire could make his mark.

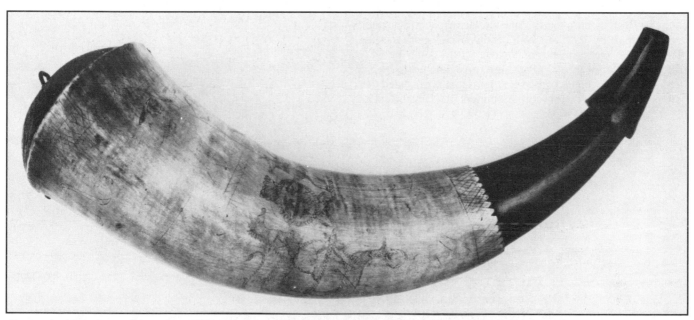

Above: An 18th century horn, circa 1755-1780, with a worked throat and spout. Engraved with a primitive version of the British coat of arms, with two unicorns instead of a lion and a unicorn. Also found on the horn is a grouse, turkey, deer and a representation of St. Paul's cathedral. Originally the horn had an extended lobe that was broken off.
Below: A small day horn with folk art engraving of fish, circa 1840-1860. (Author's collection)

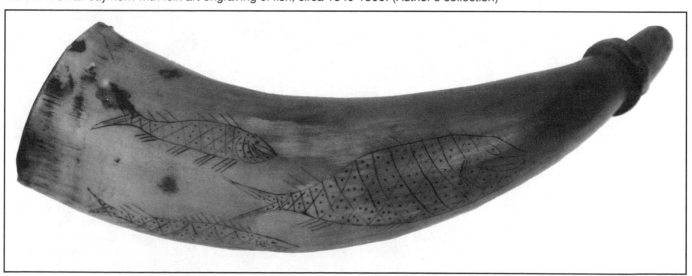

FLAT HORNS

The evolution of horn as a powder container progressed quite differently in Europe than in North America. While the Colonial American generally used a horn in its round, natural form, it was quite common in Europe to flatten or otherwise shape horn. The flask in one form or another seems to have been more popular in Europe all along, although round horns were certainly used. The flask was developed in Europe and reached its highest form there, and the craftsmanship on many of these flasks was nothing short of exquisite.

The flattened horn flask seems especially to have appealed to the Germans and Scots. These two groups developed and used them according to their own particular traditions. In 17th century Scotland, horn work played a part in the "Celtic Revival." This revival centered on some of the traditional Celtic art forms and decorative motifs. These included intricate knotwork designs, chip carving and interlacing patterns inspired at least in part by 15th and 16th century whale bone carving (Ritchie 21). Celtic-inspired powder horns could be very elaborately decorated. Highland powder horns were characteristically made of a longer horn that was heated and flattened. Horns made for more prominent individuals tended

to be carved in their entirety, while those carried by average men were more generally engraved. Traditional Celtic knotwork was commonly featured along with hunting scenes. These horns were often dated, enabling one to trace the course of the Celtic revival from the 17th century through its decline in the 18th century (Ritchie 21).

At its height several types of decoration had evolved, including concentric circles enclosing Celtic designs, bands of knotwork, coats of arms and supporters, and florals; the Scottish thistle, the English rose and the Dutch tulip were commonly used. (The tulip was inspired by William of Orange in 1689.) Gaelic writing was occasionally used as were hunting scenes and ships. Those horns engraved with ships tend to be round and are thought to be 18th century (Ritchie 21).

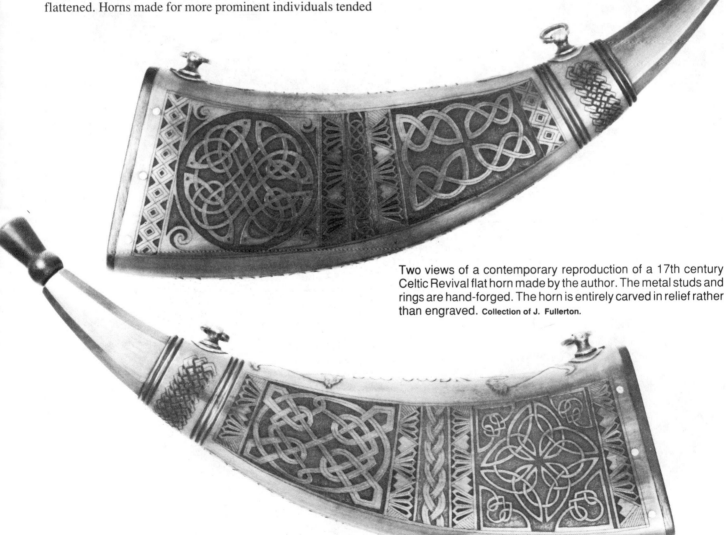

Two views of a contemporary reproduction of a 17th century Celtic Revival flat horn made by the author. The metal studs and rings are hand-forged. The horn is entirely carved in relief rather than engraved. Collection of J. Fullerton.

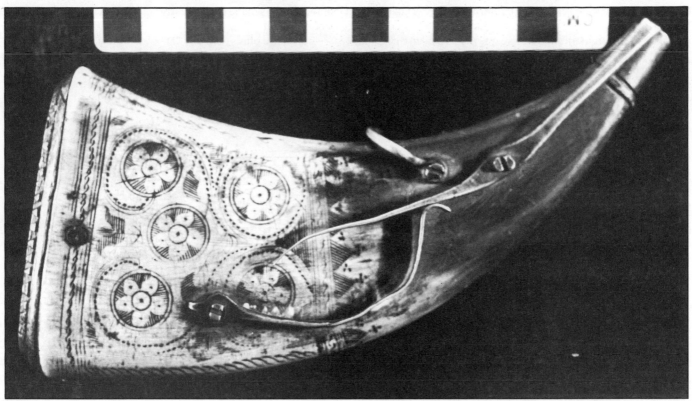

An excellent example of a mid-18th century flat horn. Hammered brass has been used to make a closure mechanism. This horn is totally engraved and has a carved base. **Collection of Jim Heck. Photo courtesy of Jim Heck.**

Two flat York County, Pennsylvania, horns. The upper horn is a screw tip and the lower is a bottle-turned or worked tip version.

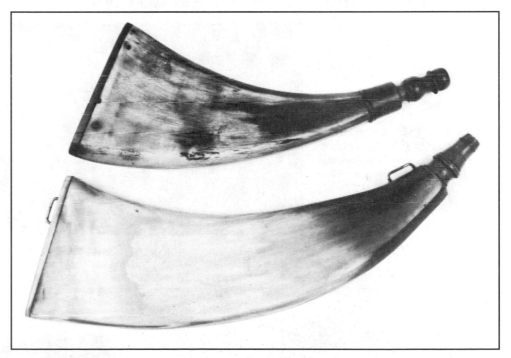

Germans also seem to have been adept at making flat horn flasks. Many early horn flasks had mountings of iron, gilt brass or bronze. These horns very often had mechanical spout arrangements. Later examples seem to lose most of the metal mountings. The horn's surface was carved as well as engraved, with martial themes, hunting scenes and florals predominating.

As Germans immigrated to North America, they brought their traditions with them and applied them to new situations they encountered. There are numerous examples of flat horns having been made in New York and Pennsylvania. Hunting scenes, hex signs, stylized florals and birds are all commonly found engraved on various horns.

In Pennsylvania, another touch was added to the flat horn. This was the screw tip, also commonly found on round horns made in the first part of the 19th century. There are examples where the tip screws onto the horn as well as the applied collar version. This type of screw-tip flat horn was rarely engraved. Bottle-turned tips were also used on flat horns.

The flat horn in this country seems to have been carried in a bag or possibly a coat pocket, although examples with staples for securing straps are not uncommon. European flat horns many times have arrangements for attaching the horn to a bag or pouch. These include metal rings or integrally carved or drilled portions on the horn and base plug itself. Many small flat horns were used as primers. The small size and flat shape of these horns made them ideally suited for a hunting pouch or a coat pocket.

The base plugs of many flat horns were also made of horn, usually over an inner wooden plug. The horn was cut, heated and flattened. The rough, flattened sheet of horn was then cut to fit the base of the flask itself and pinned to the wooden form inside. Base plugs were also made of wood and occasionally bone.

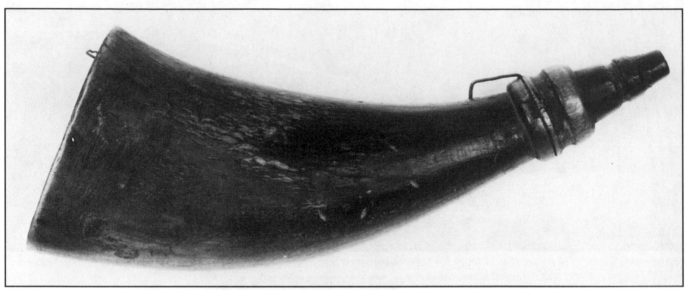

A flat Berks County screw tip. The applied collar is held in place with a staple.

This is the base of the mid-18th century flat horn pictured on page 81 showing chip carving and the date. What appears to be the initials, AVO, is actually a commonly used corruption of anno Domini, which loosely means "year of Our Lord".
Collection of Jim Heck, photo courtesy of Jim Heck.

Bases of three flat horns. From the left: A Berks County with applied collar, the base may have been altered; the middle horn is a worked tip example of a York County; and on the right is a York County screw tip. Notice how the horn base panels are pinned to the inner wooden form on the two York horns.

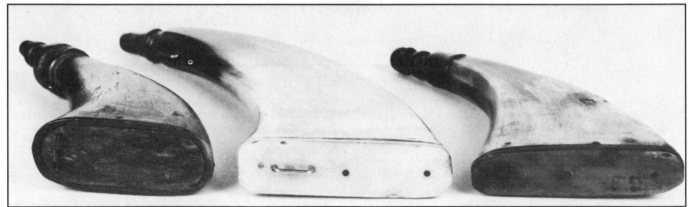

PHYSICAL CHARACTERISTICS OF POWDER HORNS

Horns were readily available, cheap and plentiful. The Bird family of Dorchester, near Boston, imported hides from Mexico, South America and the West Indies to be tanned and sold to the British Army. Horns were considered scrap and imported duty free. They cost the Birds about one cent each and were sold to the army either in the rough or trimmed and bored at a profit. These horns came from Spanish stock later known as longhorns (Grancsay 2). Horns were also obtained from Durham, Devon, Guernsey and Jersey cattle, as well as others. Oxen seemed to have large, nicely curved horns, cow horns were small and solid, and bulls carried large, somewhat straighter horns.

Horns can be classed as small, medium and large and each size had particular uses. The smaller horns were generally for priming or for use with pistols and were carried in a bag or a pocket. Medium sizes, from nine to fifteen inches, were most likely to be carried to service the rifle or the musket. The largest horns were for supply or storage and were not actually meant to be carried on the person. There were also special purpose horns, which included artillery horns, double horns, horns with internal compartments for bullets and powder, and horns with threaded finials in the base for easy filling.

Making a powder horn was a simple affair and required no special tools. First the horn was boiled to remove the core. After the core was removed, the ends were trimmed, a hole drilled for the spout and a base plug fitted. The throat was carved, making rings or a shoulder on the spout to hold the strap. Finally, the body of the horn was scraped smooth. This process produced a serviceable horn, if one chose to stop here.

In *Powder Horns and Their Architecture*, Madison Grant states:

Since the powder horn is a container, the interior of all horns performs the same function. From a mechanical standpoint the plain horn does the job as well as the most skillfully engraved piece. The so called difference in the quality of a horn then lies in the treatment of the exterior. (Intro.)

The exterior treatment of a horn comprises both the physical architecture or make-up of the horn itself and the decoration of the surface. Both of these may or may not be found on any given horn. Architecture and decoration also run the gamut as far as style, quality, inventiveness and craftsmanship.

The basic architecture or physical make-up of the horn consists of four main areas: the base plug, the body or shell, the throat, and the spout. Each of these features, in addition to surface decoration, should have consistency. In other words the horn should flow together in a cohesive manner and each element be typical of the style portrayed. The way each horn was fashioned depended upon its maker. Generally the maker followed the styles that were popular at the time, although the possible variations were as numerous as the individuals who made them. There will always be questions and exceptions concerning powder horns and their styles, however there are still major points to consider and guidelines to follow.

Horns of the 18th century were typically large, averaging eleven to fifteen inches in length. The spouts of these horns

Combination or partitioned horn. This horn has a partition pegged inside. The wooden stopper in the base can be removed to dispense balls of .40 cal. or smaller. Chester County, Pennsylvania origin, circa 1835-1860.

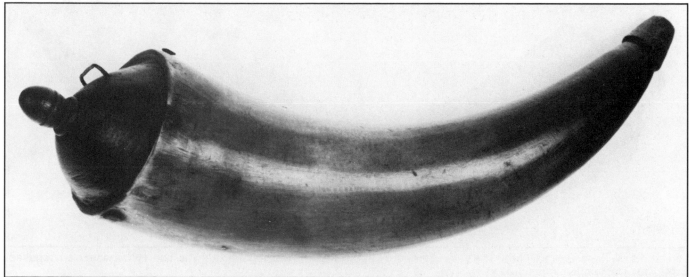

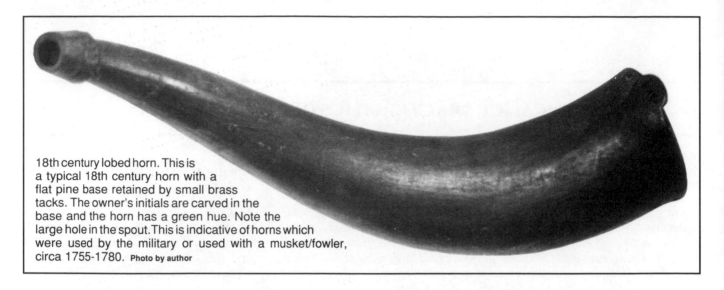

18th century lobed horn. This is a typical 18th century horn with a flat pine base retained by small brass tacks. The owner's initials are carved in the base and the horn has a green hue. Note the large hole in the spout. This is indicative of horns which were used by the military or used with a musket/fowler, circa 1755-1780. **Photo by author**

sometimes had bigger openings also. A reason for the large size could be that muskets, which were heavily used, required a larger charge of powder. Early Colonials, for the greatest part, were not well-endowed financially and used what was affordable, that being the musket. These were the primary military weapons of the French and Indian War era. An exception to size would be horns made to service the so-called Pennsylvania-Kentucky rifle. This rifle with its smaller calibers used less powder, and as it became more popular, the powder horns made to service them became smaller in size.

In addition to the larger size, 18th century horns usually had a good curve and a twist. The base plugs were flat or convex. More often than not, the plug was fitted to the natural opening of the horn, but a round turned plug would not be uncommon. The plugs were typically made of pine or poplar, since both these woods were available, easy to carve and fairly lightweight. This last point was an important consideration when one had to carry all he owned on his back. A lip or lobe often protruded from the body of the horn and was used for attaching a carrying strap. Quite frequently these lips were broken off and a staple, a nail or a screw was driven into the base plug. Also, just because a horn was damaged, its useful career was not necessarily ended. Horns were repaired with

lead patches or they were cut down. They could be returned to service in a number of other ways as well, including being wrapped in rawhide or skin.

The base plugs were often secured with small, sometimes square, hardwood pegs. Small round-headed, brass tacks were also used on early horns. Used less frequently were iron tacks.

The throat could be treated in a variety of ways including various turnings and rings. The recessed throat enabled the strap to be attached and added a decorative element as well. Engrailing or decorative carving was also popular. It is not known for sure when the recessed throat and engrailing were first introduced, but it seems likely that they were used during the first part of the 18th century (Grant 7).

The spout was also treated with panelling, or flats, and engrailed edges, and it was also carved into a classical trumpet shape. While some horns may be found with short spouts, most tended towards the longer versions.

Many early horns have black tips, which appear to have been a characteristic of some breeds of cattle. However, there are also examples where the tips have been stained. The body of the horns ranged in color from green to yellow and brown. There is much speculation concerning the color of these horns. Some think various vegetable or plant dyes were used, including

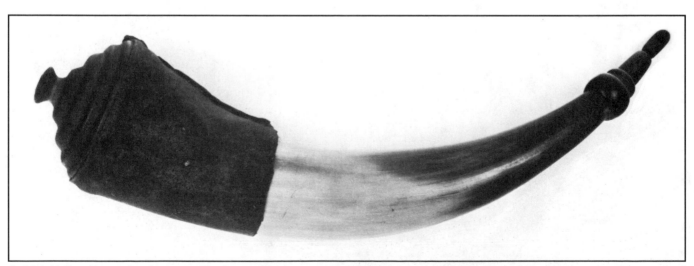

Lehigh Valley, Pennsylvania, horn. The base of the horn was cracked and was repaired with rawhide. Horns were often repaired in this way. Contemporary restoration.

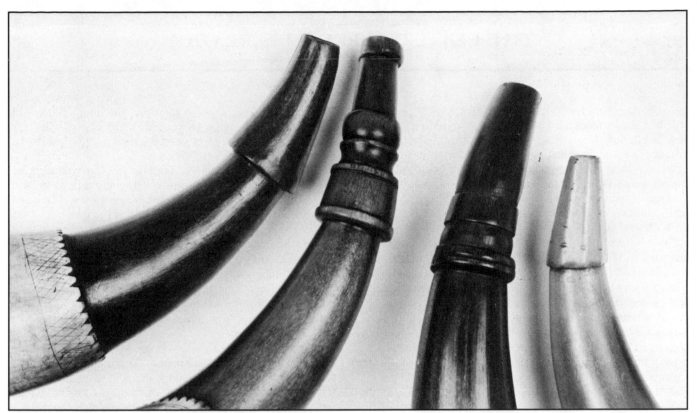

Worked spouts showing variation of treatments. From left to right: 18th century horn with engrailed edge of throat and plain spout, circa 1755-1780; horn dated 1821 by Francis Tansel with engrailed "whale's mouth" and worked spout; unidentified engraved horn, circa 1800-1830; small horn with panelled and engrailed spout from southeastern Pennsylvania, circa 1845-1860.

butternut (Grancsay 3). One theory proposes that there was a chemical reaction caused by the salt peter or potassium nitrate in the gunpowder. As the chemicals oxidized, the horn stained from the inside out (duMont 8). Still another theory with considerable merit is that horns were "dyed" more for insect protection than to color the horn. Anyone who has stored horn for a period of time can recognize the need for this. Various carpet beetles and dermestids are attracted to the protein in hair, wool, hides and horns. If these are unprotected, insects can cause considerable damage. Many old horns show that insects have been at work on them by the pits and small holes chewed in their surfaces. As noted earlier, horns were imported from various parts of the world. Transportation was slow and the unprotected horns would be fodder for bugs in the dark holds of ships. There exist a number of books and manuscripts with dye formulas for wool, silk, ivory and horn. The common factor in each of these materials is that they are animal proteins. Dyes were commonly used for many materials in the 18th century, some formulas having been used since the time of the Romans. It is speculation, but knowing that these dyes were used, it is logical to assume that they could have been applied to horns.

The yellow or amber colors on horns are thought to come from two of the most common iron dyes in the 18th century. These were ferrous sulfate, or copperas, and ferric nitrate, or nitrate of iron. Ferrous sulfate was made by reacting iron with sulfuric acid and was commonly used in household dyeing. Ferric nitrate was produced by the reaction of iron to nitric acid and its use was limited to dye houses and craftsmen such as gunsmiths.

Cupric sulfate, or bluestone; cupric acetate, or verdigris; and cupric nitrate were three common copper salt dyes. These dyes produce the various greens that are found in old horns. It is strongly suspected by some that these formulas were used to "pickle" horns, probably once they were removed from the vat used to boil out the cores. At this time such a pickling solution would enter the horn most easily and thus provide the most protection. As stated much of this line of thought is conjecture and to conclusively determine all the answers to these puzzles would require more research.[1]

[1] While much of this information is speculative, it is, however, based on fact. A number of individuals interested in historical horns as well as collectors subscribe to the theory that horns were dyed as protection from insects. Mr. William A. Knight of Reading, Pennsylvania, has been involved with the chemical industry for over thirty years and has experimented with these various dyes and the procedures necessary to dye horn. He has generously shared this information and the results of his experimentation with me. I am trying to duplicate these procedures, but more study and research is needed to come to conclusive decisions. For those interested in experimenting, the following contain recipes and processes: 1) *A Practical Treatise on the Fabrication of Volatile and Fat Varnishes, Lacquers, Succatives and Sealing Waxes.* From the German of Erwin Andres. With additions on the Manufacture and Application of Varnishes, Stains for Wood, Horn, Ivory, Bone and Leather. From the German of Dr. Emil Winckler and Louis E. Andes. The Whole Translated and Edited by William T. Brannt. Philadelphia, Henry Carey Baird and Co., 1882; and 2) *Dick's Encyclopedia of Practical Receipts and Processes.* William B. Dick, New York: Funk and Wagnall.

18TH CENTURY SURFACE DECORATION

After the horn itself was completed, scraped smooth and polished, the surface could be decorated if so desired. From the very beginning, horns have been subject to decoration. For instance an Italian horn dated 1560 in the Metropolitan Museum in New York is engraved with ancient gods, battles, ships on stormy seas, pastoral scenes, a castle and forests (Grancsay 1). Surface decoration is where the individuality of many horns really shows. Possible subjects were practically unlimited and the art found on these horns provides not only artistic interest but also biographical, geographical and historical details. The historian will find on some horns an accurate view into the past with details of flags, clothing styles, weapons, forts and towns. Names found there can be researched, providing biographical data on individuals (duMont 7).

Horns are sometimes grouped by the type of information contained in their engraving or by the area from which they originated. Some of these types are name and date horns, rhyme horns, map horns, campaign horns, naval horns, regimental horns, diary horns and location horns. There are also those that commemorate particular events such as the Cuba embarkation horns of the French and Indian War and the siege of Boston, minuteman and Canadian invasion horns of the American Revolution (Swayze 23). Many horns will carry more than one topic engraved on them such as a rhyme and a map.

While it is true that some horns of the 18th century were professionally made by gunsmiths, combmakers and professional engravers, it is safe to say that most were not and they are all different. These horns reflect the times in which they were made and the personalities of their owners and makers. Some horns had tragic themes, some were angry and some were lighthearted. Many horns carried a martial message, while still others were peaceful and were covered with vines and florals, birds, animals, ships and towns. And, of course, many map horns were made featuring towns and places that no longer exist; yet others depict actual buildings still standing today (Swayze 10).

Some horns had original sayings, verses or poems, while others carried variations on a theme. There are many horns that record the history of campaigns, expeditions and battles in which the owner participated. Some were used by more than one man and may have several names and dates inscribed.

Contemporary horn made by the author, with mid-18th century Iroquois design motifs. A lip or lobed horn with engrailed throat, this horn has typical 18th century architecture. The engraving is unique and has personal significance to its owner.

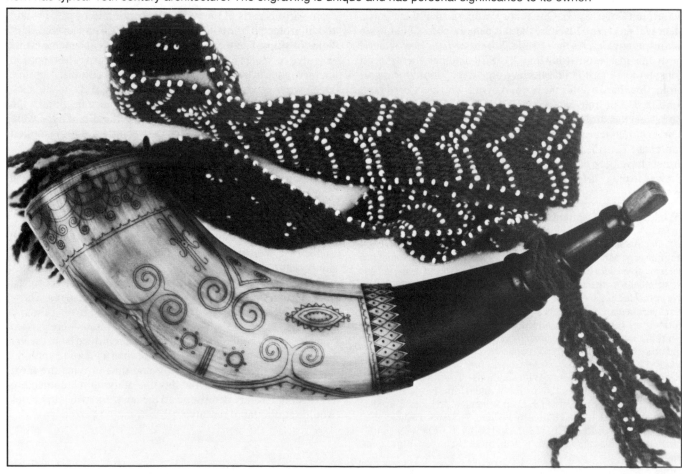

Many were handed down through families and record their use by several generations (Grancsay 5).

The decoration was sometimes planned in advance, drawn on the horn and finally engraved, but this was not always the case and mistakes are common. The design itself was engraved with the point of a knife or maybe a needle or compass. The best engraving shows signs of being done with a graver (Grancsay 3). The engraving, when completed, would be darkened or stained with soot, gunpowder dust, vegetable dyes, inks, green verdigris from kettles or vermillion red (Grancsay 3). Horns treated with these materials were termed polychrome (duMont 4).

The engraver's literacy, or lack thereof, was a primary factor in many inscriptions found on horns. Few could read or spell, therefore, phonetic spellings were common. For example: "oners" for owner's; "conker" or "konker" for conquer; and "maid" for made (Swayze 226). Many map horns from the French and Indian War had strange spellings of the names of forts and towns, such as, "Ston Rabby" for Stone Arabia and "Chinakety" or "Skenacety" for Schenectady (duMont 5).

The style of lettering was also important on 18th century horns. Capitals were commonly used in lettering and many times it was done fancifully and in an ornamental style. Often parallel horizontal lines were used so that letters would be of uniform height. Letters were often double lined and the insides cross-hatched. Some inscriptions were laid out within a given space, while others exceeded the allotted area and had to be somehow fitted to the space, often squeezing or stacking letters. Some spaces between words were marked with X's, dots or asterisks, while others were not.

By the latter half of the 18th century, American horns had developed their own styles and had evolved into a folk art unique to this continent. The skill and imagination of the engraver, whether professional or more commonly the individual with the desire, was the only limiting factor. Themes were copied from contemporary publications, period engravings or even cartoons (Grancsay 4). Among the most common themes were probably names, dates, places and rhymes. Rhymes were very popular and include religious, patriotic and humorous verse, as well as warnings. Some of the more widely known include: "I powder with my brother ball, most hero like doth conquer all"; "If I do lose and you do find, return to me for it is mine"; "Steal not this horn for fear of shame, for on it stands the owner's name" (Grancsay 37-39). There are many variations on these themes.

Diaries or travel records, in pictures as well as in words, can be found on others. In Colonial and early America, all ships sailing the seas were armed and carried powder horns. Therefore, many horns carry a nautical theme that may include ships, fish, mermaids and other fanciful creatures (Grancsay 4). Engraving of troops, forts and battles, on both land and sea, are to be found. Often, in contrast to the martial themes, many horns were engraved with peaceful memories, birds and animals, and flowing graceful florals, including the olive branch. To complement these scenes, ornamental borders often highlight areas. Sometimes cartouches are added to show important information such as a name or a date.

After the end of the French and Indian War the number of Golden Age horns made appears to fall off sharply (Swayze 19). With the onset of the American Revolution, April 19, 1775, the number again begins to increase. In this initial phase of the war, powder horns were vital, as there was no organized production of paper cartridges and their boxes (Swayze 110).

This horn is skillfully engraved with flags, banners and florals surrounding a bateau with two well-dressed female figures on board, circa 1800-1830.

While the musket was still the primary weapon of the military, the frontier rifleman with his Pennsylvania-Kentucky rifle continued to use the powder horn. These rifles were deadly accurate when loaded with patched ball and a consistent measure of powder (Swayze 11). As the fledgling American army became standardized and the production of paper cartridges and cartridge boxes was undertaken, the powder horn was less relied upon. Paper cartridges speeded the loading of muskets and the powder horn as a part of official military equipment lost much of its former importance. Of course, horns were still used and were in fact indispensable. After cartridges were shot or cartridge boxes broken or worn out, the powder horn could be relied upon again. Records of orders from Washington's headquarters show that the brigade commissaries were directed to collect all raw horns from slaughtered cattle and deliver them to the Quarter Master General to be converted into powder horns (Grancsay 9).

Contemporary horn canteen made by the author with a John Bush-style of engraving. Bush was fond of florals and his engraving style is very recognizable. The ANO over the date is a corruption of the term "anno Domini" which means "year of our Lord."

The first eleven months of the Revolution produced some of the finest horns of the war era. It appears also that most of the Revolutionary War map horns were from this initial period (duMont 7). Horns made at this time show the battles and fortifications around New York, Philadelphia, Boston and less frequently Charleston, South Carolina. A number of "Seige of Boston" horns have been found and are of great importance to historians as they show many details from the fortifications of Roxbury Camp, Bunker Hill, Castle William and Cambridge, as well as British warships in the harbor (duMont 8).

The same subjects found on French and Indian War horns, such as florals, animals, birds and martial themes, were often repeated during the Revolution. One major exception was the complete lack of sympathy for the British crown. Many horns carry patriotic rhymes and slogans championing the American cause. Contemporary publications and engravings greatly influenced the subjects engraved on these horns.

Although some makers signed their works, others did not. The styles of some engravers are quite distinctive and even if unsigned can be identified. There are horns completed by recognized hands such as that of John Bush. A mulatto, Bush made a number of Fort William Henry horns. His talented hand was forever stilled in the massacre that followed the surrender of Fort William Henry in August 1757. Other notables include Samuel Moore, Jacob Gay and Andrew Clark. Several existing horns made by Clark are totally engraved with scenes copied from publications of the time of the Revolution.

At this point it may be appropriate to mention one man who furthered the appreciation and study of early American horns: Rufus A. Grider. He was born in 1817 in Pennsylvania. In 1883, he moved to Canajoharie, New York, to teach art. He began drawing and painting scenes of local history and was soon intrigued by the early powder horns, which he drew and painted until his death on February 7, 1900.

Grider developed a method for transferring the engraving found on horns to a flat surface. His watercolors and sketches show the engraving as if the outer layer was peeled from the horn and laid flat (duMont 10). Grider's work is not exact, as he employed artistic license here and there. At times he left out material that he felt was unimportant and occasionally his renditions are somewhat different than the original horn. Regardless, these artworks are an important record and the notes that he wrote in the margins of his paintings detail known historical and biographical information associated with each horn (Grancsay 36). Grider's sketches cover a great variety of horns, including those from the French and Indian War, the American Revolution and the War of 1812, as well as Indian and hunting horns. In 1895, he catalogued 465 horns in seven classes.

There are more than 500 drawings and watercolors known to exist. The largest collection of these is owned by the New York Historical Society (Grancsay 36). Grider left a wealth of historical information for those interested in original powder horns. By studying and reviewing his drawings and watercolors, one can obtain a better picture of the styles and engravings used on early horns.

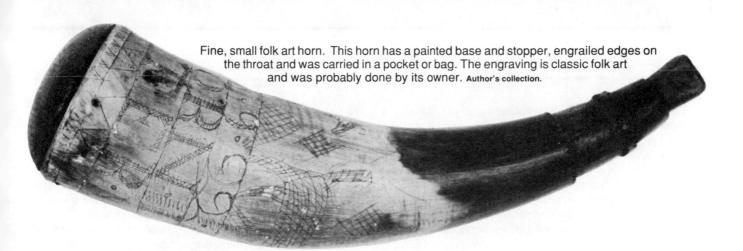

Fine, small folk art horn. This horn has a painted base and stopper, engrailed edges on the throat and was carried in a pocket or bag. The engraving is classic folk art and was probably done by its owner. Author's collection.

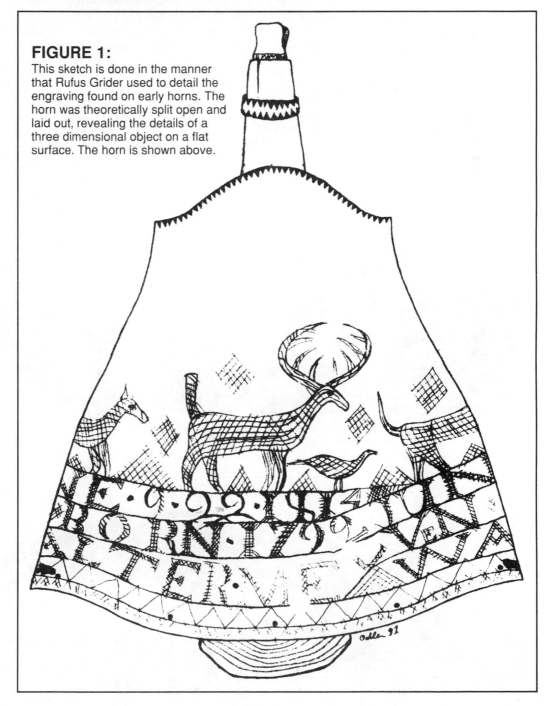

FIGURE 1:
This sketch is done in the manner that Rufus Grider used to detail the engraving found on early horns. The horn was theoretically split open and laid out, revealing the details of a three dimensional object on a flat surface. The horn is shown above.

89

19TH CENTURY POWDER HORNS

The end of the American Revolution also saw the end of the Golden Age of Horns. Beautiful horns continued to be made and engraved but the stage had been set for the coming industrial revolution and mass production. The transition from 18th to 19th century styles was gradual. Plain horns were made and used in the 18th century and highly decorated ones were made and used in the 19th century and vice versa. Unless there is an actual date associated with a particular piece, horns made from 1780-1810 may be very nearly the same in many respects (Grant 12).

With the approach of the 19th century, popular trends continued for some time as a gradual transition took place. Spouts tended to get shorter and there was less emphasis on engraved decoration. Base plugs were more likely to be turned than hand carved and the turnings were elaborate (Grant 14). Details became less intense, although early features could still

be found. This era can be hazy in regards to particular styles, and while most people with antique objects like to give them the earliest possible date, without a compelling reason to do so, one should err on the conservative side.

The 19th century itself brought many profound changes. Styles changed and so did horns. The horns themselves became smaller, generally around eight to ten inches. There is less in the way of handwork and decoration and more machine work, especially lathe turning. The fancy hand carving on the throat had disappeared, leaving a simple ring on the shoulder of the spout to secure the forward strap. The rear strap was secured at the base with a staple, an integral finial, a nail or screw (Grant 2). Horns became increasingly mass-produced and less individualistic. As early as 1800, Louis Enters of Philadelphia was supplying the government with powder horns on contract. He was paid fifty cents each. On April 27, 1815, he contracted

Lehigh Valley, Pennsylvania, horn. The turned base features concentric rings and is painted red and yellow. The engraving includes an eagle or "distlefink" with florals and the date, 1809. Also engraved is a hex wheel and the unique Lehigh Valley "Indian head." Just above the date can be seen a round hole repaired with a lead patch.

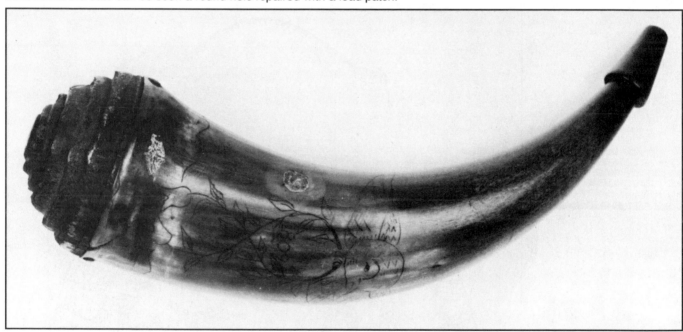

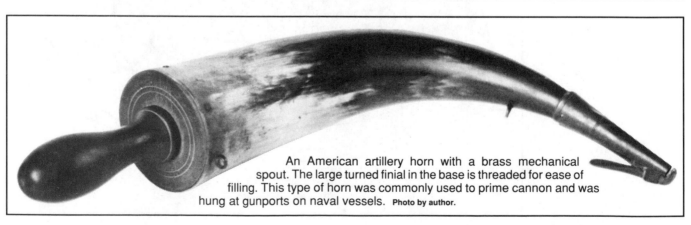

An American artillery horn with a brass mechanical spout. The large turned finial in the base is threaded for ease of filling. This type of horn was commonly used to prime cannon and was hung at gunports on naval vessels. Photo by author.

to deliver 1000 finished horns in one year at ninety cents each (Riling 87-88). Horns fitted with mechanical closures were made by and for the government. Some are marked with dates and arsenal names. Early contract horns had walnut base plugs with a threaded wooden finial and are thought to date from 1790-1812. In government records from the early 1800s, there are several mentions of orders for horns and prices paid. These horns were generally referred to as artillery gunner's priming horns or rifleman's horns (Riling 88, 89).

At this point the industrial revolution began to change America forever. Commercially made horns were introduced, and there are numerous examples of advertisements from hardware and sporting goods stores listing powder horns for sale. An advertisement run by G.W. Tryon of Philadelphia in 1819, shows powder horns for sale (Riling 17). The demand for powder horns intensified, fueled by westward expansion. By the end of the first quarter of the 19th century, commercially made horns were being produced by combmakers, factories and gun shops (Grant 38), but these commercially made horns are easily distinguished from the handmade variety. Commercially made horns don't have the individuality exhibited in handmade horns. Standardized, machine-turned plugs were placed on hundreds and thousands of factory horns from this time period.

Handmade horns were still being made, whether out of personal preference, lack of funds or inaccessibility. In some of the more remote areas and backwaters, things changed slowly and the early styles were retained longer. One notable exception to the commercially mass-produced horn occurred along the Ohio Valley in the 1820s and 1830s. Horns made during this time along the Ohio exhibited some of the earlier features, including the carved spout, rings and engrailing, along with fine engraving. These horns were very popular in the Black Hawk War of 1832.

Tansel horns are another excellent example of the resurgence of some of the 18th century styles in handmade horns. From the 1820s through the 1840s, John, Francis and Timothy Tansel made and engraved horns that can generally be recognized as their work at first glance. They can be easily distinguished from true Golden Age horns of the 18th century by the style and subject matter of their engraving. Another characteristic feature sometimes found on Tansel horns was the engrailed whale's mouth throat and spout.

In contrast to these "throwbacks" to an earlier age, most mid-19th century horns had shorter, very plain spouts, and it was common at this time to use small iron tacks to secure the base plugs (Grant 41). All in all 19th century horns generally tend to be plain and this eventually became the new standard.

As the country expanded westward, most manufactured goods came from Eastern establishments. Even in mass-produced items there were regional characteristics. These characteristics can help to identify the origins of many horns. For instance a number of southern Virginia and northern North Carolina horns are stoppered with heavy leather stoppers. Turned bone or antler tips also seem to indicate a Southern origin. The Pennsylvania Germans and North Carolina Moravians frequently used traditional designs, which aid in identification of horns from these areas. However, it is southeastern Pennsylvania that lays claim to one of the most notable characteristics found on commercially made horns. This feature is the screw tip.

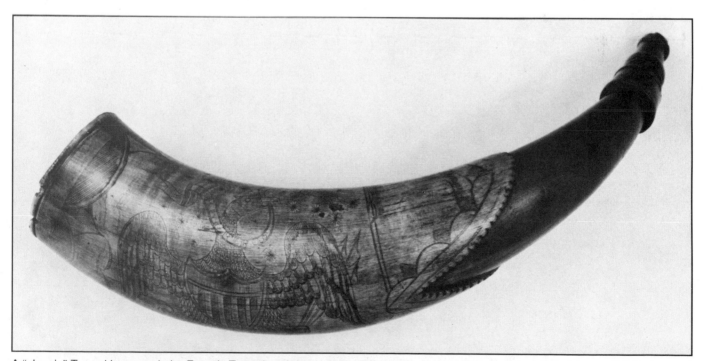

A "classic" Tansel horn made by Francis Tansel and dated 1821. The cameo cut spout is done in a "whale's mouth" design and is often found on Tansel horns. The engraving is also very typical of the Tansels with a Federal eagle, snake, deer, cannon and banners featured. It is a first-class example of horn work.

THE SCREW-TIP POWDER HORN

There are numerous examples of the 18th century powder horns which have threaded base-plug finials, but only a few 18th century tips exist. Not much is known about when the screw tips first appeared or about their subsequent development. Regardless of what had been done previously, it is generally felt that the first quarter of the 19th century produced some of the finest screw-tip horns.

The bodies of screw tips tend to be very plain although examples are known to exist that exhibit stain decoration and at least one that appears to have "factory" engraving around the base. The architecture is their primary attraction, with smooth flowing lines and an overall graceful appearance. The base plug and screw tip are subject to numerous variations and some collectors and those who study horns tend to class screw tips by these specifics in their architecture and the geographical area of greatest concentration.

York County, Pennsylvania, is one of those areas; horns originating there are considered among the best. There are several variants, but the "classic" York County horn will likely feature several elements, including a finely turned base plug made out of fruitwood such as apple or cherry. This plug will often exhibit rope and/or chip carving around a concave center that will also have a wire staple. Turned concentric rings are also evident on the domed base plug, which has its interior hollowed out. The plug will be secured to the horn with wooden pegs, often three to five in number. The body of the horn just ahead of the base will usually have two incised grooves. Another staple will often be found at the throat next to the threaded portion of the spout along with a couple of turned rings (Grant 60).

The York County's tip will always have female threads and screw onto the horn. Once again, the turning is finely done, often with three to seven grooves decorating the tip. The profile of these horns is harmonious and the lines flow together gracefully. Only the best material was used in their construction. Collectors believe the earliest screw-tip horns exhibit the best workmanship and that as time progressed some of the finer details were lost.

It is thought that comb makers and horn workers made the majority of screw-tip horns. At the time horn workers made many commonly used items (Grant 60). It is possible that the turned work, bases and tips, was contracted out to professional turners and the completed pieces assembled by the horn worker. There is a floor plan for a 19th century horn working shop in Lancaster, Pennsylvania, taken from a city map drawn up for fire protection services. This was D. Graham's Lancaster Comb Factory. It includes an open shed and a bone shed that was probably a raw material warehouse. There was a steam boiler room, a saw and a press shop, and a finishing room and a warehouse. The latter was probably for storing finished

A typical York County, Pennsylvania, screw-tip horn. This horn features the various elements that make up the York County screw tips. Included are: rope carving on a well turned fruitwood base, a seven slot turned screw tip, wire staples, and a plain but graceful shell or body. **Photo courtesy of Tom Ames.**

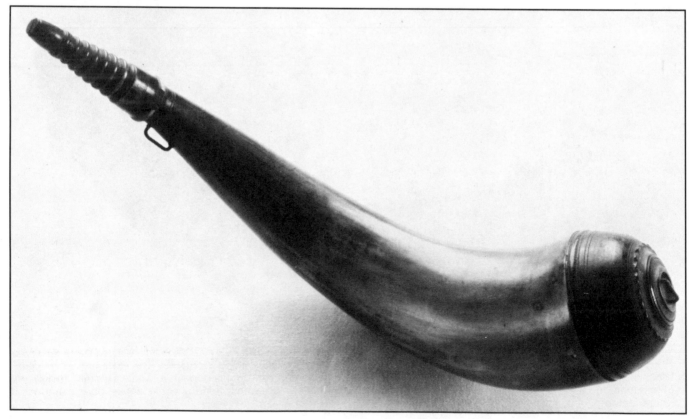

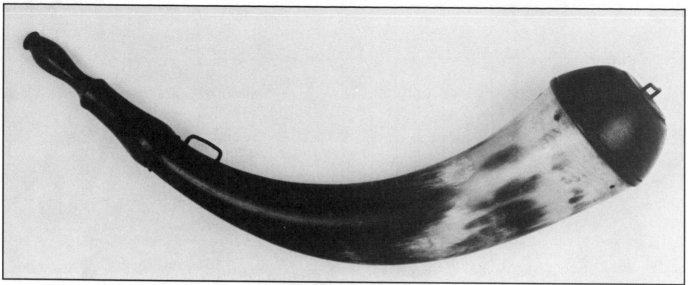

An early pattern Lancaster County, Pennsylvania-style screw tip. The bulbous apple base is retained by hardwood pins. The screw tip itself is a gracefully turned "urn" style.

A detailed comparison of Lancaster base plugs. On the left is the bulbous early style while on the right is the flatter later version with an impressed rope design.

products. The press shop included screw-type presses. While there is no specific mention of a lathe shop, no one can be sure what machinery may have been present in the finishing room.

Screw-tip horns were also made in Lancaster County, Pennsylvania, and are somewhat similar to the York County horns. Again the body of these horns was very plain and as a rule featured no engraving. Early Lancaster screw tips had bulbous fruitwood base plugs, also hollow inside. A few later Lancaster screw tips have been found that have mahogany and pine bases. Lancaster plugs were usually plainer than the York versions but were also secured with wooden pins. Later variants tended to be flatter with impressed rope or similar designs around the staple. The tips once again had female threads and screwed onto the horn. These threads were usually very fine. The early tips were long and quite graceful with careful workmanship in evidence. Lancaster tips were inclined to be less intricately turned than those on York County horns and appear smoother with few if any rings or grooves (Grant 63). The shape of Lancaster tips could be likened to that of a slender urn. Later versions of these tips are shorter. The shape of the horn as a whole seems to reflect that of the tip, being long and graceful with smooth flowing lines. As with the

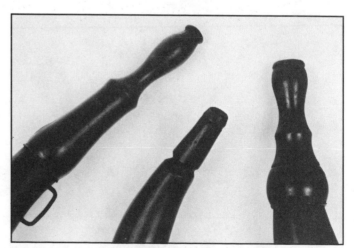

Three different Lancaster tips. The left and right tips are classic "urn" style screw tips, while the middle one is what is termed a bottle turned tip, which is not threaded and is not removeable.

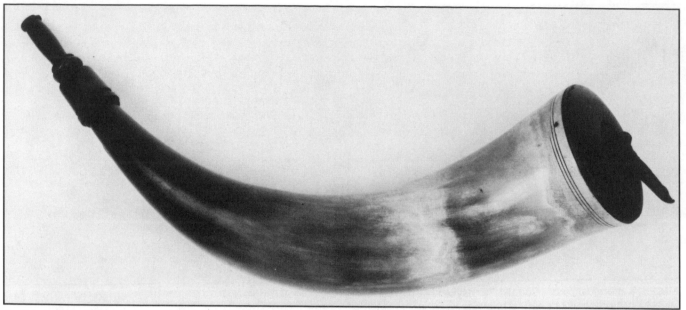

An Adams-Franklin style screw tip. This horn features a flat hardwood base retained with wooden pins. Three grooves are apparent at the base above the pins. The screw tip can be described as a deeply turned "nozzle" with female threads. There is a staple just below the screw tip.

York County horns, these almost always have a staple at the throat (Grant 63).

Another distinctive style is the Adams-Franklin County screw-tip. Common features of these include a flat hardwood or fruitwood base plug pinned to the horn with small wooden dowels. The face of the plug may also have concentric rings turned around a concave section containing a staple for attaching a strap. Usually three grooves are turned in the horn at the base. Another staple will be present at the throat. The tip will contain female threads and will have deeply turned areas or grooves looking very much like a "nozzle."

Often a Philadelphia style is included among the screw tips. The basis for this style classification is the vicinity in which they are found and their unique design features not found elsewhere. These horns are sometimes also termed

Base plugs of Adams-Franklin (left) and Philadelphia (right) screw tips. The Adams-Franklin is fairly flat and made of walnut. The Philadelphia style is more domed, made of mahogany, and features a flat brass staple.

"fancy." Mahogany seems to be used frequently in their base plugs, which often have mirrors or flat brass plates with a ring in the center for strap attachment. Mahogany was imported to Philadelphia cabinet makers and therefore common to the area. It is not known how widespread was the use of mahogany for base plugs. It is found occasionally in other styles, for example, Lancaster horns.

The late Philadelphia style had a turned base plug secured with wooden pins or at times brass or iron tacks. The plug was often slightly raised with an impressed design. The screw tip was female threaded, vaguely similar to the Adams-Franklin in style but more refined and without the deeply turned grooves.

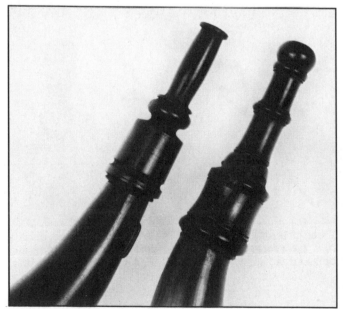

Left: A comparison of the Adams-Franklin (left) and Philadelphia (right) versions of screw tips. Fine craftsmanship is evident in both examples.

In addition to the usual iron staples to retain the strap, the use of turned brass bases with a split ring attached or even brass staples has been noted from this region.

"Associated Berks-Lebanon" is the term applied by some to another group of screw tips. Berks-Lebanon denotes a larger geographical area in Pennsylvania where this type of horn is thought to have originated. The Associated Berks-Lebanon-style screw tip seems to have been heavily influenced by the Pennsylvania Germans who settled this region. The architecture of these horns tends to be bolder and stouter, especially when compared to an early Lancaster-style screw tip. A primary characteristic of this style is an applied collar at the throat. The collar was turned, heated and applied hot to the throat of the horn. As it cooled it shrank and formed a tight fit. The collar was further secured with a wire staple that also served as a forward strap attachment. The horn was then drilled and

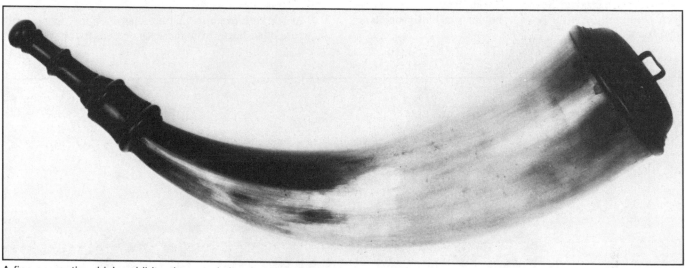

A fine screw tip which exhibits characteristics that some collectors feel indicate a Philadelphia origin. The other side of the throat has a flat brass staple.

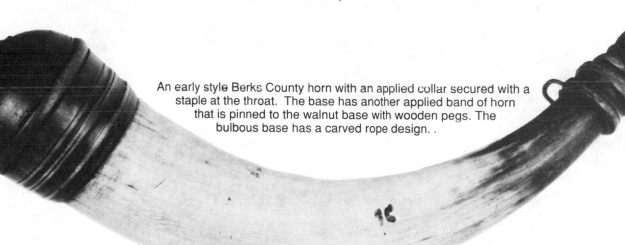

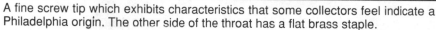

An early style Berks County horn with an applied collar secured with a staple at the throat. The base has another applied band of horn that is pinned to the walnut base with wooden pegs. The bulbous base has a carved rope design. .

An Associated Berks-Lebanon screw tip. Again there is the typical applied collar at the throat. The bulbous base has an integral wooden finial, concentric rings and chip carving that forms a "rope."

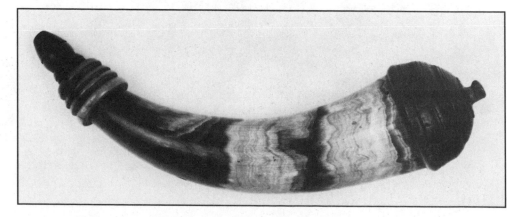

tapped, forming internal, female threads integral with the body of the horn. The screw tip was turned and male threads applied. The threads on the associated Berks-Lebanon horns are much coarser than those found on other types of screw tips. The threaded portion of the tip is usually no longer than 3/4-inch. The body of the horn typically appears as the other screw-tip styles. Walnut seems to have been a popular base plug material. The plugs were domed and the bottom edge next to the horn generally had a slight overhang. Concentric rings, chip or rope carving is also used on the plugs. For strap attachment, staples were commonly used on the base, but integral button finials are also found.

Screw tips have also been found in North Carolina and the South. They appear to be quite different than those found in Pennsylvania. The base plugs tend to be very bulbous with walnut or cherry being popular woods. A feature that seems to be indicative of Southern screw-tip horns is the frequent use of bone or antler in the construction of the screw tip. Turned bands of horn are sometimes found applied to the body of these screw tips. As with most screw tips, the workmanship is very good, although Southern horns are generally plainer with less evidence of turned decoration.

In addition to horns that are classified as "screw tips," there are other horns from these same areas that have similar

Above: Variations of Berks County and Associated Berks-Lebanon screw tips and applied collars. The collars on horns one, two and four all appear to have come from the same shop.

Below: Three different versions of Berks and Associated Berks-Lebanon base plugs.

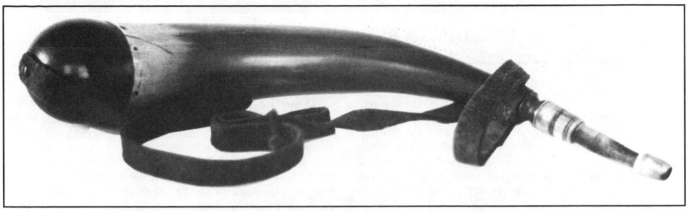

This Southern screw tip has a plain bulbous base plug of cherry. The long slender tip is turned of antler. Bone and antler tips are indicative of Southern origins. **Photo by author.**

characteristics but that do not have a threaded, removable tip. These horns have worked tips that may have been hand-filed or turned out on a lathe. These tips are often referred to as "bottle turned." These bottle-turned-tip horns will feature the same regional base plug styles that their screw-tip brethren have.

Regional characteristics, individual preferences and traditional styles have all influenced the making of powder horns. There are numerous styles and variations that are reflected in both the architecture and engraving, and these can sometimes aid in identification. When looking at an early horn, take into consideration all the different facets of its personality. Just because a horn has an 18th century furniture pull for a finial does not necessarily make it an 18th century horn. Look at the entire picture, not just one corner. It would be impossible to state absolutely the origin of each and every old horn, as there are so many variables, however, by carefully paying attention to details, one may fit a few more pieces to the puzzle.

The upper horn has a version of the bottle turned Lancaster tips while the lower horn is a flat York County-style with a worked tip.

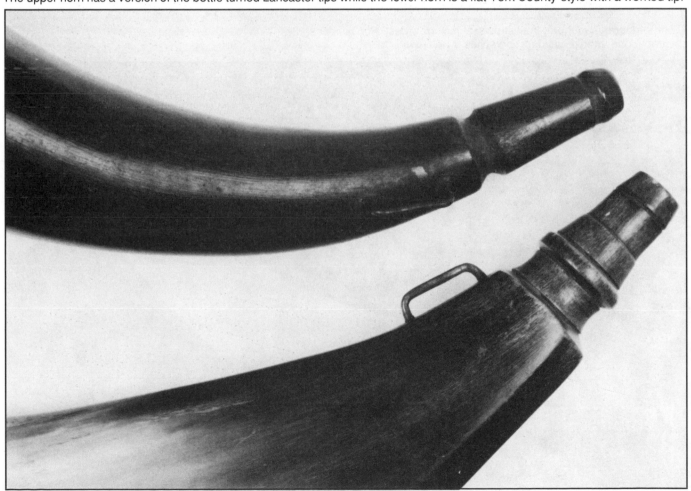

BUILDING A PERIOD POWDER HORN

For those of us who step back into history and continue to use the powder horn, it behooves us to pay attention to the small details that make up the whole of our chosen personas. Likewise, the powder horn is also made up of these small details. Other than the decorative aspects that the overall architecture and engraving of the horn can impart, these small details can add realism and enjoyment to one's horns and authenticity to one's persona.

For those interested in building a horn, Don Wright's excellent chapter in *The Book of Buckskinning II* is a good place to start. Mr. Wright covers in detail the basics of horn building that are essential to producing a functional and visually pleasing powder horn. In addition to Mr. Wright's article, the following considerations may also prove useful.

The spout hole should be drilled and the hole tapered with a tapered reamer. Anyone who has ever tried to get a wet stopper out of a straight hole in a hurry while on a deer hunt will relate to this. The stopper should also be the same taper (male to female horn). If properly made, the fit will be watertight but will allow a damp stopper to be easily removed with gentle twisting.

In securing the base plug to the horn, pay attention to the fit. Do not use glues or epoxies. If the wood to horn fit is tight, it will not be necessary. For added protection or for filling small gaps, beeswax will work just fine. For "18th century" horns, hardwood pegs add an authentic touch when pinning the base plug to the horn. These work well if an oversized square peg is driven into a round hole just until tight. Soaking the pegs in varnish or linseed oil will "set" them once they are driven into the hole. Round-head brass tacks are also acceptable. Iron tacks are usually found on later styles.

When finishing the body of the horn, whether or not the surface will be engraved, the horn should be scraped, not sanded. After examining the surface of early horns, it becomes apparent that these horns were scraped, as the marks are still there. Much has been said and written about horns scraped with glass, but it is not very effective. Glass is not hard enough and your horn, and quite possibly your hands, will be embedded with glass shards. Try it if you need convincing. Eighteenth century craftsmen used scrapers to impart a very fine finish on everything from furniture to gunstocks. A steel scraper can be made and even a knife blade will work. *Old* hand-saw blades make very fine scrapers and can be made into practically any shape needed. The scraper also leaves the grain and pores of the

A contemporary art horn that shows a mix of styles. For historical accuracy, one should avoid mixing styles. **Private collection**

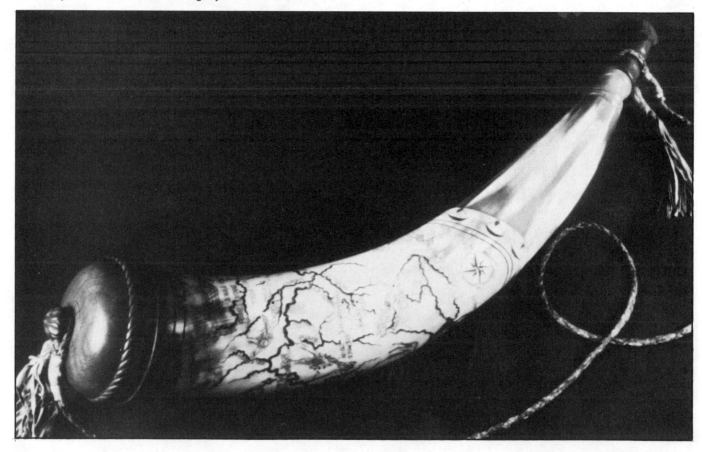

horn open so that stain will adhere better. Sandpaper was available but was used only if there was no other way to get the job done.

The use of abrasives was generally limited to the loose variety. Just as with sandpaper there were various grits, and leather was used as a backing material. The records of early gunsmiths show inventories of buffing leather. The leather was lightly oiled and sprinkled with loose abrasive, and then the surface was buffed. After scraping the horn, you could buff the surface in this manner to remove the edges of the "flats" left by the scraper. A high gloss on the horn's surface is not desirable,

and it is not necessary to remove all tool marks.

When building a powder horn, keep in mind the time period you wish to portray. Stay within this time period and don't mix styles. For instance an applied collar, Berks-Lebanon County horn would not have French and Indian War-era engraving on it, or for that matter any engraving. Strive to make all the parts of the horn—the base plug, the body or shell, the throat and the spout—flow together into one homogeneous piece. Research and forethought can make the difference between a fair piece and a really fine powder horn.

CONSTRUCTING A FLAT HORN

The construction of flat horns is somewhat involved and there are several points to consider. As in the construction of any sort of powder horn, the selection of the horn itself is of prime importance. The adage "you can't make a silk purse from a sow's ear" holds true in most work. You owe it to yourself to be selective in the material you decide to use. Practice with the poorer quality pieces and save the best horn for finished work. Look for horn with good, consistent quality and even texture. The horn should not have any twist, as this will needlessly complicate matters. The horn should not be too thick nor should it be paper thin. For the base end, just under 1/8-inch is about right. Remember, most horn gets progressively thicker closer to the tip. Steer horns seem to have a fairly consistent wall thickness until one encounters the solid tip.

Avoid horns with obvious defects, which may include cracks, dents or cuts. Remember to check the inside of the horn also. Any horn can be flattened, however, some just seem to lend themselves better to this sort of thing. I personally prefer amber or light colored horns. Black horn and horn from beef cattle tends to be coarser and the surface will often contain flaws after the horn is pressed.

As far as size is concerned, most of the original flat horns I personally have seen have been around seven to nine inches long if measured around the curve. I don't recall seeing any over twelve inches long. Naturally the smaller the horn, the easier it is to press. To start with, it may be advisable to use a horn around five or six inches long.

This may be a good place to once again refer one to Don Wright's chapter in *The Book of Buckskinning II*. I strongly suggest that one know how to build a "round" horn prior to undertaking a flat one. Mr. Wright covers the subject in detail and many of the tools and techniques will be the same. The only other tool necessary to build a flat horn is a heat source. This could include anything from the kitchen stove to a charcoal brazier or a kerosene heater. The only sources I am aware of, pertaining to the heating of horn by original hornworkers, describe the use of charcoal grills or braziers. It was usually an apprentice's job to actually "roast" the horns or sections thereof, depending on the job at hand. As to boiling the horn, it can be done for smaller, thinner pieces but will not sufficiently heat larger or thicker horn to the point necessary to adequately soften it. Boiling takes longer to soften horn and the horn must stay clamped until completely dry to prevent its "memory" from returning it to a partly round state. Dry heat is faster, but

the potential for burning or overheating the horn is greater. I do not know specifically what the temperature has to be in order to soften horn. I would *guess* it to be around 300-350 degrees. I use experience as my guide and carefully observe the horn that I am heating.

You will need smooth, hardwood boards or better yet metal plates to sandwich the horn when pressing. It is important to remember that heated horn is very plastic, and it is easy to emboss any surface texture into the horn's flattened surface. I have found that smooth metal plates of sufficient thickness so as not to bend are the most effective. I heat these plates prior to pressing the horn as further insurance that the necessary heat is present to complete the process. Hardwood boards will work but they cannot be heated, and generally the grain will be embossed into the surface of the horn.

Before actually heating and pressing the horn, there are several steps that if followed will make for a better finished piece. After selecting a suitable horn, file or scrape its surface smooth and free of scale, cracks, dents, cuts, bumps and other minor surface imperfections. If you press the horn with these on the surface, the finishing process will be much more difficult. I generally trim the base and drill an undersized hole

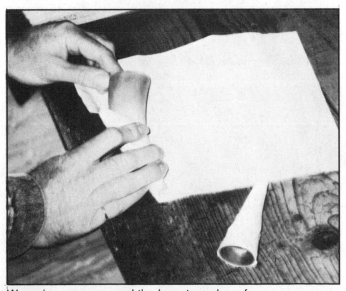

Wrapping paper around the horn to make a form.

99

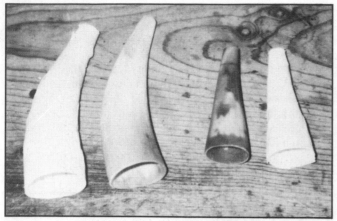

The horns with their respective paper forms.

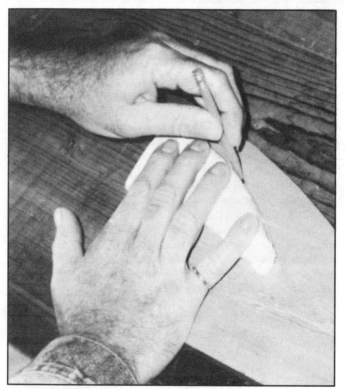

Flattening the paper form and tracing around it on pine.

for the spout at this time also. I drill a smaller hole than will be used in the finished horn because the hole will often be deformed in pressing and will have to be re-drilled and tapered anyway.

The next step will help to make the flattened horn evenly pressed and the base form properly. Take a sheet of paper and wrap it around the horn. It doesn't have to be perfect nor does it make any difference if it wrinkles. Wrap it as tightly as possible and tape it so that it doesn't come undone. Trim the paper even with the base of the horn. The horn should slip out of this paper form easily. You now have a paper mold of the horn that will be used to make an inner wooden form. This inner wooden form helps to make the base properly shaped and prevents the body of the horn from collapsing when pressed.

I use scraps of 1" x 12" pine sheathing for the inner forms, because it is easy to obtain and work. Choose a clear piece of wood free of knots or cracks and lay your paper form on top so that it follows the grain. Determine how thick the flattened horn is to be and gently flatten the paper so it is about the same. It doesn't have to be exact. Remember the tip of the horn is fairly solid and that most of the flattening will take place on the body of the horn. Trace around the pressed paper form. You now have a shape that can be sawed out. This rough blank needs to be profiled in order to make it useable. Either file or saw the blank evenly on both sides to make a flowing taper that will fit inside the hollow horn after it is heated. All edges of the form that will contact the inside of the horn should be rounded and smooth. It takes practice and experience to get this just right, and I often have to do some alterations.

After you are satisfied with the form the next step will be to cut kerfs that follow the shape of the form. These should extend at least half the length of the form from the base toward the tip. Next, cut small wedges that will fit into the kerfs but will not be wider than the form is thick. Wax the form all over with paraffin so that it can be easily removed once the horn is flat and cool.

You are now ready to proceed with the actual flattening of the horn. Have all your materials at hand so vital heat will not be lost while you search for something. The horn can be flattened with a vise, C-clamps or any other suitable type press.

Several inner forms with kerfs cuts following the shape of the forms. Also note the pile of wedges cut to fit into the kerfs.

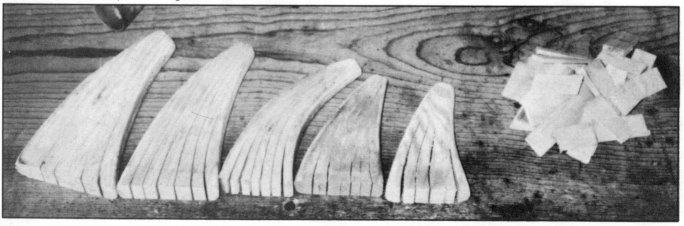

The author's horn press. For pressing horns, metal plates are placed above and below the horn to be pressed.

I use a small printer's block press. This type of screw press is very easy to construct and use. Once again, the heating of the horn is a matter that takes practice and experience. When the horn is hot enough, it will be very obvious, because it is quite malleable and will bend easily. Keep the horn several inches from the heat source and heat it evenly. The thinner base will heat faster than the tip, so it is advisable to start heating from the tip backward. Heavy gloves are a must as the heat will be uncomfortable. Watch and listen closely! You can see and hear a horn start to char and you don't want that to happen. Overheating takes the "life" or plastic nature of the horn away and makes it brittle.

When the thicker parts of the horn are hot and easily molded, remove from the heat and quickly insert your prepared form. It should fit, but if not, take note of any corrections to be made and try again after reshaping the form.

Heating the horn using dry heat. Start at the thick neck area and heat toward the base.

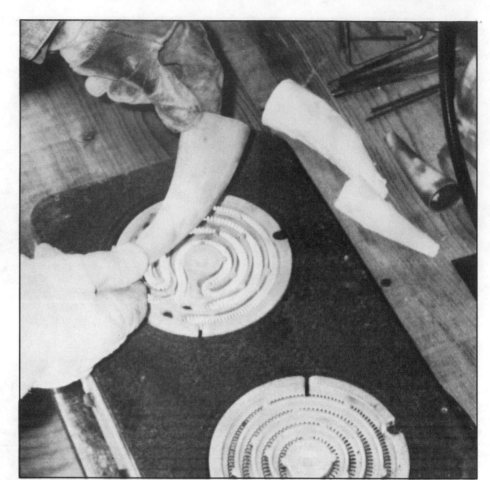

After the horn is thoroughly heated, push the inner form into the base, then press the horn flat.

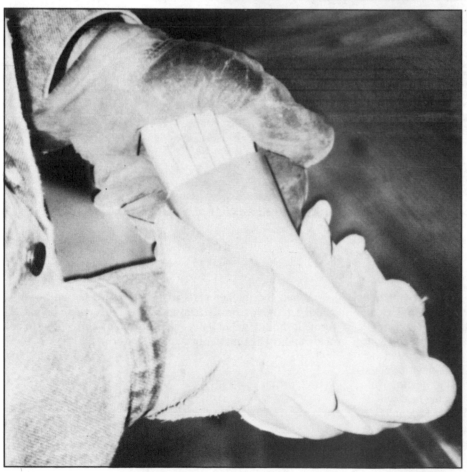

The heated horn with inner form in place has been flattened in the press and the wedges driven in.

Push the form inside as far as it will go and immediately put the horn into the press between the pre-heated metal plates. Make sure that the horn is centered and is getting even pressure. I usually try to center the pressure over the middle of the horn and the ends will follow suit. You only need enough pressure to flatten the horn to the desired thickness, no more. Proceed quickly and insert the wedges into the kerfs. Tap the wedges up tight. This helps to make an evenly formed base for the finished shape.

At this point everything needs to be correct. Once the horn cools, that will be its final shape unless the process is repeated. All that is needed now is time for the horn to cool. Several hours should suffice, however I usually leave the horn in the press overnight if possible.

When cool, remove the horn from the press, take out the wooden form and proceed with fashioning the base plug. I recommend fitting the plug as soon as possible after removing from the press. The horn will still have some amount of "memory." The wax on the form should aid in removing it from

Two examples of flattened horns with inner forms and wedges in place.

103

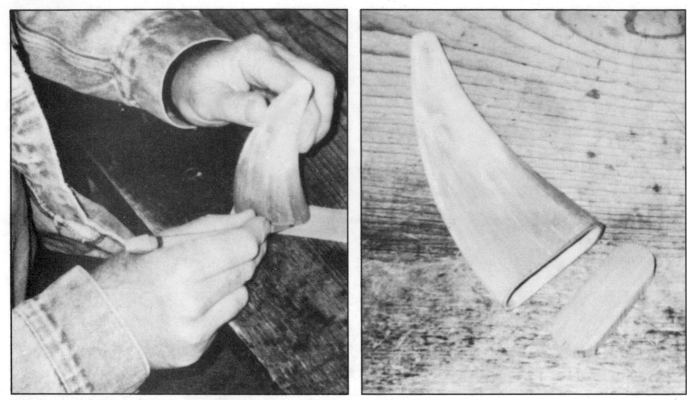

Left: Tracing around the horn for a base. Right: Preparing to carve and install the wood base.

The base has been fitted and pegged and a stopper made.

the horn after the edges have been taken out. A wooden plug can be carved to fit the base opening. This was probably the most commonly done. A "cap" of horn, as seen in the bottom photo on page 82, can be pinned over this wooden plug if desired.

After the base plug is installed, the rest of the horn may be worked to suit the owner's taste. The architecture of most early American flat horns was fairly simple and rather plain, however there are some examples of fancily carved flat horns. Panelling was commonly found and is well-suited to the shape of the horn. If the horn has enough material at the tip, a screw tip may be fashioned. However one chooses to finish the flat horn, remember to keep it historically accurate. So, it is hoped that by following these simple instructions and with practice you will be able to make a well-formed, serviceable flat horn.

Once the base plug has been installed and pinned, it's time to finish the horn.

The final scraping on the body of the horn.

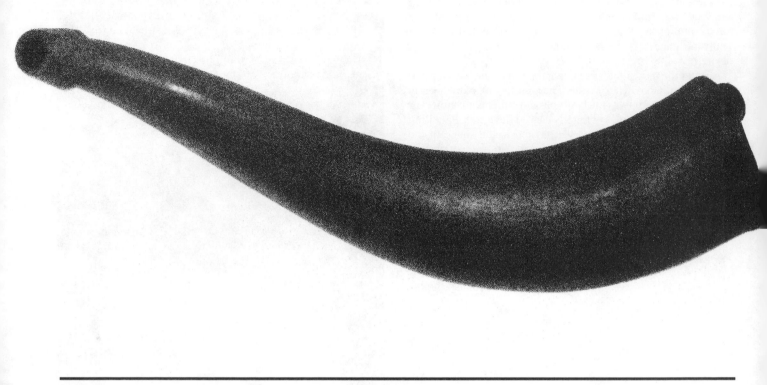

CONCLUSION

Many thousands of horns were manufactured commercially in the first half of the 19th century. By the 1830s, metal flasks had become popular, bringing the evolution of the powder container full circle. Even so, hardy individuals still carried horns and various sporting goods and hardware stores continued selling them on into the 1870s. The Civil War was fought with many soldiers carrying flintlock and percussion firearms with the necessary powder horns accompanying them. The development of breechloading weapons ended the general use of the powder horn.

Powder horns served equally masters both rich and poor and those with intentions both good and evil. Horns have shared a long and colorful history with their companions, muzzleloading guns. They have been made in a variety of shapes and sizes, plain and fancy. By studying the history of horns, we can study our own history. Powder horns connect us to times past.

I hope this chapter has helped to shed light on the history, some known facts and details that make 18th and early 19th century horns what they are. I have only touched on just a few areas. For those who are interested, I highly recommend Madison Grant's book as an excellent resource. Mr. Grant's book *Powder Horns and Their Architecture* goes into much detail and shows many more examples of the possibilities one can explore in relation to horn work than the scope of this chapter will allow.

As we continue our search, we may learn some of the answers concerning styles in the architecture and the engraving of horns. Although some of the questions may never be answered, the search for clues and knowledge can prove a fascinating quest. We must remember that understanding the powder horn in an analytical way is still in its infancy. Many collectors have varying opinions based on years of studying regional characteristics. My studies and observations are merely an extension of some of these ideas. In our efforts to advance the powder horn to the status it so richly deserves, we are just

now beginning to understand and develop specific knowledge and ideas relating to the construction, decoration and origin of these unique pieces of Americana. Therefore, this chapter is in no way meant to be conclusive. One thing of which I have become aware is that the more I learn the more I realize how much more there is to know.

If I did not thank all those who have helped me in my search for knowledge and who have given me support and assistance, this chapter could not be complete. I would like to thank Bill Scurlock for this opportunity and Bill Knight for generously sharing his knowledge of 18th and early 19th century chemicals, dyes and various other useful tidbits of information. I would especially like to thank my brother, Tom Ames, who has patiently helped and given his endless support to me over the years. Last, but not least, I would like to thank my wife, Anna, for her tireless efforts and for her understanding.

APPENDIX A: WORKS CITED

duMont, John S. *American Engraved Powder Horns: The Golden Age 1755-1783*. Canaan, NH: Phoenix, 1978.

Grancsay, Stephen V. *American Engraved Powder Horns*. New York: Metropolitan Museum of Art, 1946.

Grant, Madison. *Powder Horns and Their Architecture*. York, PA: Madison Grant, 1987.

Houze, Herbert G., ed. *The Sumptious Flask*. Cody, WY: Buffalo Bill Historical Center, 1989.

Riling, Ray. *The Powder Flask Book*. New York: Bonanza, 1953.

Ritchie, Carson I.A. *Bone and Horn Carving: A Pictorial History*. New York: Barnes, 1975.

Swayze, Nathan L. *Engraved Powder Horns of the French and Indian War and the Revolutionary War Era*. Yazoo City, MS: Gun Hill, 1978.

APPENDIX B: WORKS CONSULTED

Grant, Madison. *The Kentucky Rifle Hunting Pouch*. York, PA: Madison Grant, 1977.

Guthman, William, ed. *Guns and Other Arms*. New York: Mayflower, 1979.

Neumann, George C., and Frank J. Kravic. *Collector's Illustrated Encyclopedia of the American Revolution*. Texarkana, TX: Rebel, 1989.

Photos by Tom Bryant.

A horseback trek such as described by Bob Schmidt on page 46 is a great adventure for modern-day mountain men. In their chapter Bob Schmidt and Tom Bryant describe 18th and 19th century saddles and tack.

I

Above: Various historic leather work reproductions made by Steven Lalioff including trunks, portmanteaus, fire buckets, pouches, saddlebags, and 18th and 19th century folk art leather items.

Right: Closeup of reproduction triple heart pouch, a fine example of early 19th century folk art. The heart insets are rawhide deer skin with some hair still on.

All photos pages II and III by K. Abercrombie.

Above: This spider web pouch measures just seven by four inches, but small bags were not uncommon. Only the most basic tools would have been carried in here. Extra accessories would have been carried in a pocket or possibles bag.

Below: This dew claw pouch combines elements found in two original pouches. Measuring 8" x 9-1/2", this bag is representative of mid 18th to early 19th century pouches.

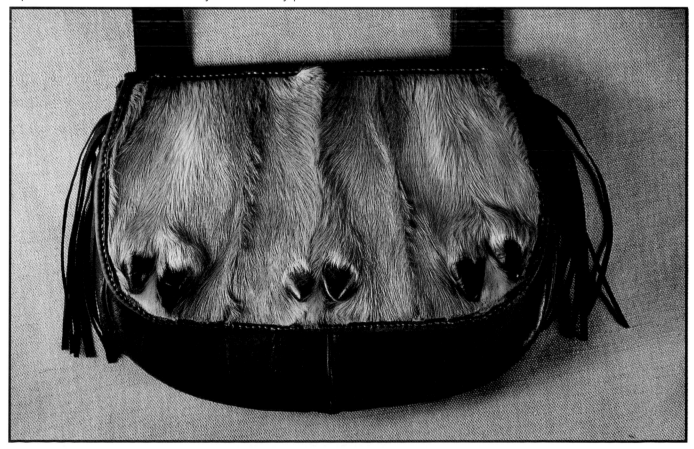

Photos by Robin Worline.

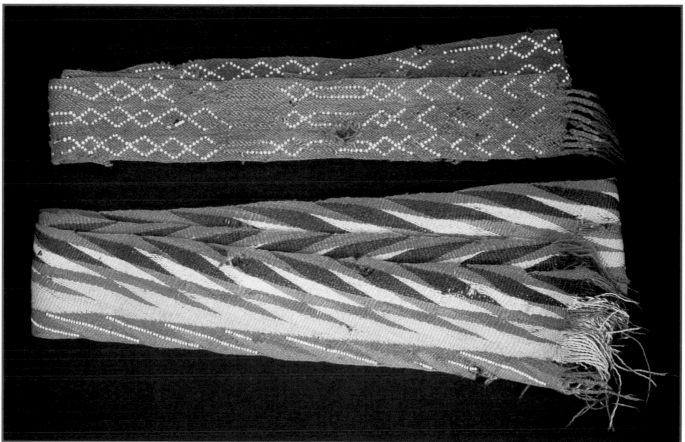

Above: Original sashes, probably Mohawk. The top one is a common Iroquois design, oblique weave, red with white beads. The bottom one illustrates the arrowhead design.

Facing page: (Upper left) A reproduction sash from a French collection. It was collected during the French & Indian War but no information is available on its provenance. (Upper right) A representation of a typical woodland-style bag of the 18th century. (Lower) The garters on the left contain a design element used throughout the Great Lakes and woodlands areas to represent thunder. The pair on the right was reproduced from Benjamin West's painting of Guy Johnson and are probably Iroquois style, 18th century.

Below: A tumpline of moosehair embroidery. Notice the little men embroidered into the design.

Above: A reproduction of an original collected in Virginia. The style and designs incorporated in this pouch exhibit a strong English influence. This bag measures twelve by ten inches. This pouch could have been made in the late 18th or early 19th century.

Photo by K. Abercrombie.

Below: A comtemporary horn using mid-18th century Iroquois design motifs made by Mark Odle. The strap, made by his wife, is finger woven of natural-dyed wool with beads interwoven.

Photo by Chuck Connors, Tantra Photographic.

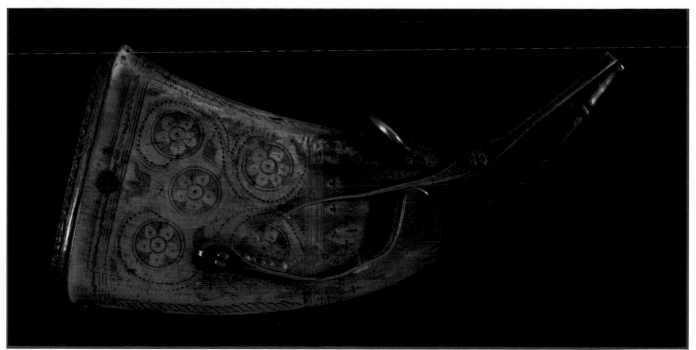

A beautiful mid-18th century flat horn. The mechanical closure is fashioned from hammered brass. This horn is entirely engraved on both sides. Inset: The carved base features the date, ANO 1766, and a chip carved border. ANO was a commonly used corruption of "anno Domini," which loosely means "year of our Lord."

A contemporary reproduction of a 17th century Celtic Revival flat horn. The entire horn is relief-carved, and the rings and studs are hand-forged.

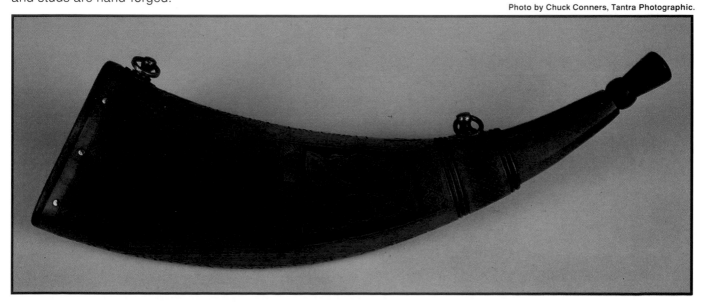

A modern-day brigade on a 19th century cross-country ride. It's fun to get all the horse tack together for use at local rendezvous, but a ride of five or more days tests the usefulness of your gear.

Frontier Trail Foods

by Edward C. Maurer

Ed Maurer has loved the outdoors since he was a young boy raised on the edge of the Florida Everglades. He learned the values of self reliance, conservation and woods lore as he went out on solo trips into the swamp with its meandering waterways and chest-high saw grass occupied by alligators and water moccasins.

Ed has been in the United States Air Force since 1975 when he enlisted "on a whim," as he puts it. He didn't see mountains or snow until he was in his early 20s when he was transferred to Elmendorf Air Force Base, Alaska. That was also where he got his first exposure to buckskinning. "I went camping with a local party from Anchorage. I went out to help collect wood and had the misfortune to ask how I could tell the difference between a dead tree and a dormant one. I hadn't ever seen snow; in Miami if a tree doesn't have leaves, it's dead! I think I've got it straight now."

Ed has written several articles for *MUZZLELOADER* magazine, including "Developing A Persona: The First-Person Impression," "Advantages and Use of the Smoothbore in the Wilds of America," and "Stay Alive— Be Prepared."

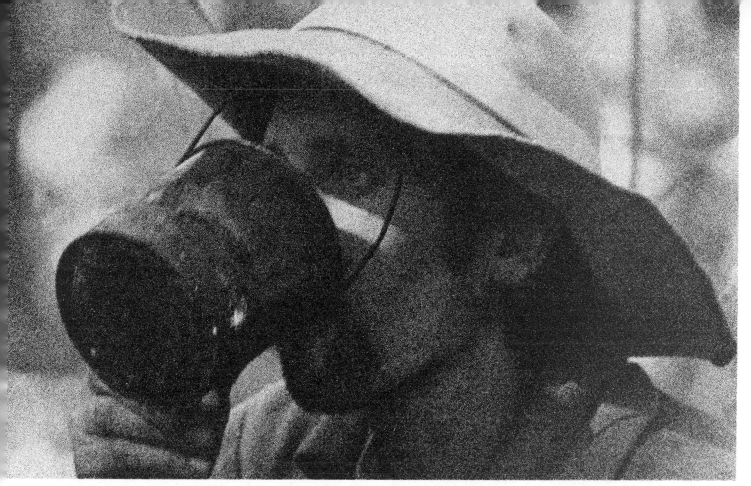

The woodsmen, Indians and other travelers in the uncivilized reaches of our young country had a wide variety of foods to eat while they were on the trail. These days we too can have pretty much the same variety when we take to the trail, whether it leads us on a journey into the mountains or just to rendezvous. We can buy this food at the corner market, or we may want to grow our own. We can even learn to forage for ourselves when beyond the reach of asphalt and glass. In this chapter I will address some of those foods that are readily available and identifiable to most of us and discuss some options for those times when we need to live off the land.

Of the many recipes available to the modern reenactor or buckskinner, few are written for use on the trail. In spite of that, we still must feed ourselves whether we're out for one night or a week or more. Naturally, the longer the stay the more food you need, and unless you've got a pack animal, it has to be carried on your back.

You can always hunt small game or catch fish, right? No, not necessarily; we frequently find ourselves unable to forage. Game regulations, proximity to populated areas and environmental conditions determine our opportunities. In addition to these problems, large groups generally are best-served these days by carrying their own food. Availability of natural resources to feed a large group is a concern, as is the environmental impact of such a venture.

My first attempt to feed myself solely from mother nature's bounty ended up being a trip with no meals. I spent three cold, winter days in the mountains with no more than hot water to keep me going. I decided then and there that I would learn all I could about keeping myself fed on the trail. That was a long time ago and I've learned a lot since then, including how to pack lightweight, "period" foods that won't readily spoil. I want to stress that I am referring to *period* foods for a couple of reasons. To begin with these are the types of foods that were used by our ancestors, and we should try to be authentic whenever possible. Also, since our modern methods of food preservation did not exist then, they used their own age-old methods of keeping food edible for extended periods of time, methods that will work just as well for us today.

Our predecessors didn't have hot dogs and canned chili, but they did have a lot of good, perfectly healthy foods. After reading this chapter, you shouldn't have any reason for carrying canned beans on the trail. You may even start leaving the cooler home when you go to rendezvous!

My primary food on the trail is dried corn and jerky. Now for some of you that can get old in a hurry, and it sure can motivate you to catch fish or get a bunny for the pot. It will also motivate you to find other foods that are wholesome, resistant to spoiling, lightweight, compact and authentic to your period. All of these needs can be satisfied by using the same or similar foods, foraging and preservation techniques used by the Indians and frontier folks.

A BIT OF HISTORICAL BACKGROUND

It pleased God, after a while, to send those people which were our mortal enemies to releeve us with victuals, as Bread, Corne, Fish, and Flesh in great plentie, which was the setting up of our feeble men, otherwise, wee had all perished. Also we were frequented by divers Kings in the Countrie, bringing us store of provision to our great comfort. (Robinson 9)

To begin with the Indians knew what they were doing. And it was from them that the white explorers learned how to fend for themselves. In the early years of the European invasion, the parties of exploration would generally carry enough food for the entire trip. As you might guess, a few men would have to pack hundreds of pounds of food for just a few weeks. Consider this quote concerning Col. Byrd's trip to establish the border between Virginia and North Carolina in 1728:

[The surveying party from North Carolina consisted of three or four men who brought] *five hundred pounds of bacon and dry'd beef and five hundred pounds of bisket.* (Arnow 98)

This party turned back because they ran out of bread! Maybe the venerable Col. Byrd should have brought along a cook too; one of their meals consisted of bacon cooked in rum.

The "cooks" then drank the rum and fat solution with their meal. Mmmm, corn and jerky sounds good right about now, doesn't it?

Those early explorers, especially the English, were usually incapable of living off the land, and many a party of exploration was disbanded because an Indian could not be hired to hunt for them. After more white men had the opportunity to travel into the unexplored regions of the country and learn from the Indians, a type of individual developed that could endure; he would be the one to provide food for those otherwise capable explorers. Thus was born the true American frontiersman, who would be relied upon throughout the rest of our exploring history to feed the fur traders, frontier outposts and wagon trains.

It is said an army travels on its stomach. That doesn't imply that they have to crawl everywhere but rather addresses the importance of feeding the troops. When in settled areas, the armies of the time would forage; the military use of the word meant stealing food from the local inhabitants. But when venturing into the wilderness, they had to carry along their own rations. On April 24, 1757, the Earl of Loudoun gave the following orders to Col. Henry Bouquet, the commander of His Majesty's 62nd or Royal American Regiment. It reads:

A hearty meal is especially important in cold, wet conditions. Fred Gowan tends a fire over which hangs small copper kettles.

The allowance of each person victualled by the contractors for one week is as follows:
7 lbs. bread, or in lieu thereof, 7 lbs flour
7 lbs beef,   "   , 4 lbs pork
3 pints peas, l lbs cheese, or in lieu thereof, 6 oz butter
l lb flour, or in lieu thereof, 1/2 lb rice

(Bouquet 85)

Even with the ability to fend for themselves, both the frontiersman and the Indian left his respective settlement with a certain amount of provisions:

On this day came again the savage.... They brought with them in a thing like a bow-case (which the principle of them had about his waist) a little of their corn pounded to powder, which, put to a little water, they eat. (Mourt's 53)

Their provisions may have been just a bag of jerky or a sack of corn, but whatever it was, when it ran out, he would live by his wits. He may have had the chance to obtain food at various villages and settlements, either with or without the residents' permission, or he could help himself to the food of a vanquished foe. Hunting and gathering was of course an option, and unless it was unwise to do so, the hunter's instinct usually prevailed.

FORAGING IN YE SUPERMARKET

A number of different types of meat for the trail can be found at almost any market. This runs the gamut of fresh and frozen meats to sausage, salt pork and other products that are artificially preserved. I have used a wide variety of these meats, and with a little care, you can find a good, affordable selection.

I usually select a lesser grade of very lean beef for the trail. Quite often leaner meats, like round or chuck, are more affordable because it is the fat in domestic meats that makes them flavorful. Leaner meats are also easier to preserve by drying or cooking because of their lack of fat. Avoid pre-cooked meat from the store! It is generally full of spices and is always expensive. This also goes for store-bought beef jerky, which is soaked in salt brine and costs a king's ransom. This type of "jerky" isn't really jerky, and if you look carefully at the package, it will usually recommend refrigeration after opening. Later on I'll tell you how to make real jerky that will last a very long time and isn't laced with chemicals.

Pork can be treated like beef, but it is often fattier. The salt pork available today is also different than what they had historically, much the same as with the jerky. Both pork and beef were stored in barrels of salt to preserve them. Smoked pork is, of course, very popular. As with other smoked meats, if you buy it that way, make sure it doesn't require refrigeration.

The store is full of fish. Buy the biggest, thickest one you can find. Once smoked it will be about the best-tasting thing you will ever carry on the trail, and if done properly it will last quite awhile. No, shrimp, clams and crab legs aren't fish.

Most any type of bird can be smoked, dried or otherwise preserved for the trail; I've had smoked turkey I would kill for. 'Round about Thanksgiving stores practically give whole turkeys away. Another type of bird well worth getting is a

FORAGING LIST

A selection of authentic foods that can be readily bought in the store, grown at home or foraged on the trail. Once obtained you should now be able to preserve, package and carry them on your next outing, whether it's on foot, a horse or canoe trip, or even a rendezvous. Leave the hot dogs and canned chili at home and eat the foods our forefathers did. You'll be challenged and will come to appreciate even more the abilities of the native peoples of this country and the explorers, trappers and pioneers who followed in their footsteps.

ANIMAL	VEGETABLE	BERRIES
Meat	Corn	Blackberries
Fish	Beans	Blueberries
Fowl	Squash	Chokeberries
Hard Cheese	Pumpkin	Wild Red Cherries
	Turnips	Cranberries
	Cucumber	Currants
		Elderberries
		Gooseberries
		Hawthorns
NUTS	**SPICES**	Huckleberries
Butternut	Dried Mustard	Serviceberries
Hickory Nut	Red Pepper	Red Mulberries
Chestnut	Sage	Black Plums
Acorn		Raspberries
		Strawberries

capon, which is a rooster that was "fixed" sometime during his life. They get real big and are reasonably priced. Game hens are also good, and they are easy to pack for a short trip. Skip the expensive stuff, because once you've preserved it, you won't know the difference.

As with other meats, there are different types of sausages available. The trick to selecting a preserved sausage for camp is to avoid any that are in factory-sealed, plastic packages. The best kind is a dried sausage that looks like a pepperoni. These are easily recognized by their shriveled paper or gut wrappers and are hanging in the store un-refrigerated. This stuff may outlast mankind itself. Another type of sausage is an uncooked type found in the cooler. It is often an Italian type, usually in a gut wrapper and looks like a pale, fat hot dog. This sausage is good if completely dried or smoked. These may contain a lot of fat and must have the skins punctured to let the oil run out while smoking and drying.

FORAGING IN YE WOODS AND STREAMS

The greatest test of one's ability to truly exist as our ancestors did in the wilds is to actually live directly from nature's bounty. I have fed myself reasonably well ever since that first winter trip, when I lived for three days on warm water. I have learned different techniques for hunting, fishing and trapping, and I would like to present to you a number of these tried and true methods. Many of these I have used, some I have not. But all have been used by experienced woodsmen at one time or another. Some of these methods may be illegal in your area and should only be used if you have received special permission from the appropriate authorities or you are actually in a jam and need the food *very* badly.

If I am to hunt for my food, I generally prefer to rely on small game, such as rabbits, squirrels and birds:

In the forests here there are many partridges, heath-hens and pigeons that fly together in thousands, and sometimes ten, twenty, thirty and even forty and fifty are killed at one shot. We have here, too, a great number of all kinds of fowl, swans, geese, ducks, widgeons, teal, brant, which sport upon the river in thousands in the spring of the year, and again in the autumn fly away in flocks, so that in the morning and evening any one may stand ready with his gun ... and shoot them as they fly past.
(Leach 84)

While we haven't seen birds in those numbers in many years, small game is generally plentiful. In addition, taking small animals like rabbits, squirrels and birds is generally less wasteful and has less impact on the environment than harvesting a large animal like a deer. Small game is also easier to clean, preserve and carry.

The most crucial part of hunting and trapping is determining what animals are native to the area you are in. This is best done by observing nature, which is one of the reasons many of us go into the woods. But how many of us actually *see* what's around us? Are you the type to go barreling into the woods willy-nilly hoping to see something, or are you taking time to stop and smell the roses? In order to actually see what is around you, my best suggestion is to stop, sit down and shut up. When you are stationary, relaxed and quiet, you are the least obtrusive and will cause the least amount of disturbance. It is then that you will have the best chance to see even the most wary animals. You will be able to see that rabbit crouching under a bush nibbling on grass or hear a squirrel breaking open an acorn. Once you have learned to become *part* of the scene instead of intruding upon it, you will not only see more animals, but you will also appreciate your surroundings and environment to a greater extent.

All animals, including mankind, have the same basic

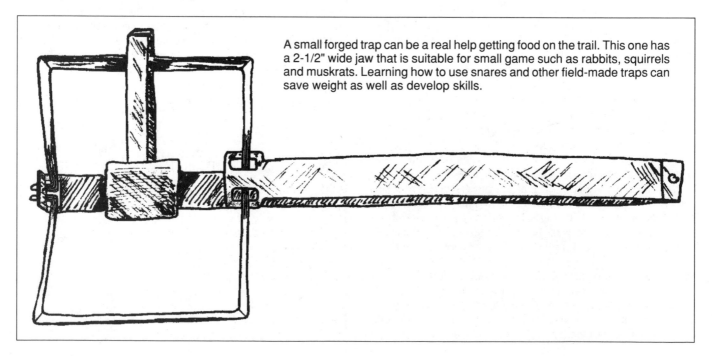

A small forged trap can be a real help getting food on the trail. This one has a 2-1/2" wide jaw that is suitable for small game such as rabbits, squirrels and muskrats. Learning how to use snares and other field-made traps can save weight as well as develop skills.

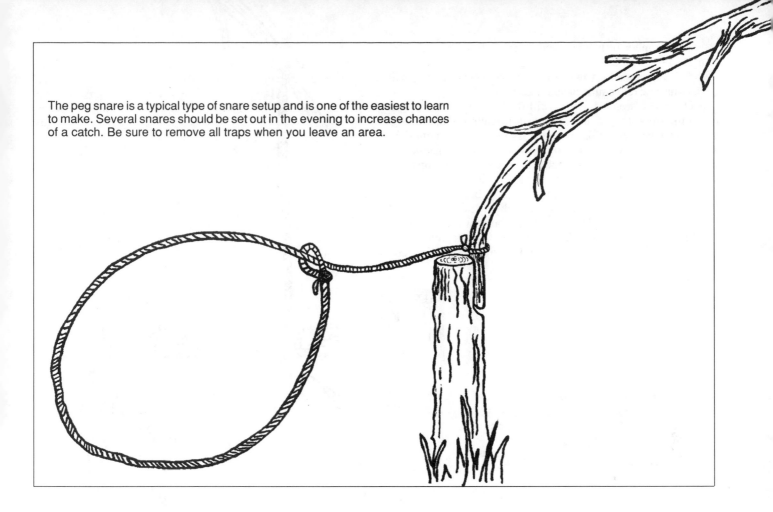

The peg snare is a typical type of snare setup and is one of the easiest to learn to make. Several snares should be set out in the evening to increase chances of a catch. Be sure to remove all traps when you leave an area.

survival needs: food, water, and shelter. You will be able to find places where your food supply will most likely be at any given time by determining which of these they will need to satisfy the most. If it is hot, animals will be the most active in the morning and evening and stationary during midday. When it is dry, they will be seeking water, and when cold, they will be searching out warm, sunlit areas out of the wind. A basic rule of thumb is that whatever you feel driven toward at any given time is what the animals will most likely be seeking as well. Plan to hunt near these areas but not too close. A gunshot will spook the game for a short while, but the smell of death may keep them away or even make them move on. Don't contaminate a prime area with that smell if it's avoidable.

There are a number of simple traps that can be set near these prime areas as well. The following description of Cree Indians using a deadfall trap is found in *Five Indian Tribes of the Upper Missouri* by Edwin Denig:

Wolves are trapped and killed in many ways by these [Cree]. *The most common is the deadfall, constructed by small pickets driven in the ground and a trigger baited with meat supporting a heavy log. The wolf in endeavoring to get the meat displaces the prop and the log falling upon him breaks his back.* (119)

The best trap sets will be made along passageways the animals use to travel to and from feeding, watering and hiding areas. Look for trails that are heavily tracked or have a lot of droppings, since these trails are frequently traveled and make for prime trap locations.

Snare traps are spring-loaded traps that are designed to catch an animal about its neck and kill it by strangulation or snapping the animal's neck by the shear force of being caught. One of the best types of snares is the spring snare. The snaring action is provided by a bent sapling or tree limb. The action of the spring is so sudden that it will not spook the animal, and the sheer power of the release will break the neck of many small animals. A second type of snare is the lever or dropping-weight snare. The snaring action is provided by a lever or counterweight causing the snare cord to catch the animal fast. A very important aspect of any snare is to ensure that it will raise the animal off the ground when caught. This will help keep other animals from getting to your catch and will ensure that your animal will not be able to escape if it is not killed immediately.

The peg snare is a very simple snare to make and because of that is one of my favorites for small animals. The action is provided by a sapling or branch held in place by a stout peg driven into the ground. The contact spot of the peg and spring should be shaped to prevent the two of them from slipping apart at the wrong time. This can be accomplished by carving a small notch in either or both pieces or just cutting a flat spot into one of them. Exactly what is needed will be determined by the materials used and the relationship of the pieces.

The pencil snare, like the peg snare, can use a sapling or limb as a spring. It is also very effective as a falling-weight snare. The snare cord is attached to both the weight or spring and the trigger. An animal moving along a trail will dislodge and activate the snare. I found this to be a useful snare when placed in the slide area where muskrats enter and exit the water. This is a very fast trap and can be very sensitive.

Any number of triggers and springs can be used for the tunnel snare. The trick here is to place it at the mouth or just within a tunnel or burrow. This is good for rabbits but will occasionally catch squirrels and badgers.

Deadfalls are designed to kill the animal by crushing it under the weight of a heavy object such as a large stone or log. These can be very effective and require only a minimum amount of work. Unlike the snares most deadfalls require no cordage. Of primary importance is the selection of a proper log or stone. It should be large enough to kill the animal quickly but not so heavy as to damage too much meat or burst the animal's intestines. For small animals such as rabbits, a deadfall of about five pounds should be ideal. It is also important that the falling height be sufficient to be effective as well. On soft ground such as sand or mud, a hard object should be placed on the ground

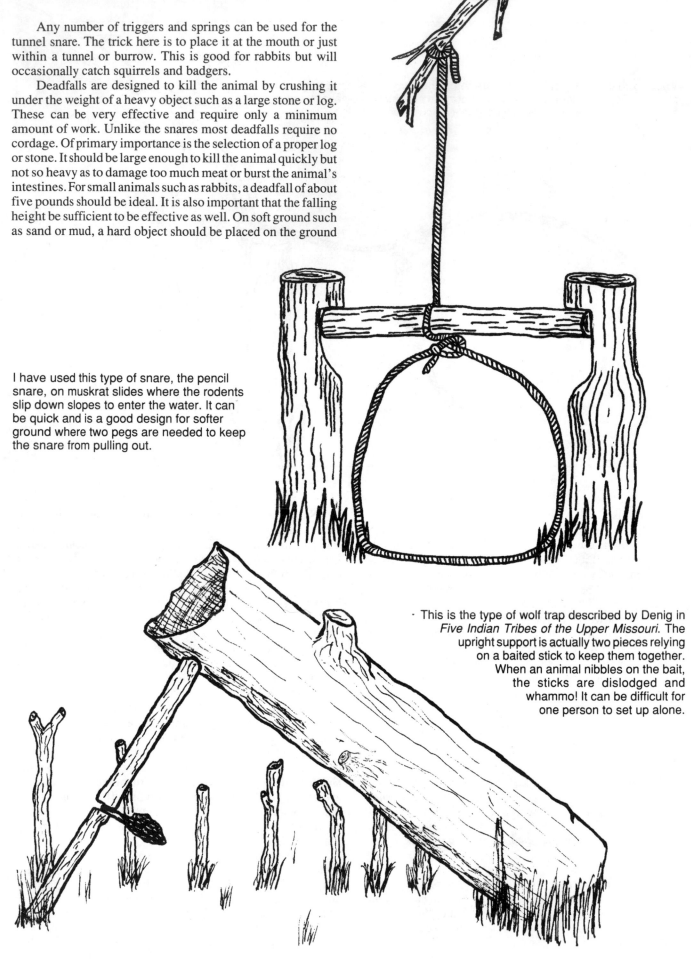

I have used this type of snare, the pencil snare, on muskrat slides where the rodents slip down slopes to enter the water. It can be quick and is a good design for softer ground where two pegs are needed to keep the snare from pulling out.

This is the type of wolf trap described by Denig in *Five Indian Tribes of the Upper Missouri*. The upright support is actually two pieces relying on a baited stick to keep them together. When an animal nibbles on the bait, the sticks are dislodged and whammo! It can be difficult for one person to set up alone.

114

Hawk Boughton demonstrates setting a snare while camping in Kentucky.

beneath the fall to act as an "anvil" to improve its efficiency. This will decrease the likelihood of the animal being maimed and crawling away.

Small, forged iron traps can also be carried. One trap should be sufficient to feed one or two men. Take care that

The product of an enjoyable day of fishing. One of the best parts of a trek is practicing a period skill while in camp. These trout represent a day spent not traveling but taking time to stop and "smell the roses."

The author's fishing kit consists of an enameled tin that contains split shot, snelled hooks, toggle hooks and a deerskin fly line with sinew leader.

you don't end up carrying too much additional weight though. If you are proficient at building your own traps out of natural materials, you will save yourself from carrying a lot of extra metal.

Fishing is one of my most pleasurable pastimes and I plan most of my trips for the express purpose of being able to fish for my own food. I often catch so much that I throw back most of what I get, keeping only the fish I need for that day's meal. The early Americans also had great success fishing, as evidenced by this quote from *The Siege of Quebec*: "Our men take great quantities of fish over the ship's sides; they are chiefly mackerel and pollock" (Knox 27). Fishing is also a good way to obtain a fair quantity of food that can easily be preserved and carried on the trail. Pound for pound fish is higher in protein than red meat and when dried is light and easy to carry. Aside from fish one can also catch or trap eels, crawdads (crawfish) and clams.

My favorite method of catching fish is with hook and line. Several different materials may be used for lines; I have tried silk, linen, sinew and deerskin. I have also used a deerskin line with a sinew leader and found it to be very effective under certain conditions. An enterprising person could also make his own cordage and, with a leader of sinew or thin but strong plant fiber, could do very well. Most naturally occurring materials will not spook a fish. I've had trout strike a hook that was tied

to a sinew line with the excess line still remaining on the hook. I guess it looked something like a worm.

Sinew used for a line should be soaked in cold water to separate the fibers. (Don't get in a hurry and try to soak it in hot water; you will only cook and ruin the sinew.) Thinner strands can be held in your mouth to soften like the Indian women did when sewing. While hunting for bait, I do this with the lines that I have already made up. Once separated into strands about the thickness of a kite string, the segments can be tied together to make up a line as long as you find necessary. The last few segments should be progressively thinner, with the last section to be tied to the hook as thin as possible without breaking too readily. It will be easier to tie to the hook and will be less disturbing to the fish. Wet sinew does not hold a knot very well, so you will have to find one that will work. Don't bother twisting the sinew into a cord; it will probably just uncoil once it gets wet anyway.

One of my more successful lines is a deerskin line about 25 feet long with a sinew leader of about 3 feet. This skin line is a single, continuous piece made by cutting a piece of skin in a circular fashion. Once cut I greased the line with a combination of bear grease and beeswax to help it shed water and float. I have used this line as both a fly line and a floating line when fishing on the surface with bugs. I can place a bug on the hook

117

and float it downstream to waiting trout. It works especially well in tight areas where the bait must be presented on the surface but must also float under a bush or overhanging limb. I used this once in Montana and had lunch before my partner could catch another moth to use as bait. Now that's effective!

Silk suture material from surplus military medical kits makes very good line as well. If you cannot find that, try heavy silk sewing thread, which is available at better fabric shops. Silk is extremely strong and if properly dried will last very long.

I found a thin, waxed linen cord used for leather work that also works very well. It is strong, easy to obtain, affordable and has many uses. It seems to fill the ticket for an item to be packed into any haversack. You may need to use a short piece of sinew as a leader, especially when using small, trout-size hooks.

Split-shot sinkers are easy to make and have been found in archaeological sites. As the name implies, these are simply buckshot that have been split about halfway through. I normally carry ball and shot on the trail and some of the shot is .32 caliber buckshot. I split the shot partway through with a knife to make sinkers. To split it without making two little half moons is easy if you take care. First, place a shot on a hard surface like a flat rock or piece of wood. Then place the edge of your knife on the shot like you were going to cut it into two. Tap on the back edge of the knife with another piece of wood, driving the edge into the shot about halfway. Do not try to push the blade through the

shot; this will most likely produce two pieces of shot instead of one sinker. With a little practice, you can quickly turn out a lot of sinkers with a minimum of wasted lead. The split shot can be easily pinched onto the line or removed as needed. Use only the amount of weight required to control your line. Too much will dampen the feel of a strike, especially from smaller fish.

Early fish hooks were much like the ones we have today, except that they had no eyes for tying on the line. Instead of an eye, they had a flattened spot at the end of the shank. This flat spot would prevent the line, which was tied around the shank, from slipping off the hook. Apparently, this type is still pretty popular in Europe and the Orient. Another type of "hook" is the toggle hook. This is fashioned by shaping a piece of wood or bone into a small bar sharpened at each end with a groove worked around its middle. The line is tied in the groove. The idea is to make it small enough for a fish to swallow, getting the toggle wedged in its mouth or throat.

Since a bare hook or toggle will not generally catch fish, one must have bait that will entice a fish into striking. The availability of bait will vary with the area you are in and the type of fish you are most likely to catch. If you have been lucky enough to kill game, the organs will make good catfish or carp bait.

Other types of naturally occurring bait are almost always available. If you know where to find them and how to use them, you will usually catch fish. Worms are the most common type

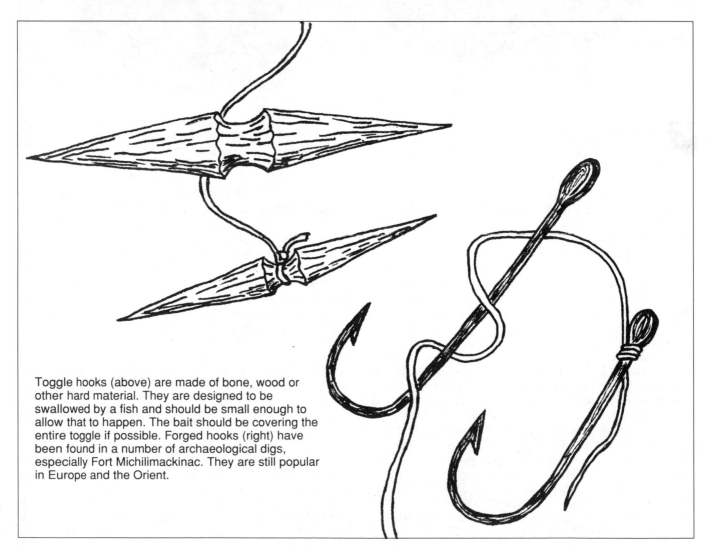

Toggle hooks (above) are made of bone, wood or other hard material. They are designed to be swallowed by a fish and should be small enough to allow that to happen. The bait should be covering the entire toggle if possible. Forged hooks (right) have been found in a number of archaeological digs, especially Fort Michilimackinac. They are still popular in Europe and the Orient.

Although a fishing pole is not always necessary, it is sometimes essential for the proper presentation of the bait. Here the author uses his gun's ramrod to get the bait out past the weeds.

of live bait, and I have found them from Florida to Alaska and many places between. Worms can be found under logs, rocks or piles of debris, especially after a rain. They can also be dug or found by an old method known as "grunting." I have used this method in Georgia, and there's no reason it wouldn't work elsewhere. It is called other names in different parts of the country; you might recognize it. Find a piece of wood two to four inches in diameter and about three feet long, then drive it into the ground about two feet. This is best done in a damp, grassy area. Once the stake is driven, start tapping on its side or rubbing a stone or axe head across the top to cause a constant vibration. This will bring the worms to the surface up to eight feet or more from the stake, depending on the conditions.

Worms are not the only kind of natural bait that can be used to catch fish. You may also be able to find crickets, grasshoppers, slugs, grubs and leeches. Frogs and lizards work too; whatever is available and small enough for the fish to eat will usually work if you are in a pristine area, unadulterated by humans and their pollution and crowding.

Another tried and true method of catching fish is with the use of a spear. Spearing is most successful when the fish are in a position that gives you an advantage of position over them, or they are crowded into a small area like the base of a waterfall or a narrow spot in a stream. Native peoples have caught fish like this for millennia, and I have found it to be very successful under the right conditions. Consider this quote from *Scoouwa*, James Smith's story of Indian captivity:

... we came to the little lake at the mouth of Sandusky...we diverted ourselves several days, by catching rockfish in a small creek, the name of which is also Sunyendeand, which signifies rockfish. They fished in the night, with lights, and struck the fish with giggs or spears. (Smith 114)

Fish can also be caught in traps. There are many different types, but I think one of the easiest is the basket trap. This is simply a cone of long, straight sticks, such as those from a willow or cane, submersed in the water. A very effective method is to place the trap into a narrow spot in a waterway, preferably facing upstream. By herding the fish downstream, some of them will swim into the trap and all you need to do then is lift its open end out of the water with the trapped fish inside.

All the brooks in Canada contain crawfish....The French are fond of eating them and say they have vastly decreased in number since they began to catch them. (Kalm 479)

Wow, can you imagine catching so many crawdads that you can actually tell that their numbers are dwindling? Crawfish are easy and fun to catch and provide both food and bait. Crawfish, also known as crawdads or just 'dads, can be caught in baited traps or gathered by hand. I find the early morning and evening the best time to find these little guys hiding in the water under stones, immersed logs or just crawling about looking for something to eat.

Meat has to be smoked, dried or salted to keep it from spoiling. The most common of these that we are familiar with is jerky or jerk. Smoked or dried jerk was typically made from deer, elk, bison and, later on, beef. Other meats were also preserved this way, including bear, birds, fish and pork. I would not recommend dried or smoked bear unless you are sure that it is free of the parasite that causes trichinosis. This parasite burrows into the muscle and lays eggs that are protected by a tough "capsule" that is frequently unharmed by smoking or drying. Pigs are close kin to bear and may be infected with this little critter as well.

Jerky is relatively easy to make. Forget soaking the meat in brine or any other concoctions. They will just ruin it for use as a constant diet on the trail. The addition of spices to the meat will also make you thirstier. I find that slicing the meat across the grain in very thin strips allows the meat to dry very quickly. The thin slices will also help to keep flies from laying their eggs in the meat. Hang these slices on racks or tree branches that get a lot of sun or over a warm, smoky fire. If they are not dry by the end of the day, take them in before they begin to cool and re-hang them the next day to continue the drying process. At home, one can dry the meat in a dehydrator or in a warm oven.

If you are going to be in one camp for awhile, you can build a smoke house. Construct a covered tube or a rectangular structure out of reeds, willow twigs or bark. Place this about two or three feet from a small fire pit dug into the ground. Between the two structures, construct a chimney that will carry the smoke from the fire into the smoker. This chimney should be long enough to allow the smoke to cool before it enters the smoker. This affair is best built on a hill side so that the smoker can be uphill of the fire. Make a small fire using hardwood if available, and when the fire dies down, add damp wood to create a lot of smoke. If properly constructed the smoke should be drawn through the chimney and into the smoker. While smoking your meat, it wouldn't be a bad idea to re-smoke your leathers. Keep a close eye on the smoker; you wouldn't want to overdo your meat, or your skins.

[Lieutenant Governor] *Sinclair detached a sergeant and six privates to fish....They caught enough to feed all the Michilimackinac Indians and had a surplus of about a thousand pounds to ship to Niagara. The cleaned trout were salted down for one night and then smoked with juniper.* (*At the Crossroads* 133)

Hundreds of pounds of smoked and dried fish were stored at Fort Michilimackinac for winter provisions (Armour 133), and only a few years ago, when I was living in Iceland, I saw acres of fish drying on racks in the sun. The temperature never reached 70°F but the fish dried hard in just a matter of hours. I have carried smoked fish on trips and it sure is a nice change from regular jerky. "Tinned" fish was not readily available until the 1830s and it was pretty unusual and very expensive.

There are also a great variety of fruits and vegetables available to us that are the same as those eaten by the Indians and frontiersmen. All of these can be found in the store, picked in the woods or grown in your own garden. (By the way food gardens were called "truck patches" and their products were "truck.") As with meat those vegetables that are normally moist, like squash or corn, must be dried not only for preservation but also to cut down on weight and the room they take up in your haversack or pack. Small truck like beans and peas can be spread out and dried. Larger foods like squash need to be sliced thin, strung on a cord and then hung to dry. If they turn brown, don't sweat it; that's normal and won't affect the taste. They

← **Bark-covered frame structure with meat racks**

← **Meat in smoker (cut away view)**

Stones cover the pit to control air flow

Underground chimney leading to smoker

A smoker can be used to preserve fish, fowl and meat. It is very important that the smoke flow through the smoker without creating enough heat to actually cook the meat or set the smoker afire! This one is made of bark, but any covering that retains the smoke without burning will do.

The author's entire set of cooking gear with food sacks, salt horn, tin cup and pot, horn spoon and penney knife. Note that the penney knife is carried separate for general use on the trail and in camp.

just won't be as pretty. Again, there are several methods useful for drying your food. A hot, clean back porch works for me at home, and a food dehydrator works well, too. Actually, any clean surface that gets plenty of sun and warmth will work. Just keep the flies and the dog away from it.

The three sisters of the Iroquois were corn, beans and squash:

Ears of corn twenty inches long or more, growing on stalks as high as eighteen feet. Pumpkins and squash grew to enormous sizes...weighing as much as eighty pounds apiece. Potatoes...beans, turnips, cucumbers, watermelons, parsnips and other vegetable crops....As agronomists, the Iroquois could obviously teach the whites a great deal. (Eckert 447)

The term "three sisters" covers a wide variety of foods that can be carried on the trail:

The French when making their journeys far up into the country to visit the Indians have as a rule during that long period of from one half to three years nothing else to live on than the hulled corn as described before, the fat of various animals which they mix with the corn and boil, and the game

which they shoot in the forests. This is actually all the food they live on for such a long period....It was on this account that the people of Canada considered corn a kind of grain which ought to be highly prized. (Kalm 574)

The two most common types of corn grown by the Iroquois were what we now call "white dent" and "white flint." Only rarely was the red, multi-colored "Indian corn" found. White dent, known also as Tuscarora or squaw corn, was generally hulled or eaten on the cob (Lyford 16). It did not seem to be the corn of choice for most uses, but it had its place alongside the more widely used and versatile flint corn. White flint had a wide variety of uses. When coarsely ground it could be used for plain mush or mixed with meat to make a more substantial meal. It was also used as the main ingredient in unleavened bread.

Hominy, made by soaking shelled flint corn in lye until the hulls slip, could be used to make soup or combined with beans and meat. A type of boiled corn bread was also made of hulled corn and beans. Another way of processing corn was to roast it until dry. In this dried state, it would last for years and could be eaten cooked or uncooked. Dried corn that was pounded fine and mixed with maple sugar was a very popular type of trail food. Eaten as is by the handful or baked into cakes, it could be a staple for a man on the trail.

The Indians knew ten or more types of beans (Lyford 16). As a replacement for meat, beans could carry a family through a hard winter. This was true throughout the American experience. We have all heard the Cavalry phrase, "40 miles on beans and hay." Even some college students have had to choose between beans and hunger when the old money well ran a little dry.

We have about six varieties readily available to us. These include both purple and white kidney beans, string beans, lima beans, white beans (the small kind) and pole beans. All of these can be dried and easily carried on the trail. That's about all I have to say about beans right now. What the heck, beans is beans!

The Indians cultivated several varieties of squash, all of which can be sliced and dried in the sun or stored in rock-lined, underground cellars. Hubbard and crookneck squash and pumpkins were planted in mounds that could have been tended or left to grow wild. One of the advantages that I have found in squash crops is that they will produce for many months and will continue to do so until killed by a hard frost.

Berries were gathered by the bushel. Of all the berries that the Indians had available to them, we can readily find 15 different types. These can be picked while in camp or on the trail or purchased at the store or fruit stand. Berries cannot be packed very well when fresh, but when dried they are a good source of vitamins and can add some variety to many of your meals. They can be used in a wide variety of breads and stews. When mixed with pulverized jerky and a small amount of suet, they give us pemmican. The complete list of berries, along with other veggies, are included in the foraging list accompanying this article. A few of the berries in the list are cranberries, raspberries and, my favorite, blueberries.

With the emphasis placed on the importance of berries to the Indians, it is curious that there is no evidence of their purposely cultivating berries like they did corn or squash. This would lead us to believe that the woods were literally full of wild berries. As a point of interest, the Viking sailors that landed in the New World called it "Vinland," suggesting the presence of large numbers of berry or grape vines.

A diversity of nuts was also available to the wayfaring explorer or Indian. I have found six that were common in the Eastern forests. These are beechnuts, butternuts, hazelnuts, hickory nuts, chestnuts and of course acorns from a number of different oaks. With the exception of acorns from the white oak, all of these nuts can be eaten raw or after being roasted in a bed of coals. The acorns from the white oak need to be crushed and thoroughly rinsed to leach the bitter-tasting tannic acid out of them. The resulting meal can then be roasted as is or made into cakes and baked.

A seventh nut (I guess we can call it that) is the pine nut. These can be found in the cones of a number of different pines throughout the country. Generally, the larger cones have the nuts that are worth the trouble of harvesting. Collect a bunch of cones and break them up to retrieve the nuts; with a bit of care, you can collect several pounds without destroying too many. These can then be roasted and eaten at your leisure. If all you can find are cones that have dropped but have not opened, place the cone near a fire and the drying process will cause them to gradually open up. If you are lucky enough to be out West where there are pinon pines, be sure to collect and roast these; they are the absolute best.

The Indians and frontiersmen also had turnips, wild cucumber and a variety of edible fungi such as mushrooms to choose from when in the woods. I highly recommend *against* eating any wild mushrooms unless you are *absolutely sure* they are edible. Many poisonous varieties look similar to edible

Two tin military cups. The large one on the left has been made into a "corn boiler" with a bail and lid. I have not seen any authentication for this style prior to the Civil War.

mushrooms; the wrong choice can mean not having to concern yourself with trail food ever again!

The frontiersmen and the mountain men descended from them were notorious for their sweet tooths. The most available sweetener in the hardwood forests was, of course, maple sugar. Maple sugar is procured by "tapping" a maple tree. This is done by boring a hole into the tree while the sap is running. The sap will run out of the bore hole and into a waiting container. The gathered sap is then boiled slowly, rendered if you will, until nothing but sugar remains. A Yankee friend of mine relates how she would pour partly-rendered sap on the snow and eat it after it was frozen. Gee, being from Florida, I only had piña coladas. The frontiersman also had the occasional luck to find a beehive and its precious honey. Both of these sweeteners could be mixed into a variety of cakes and dishes such as mush.

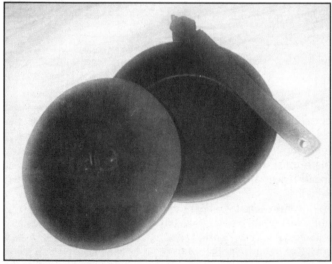

A sheet steel frying pan with lid. This version of the folding handle, which is commonly found on molds and cookware, rotates on a hinge pin to save space.

Lest I forget, rice was available in the Great Lakes region. It's not the all too familiar white rice but the healthy wild rice that can be found in most stores. White rice is a whole lot of starch and not a whole lot of nutrition. For food, use wild rice; for starch, cook the white stuff and use the water for starching your petticoats. But don't bury the solid parts; it could be an EPA violation.

I found an interesting, if not disturbing, comment while reading Rev. Joseph Doddridge's *Notes on the Settlement and Indian Wars of the Western Parts of Virginia and Pennsylvania*. In this book, which is not appreciably longer than its title, the Reverend states that drinks such as coffee and tea were called "slops," since they would not "stick to the ribs!" At least one of his sources said, "A genuine backwoodsman would have thought himself disgraced by showing a fondness for those slops" (140). But thankfully that was just one man's opinion, I hope. Actually, to come clean, I personally am not fond of those slops myself. I just drink them to fit in. Really.

Speaking of slops, I have found that coffee is just too bulky to carry any more than just a few days' worth. When on the trail, I now carry block tea. A small block of compressed tea only a couple of inches square will easily provide a week's worth of tea. Not only is the block tea convenient to carry, but it is also less prone to moisture damage than loose tea. Tea can be brewed as dark as coffee, which is the way I do mine. The faster the water is boiling, the darker it will brew without becoming too bitter.

The white settlers also grew crops, some of which were brought over from Europe. Initially the English, ignorant fools that they were, came over to grow cash crops like tobacco and relied on shipments of food from Britain. The French, Dutch, Swedes and others, even the English after awhile, grew their own food crops. The Europeans introduced peas, wheat, apples, peaches, pears and another variety of cherries. The settlers also grew native crops like corn, pumpkins, squash, beans and potatoes in their truck patches.

COOKING AND EATING ON THE TRAIL

Once you have dried or otherwise preserved your trail food, you will need to pack it in some sort of container. I have found cloth sacks to be about the best for a number of reasons. A cloth sack will not retain moisture like one of leather and should it get wet will dry quickly. Dried foods can be wet and re-dried without going bad. Simply spread the food on a clean, sunlit surface and it will soon be dry. I have gotten my food bags wet and just hung them up in the sun to dry without concern for spoilage. You will find that most dried foods are pretty much water resistant and will not soak up water very quickly. I keep my jerky in a sack with some salt to attract the moisture that the jerky might otherwise draw, and it also helps to retard spoilage.

As for how much food you should carry, well that depends upon your eating habits. I carry my food sack of dried corn in my tin kettle, which holds about 4-1/2 cups. This, with a like amount of jerky, will last me over a week without having to supplement it by hunting or fishing. A small amount in the morning and the same amount in the evening will generally suit me just fine. Even with this "take-along" food, I try to forage so I don't have to rely on my stores. Fresh meat is almost always better than dried anyway.

All that is generally needed to cook most trail food is a small kettle or large cup. A sheet iron frying pan will also work but is not nearly as efficient as a kettle. As a matter of fact, there are no trail foods that absolutely must be fried. Carrying oil or grease is a waste of space and the resulting weight is excessive, especially if you are on foot. If you are traveling by water or with a pack animal, it's not such a problem. But I have not seen many accounts of frontiersmen frying food and prefer not to do so myself. Rancid oil or grease can ruin a trip. Even George Washington advised against frying and recommended broiling and roasting, feeling it was healthier for the troops.

I commonly carry only a small tin cup and a tin kettle with a lid and bail. I have used a sheet metal frying pan with a lid and have gone back to the kettle since food cooks much quicker in the kettle, especially at high altitudes. Coffee or tea is easier to

Two tin pots. The one on the right is a copy of a Colonial period piece and holds about 4-1/2 cups. On the left is a commonly available "beer bucket" type supplied by many of today's suppliers. Both are very light, but the larger will not readily fit into a bedroll or haversack.

make in the kettle as well. Since losing my fork somewhere in the mountains, the only eating utensil I carry is a spoon. The only time I feel that a cast iron pot or fire irons of any size makes sense is when you are not concerned with carrying the extra weight. At a rendezvous or when traveling by canoe or with pack animals, the extra weight is easily managed. But when on foot, the weight is an unnecessary burden that is best avoided. A pound here or a few ounces there adds up quickly. Walk a few miles in rough country, try uphill at an altitude of 6,000 feet, and you'll start getting my message real quickly!

Of course, many foods can be cooked without utensils. If you learn a few of these simple techniques, you will find that you can do without most of the cooking gear you are accustomed

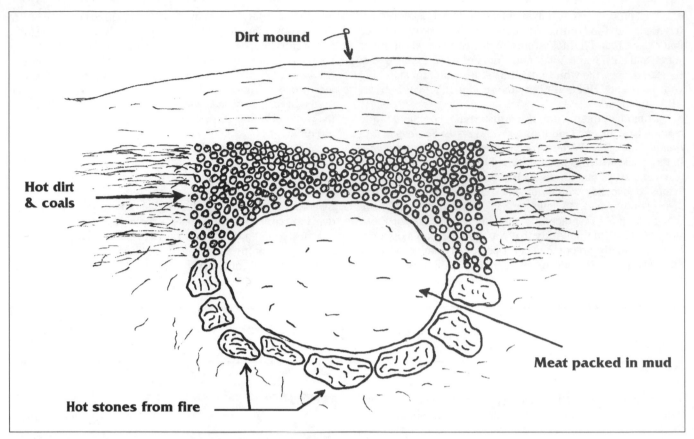

Dirt mound

Hot dirt & coals

Meat packed in mud

Hot stones from fire

A well-made pit fire can cook your food while you are away from camp, and it helps to fool the camp dogs. It's important to have enough insulating material around the food to keep it from drying out and burning.

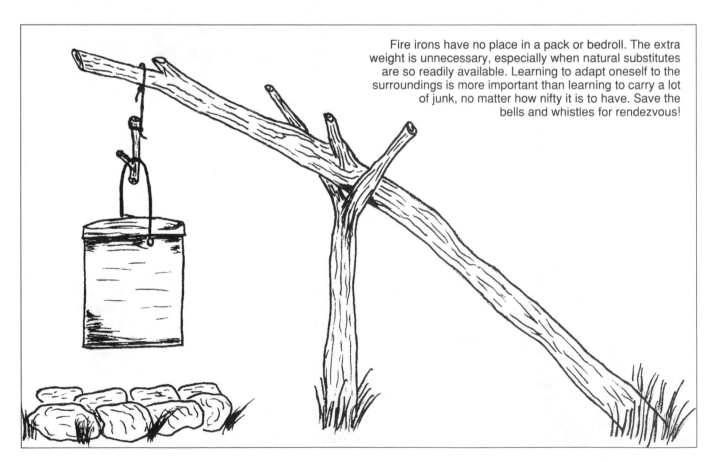

Fire irons have no place in a pack or bedroll. The extra weight is unnecessary, especially when natural substitutes are so readily available. Learning to adapt oneself to the surroundings is more important than learning to carry a lot of junk, no matter how nifty it is to have. Save the bells and whistles for rendezvous!

These copper kettles, made by Westminster Forge, are designed to "nest" or fit within one another. A nested set of pots or kettles is just right for carrying on a pack horse or in a boat. When a number of people are traveling in a party, the nested set can be carried by one man while the others carry the food. Keep the set from rattling by separating each piece with grass or sections of fabric that can double as pot holders.

to having on an outing. The easiest way to cook most fresh meat is to roast it. I have cooked small game and a lot of fish this way, and it requires almost no preparation. Find a rock that is flat enough to support the meat and clean the dirt off of it. Place this rock in the fire until it is hot enough to cause a few drops of water to sizzle when dropped upon it. Move it to one side of the fire and place your game on it and allow it to cook. Be sure to turn the meat over frequently enough to keep it from burning.

Another cooking method with rocks is to construct a rock oven. This should be built before the fire is burning if possible. All you need to do is build with flat stones a small rock cave that is just large enough to hold your food. Make sure the mouth of the oven is facing the fire. Place your meat inside and allow it to cook. If you wish you can pile hot coals on top to quicken the cooking. Make sure that you do not use any rocks that have been in the water or buried in wet ground. Chances are that they retain moisture, which will expand rapidly when heated and cause the rocks to explode.

Food can be cooked in an underground pit as well. I like to dig a hole under the already burning fire and place my food inside. Once covered by a sufficient layer of coals and soil, your meat will cook very nicely. Larger pieces of meat and

whole birds can be cooked like this. Cover the meat with a thick layer of wet leaves and mud and it will be less likely to dry out and burn. Cooking time will vary according to the temperature of the fire, dampness of the ground, depth and size of the food. This will take some firsthand learning. Once this technique is perfected, you can get a lot of other things done while your food

is cooking unsupervised. It also defeats all those "camp dogs" that seem to find their way to *your* place when they smell food cooking.

Another form of roasting, spit cooking, is pretty successful too. This works well for meat or birds, but I prefer not to hang fish from a spit because of the different cooking time required for the thinner and thicker sections. Be sure to turn the meat when on the spit to keep it from cooking unevenly.

All your veggies can be boiled, and some, especially the fruits, are good raw. A word of caution on the dried fruits: too much at one time is a good cure for constipation. 'Nuff said. The easiest way to cook your dried goods is to let them soak in water to reconstitute. They will soak up a lot of water if left immersed while you go about the business of setting up camp, cutting firewood or just fooling around at rendezvous. If you are not changing camps that day, such as at rendezvous or a non-traveling day on the trail, set your stuff to soaking after your morning chores are done. The longer dry foods are soaked, the less you will have to cook them.

It is a good idea to carry a certain amount of food that doesn't require cooking. If you're caught in a storm and can't make a fire, you'll come to appreciate this idea. I have done this for years, and it's proven to be a wise decision. Dried meats, including fish, can be eaten cooked or uncooked. Uncooked, they are a handy source of energy and will help ward off those hunger pangs when sitting along a deer trail. Any of the dried meats can be shredded, crumbled or ground and slowly cooked. I have found that dried meat added to beans, peas or corn makes a hearty stew that can keep you warm in even the coldest weather.

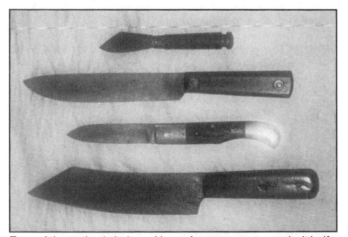

Four of the author's knives. He prefers to carry two: a belt knife with a stouter edge for heavy work, and a folding knife for finer work requiring a thinner blade. He currently carries the folding "penney knife" at top and the simple but well-made butcher knife below it. Below the butcher knife is an English folding knife of the late 1700s. At the bottom is an original butcher style made in the 19th century.

CONCLUSION

The true American frontiersman, whether he was a long hunter or the Western trapper that followed, was totally self-sufficient. He could hunt and fish or trap fresh meat. He could also gather wild food plants, many of which I have not even mentioned here. He also knew where to find crop foods planted by others. With a little experience, the modern reenactor or buckskinner can also keep himself (or herself) well-fed on the trail.

Now a final word about conservation and its impact on what we do. If you haven't picked up some of my subtle hints, most of your success in hunting, fishing and just generally being able to exist in the woods depends on how we treat our environment. It never ceases to amaze me when I'm up in the mountains fly fishing and I find beer cans and candy wrappers. I've been on 9,000 foot mountain peaks only to find trash. And all this time I thought pigs lived on farms, not mountains. We must take an active role in protecting our environment if our children and others who come after us are to be able to hunt and fish as we have. Carry out your trash. After reading this chapter, you shouldn't have any need to take it into the woods anyway.

Appendix A: Works Cited

Armour, David A., and Keith R. Widder. *At the Crossroads: Michilimackinac During the American Revolution.* Mackinac Island, MI: Mackinac Island State Park Commission, 1978.

Arnow, Harriett Simpson. *Seedtime on the Cumberland.* New York: MacMillan, 1960.

Bouquet, Henry. *Papers of Col. Henry Bouquet.* First American Frontier Series. Salem, NH: Ayer Company Publishers, 1972.

Brown, Tom. *Tom Brown's Field Guide to Nature Observation and Tracking.* New York: Berkley Books, 1983.

Denig, Edwin. *Five Indian Tribes of the Upper Missouri.* Norman: University of Oklahoma Press, 1977.

Doddridge, Joseph. *Notes on the Settlement and Indian Wars of the Western Parts of Virginia and Pennsylvania from 1763 to 1783.* Albany, NY: Joel Munsell, 1876.

Eckert, Allan. *The Wilderness War.* New York: Bantam, 1982.

Heath, Dwight B., ed. *Mourt's Relation: A Journal of the Pilgrims at Plymouth.* Boston: Applewood Books, 1986

Kalm, Peter. *Peter Kalm's Travels in North America.* Ed. and trans. Adolph B. Benson. New York: Dover Publications, 1987.

Knox, John. *The Siege of Quebec (1757-1760).* Palo Alto, CA: Pendragon House, 1976.

Leach, Douglas Edward. *The Northern Colonial Frontier 1607-1763.* Albuquerque: University of New Mexico Press, 1966.

Lyford, Carrie A. *Iroquois Crafts.* Ontario: Iroqrafts, Ltd., 1982.

Robinson, W. Stitt. *The Southern Colonial Frontier 1607-1763.* Albuquerque: University of New Mexico Press, 1979.

Smith, James. *Scoouwa: James Smith's Indian Captivity Narrative.* Columbus, OH: Ohio Historical Society, 1978.

Appendix B: Reccommended Reading

As with all things new, we need to learn from more than one source to gain a well-rounded, broad knowledge of the subject. I have many books that I use for references, both for this chapter and my general woods' lore. It's not all learned by experience; a lot of it has to come from someone else first. What follows is a recommended reading list for those of you who would like to learn more about living off the land and applying old technologies similar to those of our ancestors. I hope these books help you as much as they have me:

Tom Brown's Field Guide to Wilderness Survival. New York: Berkley Books, 1983. ISBN #: 0-425-10572-5.

Tom Brown's Field Guide to Nature Observation and Tracking. New York: Berkley Books, 1983. ISBN #: 0-425-09966-0.

Tom Brown's Guide to Edible and Medicinal Plants. New York: Berkley Books, 1985. ISBN #:0-425-10063-4.

The Foxfire Series. Garden City, NY: Anchor Press—Doubleday.

The Book of Buckskinning Series. Ed. William H. Scurlock. Texarkana, TX: Rebel Publishing.

Old-Time Shooting Matches

by George D. Glenn

Much as he hates to admit it, George Glenn (seen here contemplating the error of his ways at a Revolutionary War reenactment) has been involved in muzzleloading, buckskinning and reenacting almost long enough to be considered an "old timer." His interest in old guns and all that goes with them was first kindled when his father gave him a Civil War Enfield musket at the age of 13 in 1951. He did not come from a gun or shooting-oriented family—only God knows what possessed his father.

After George married he built a flintlock longrifle from Dixie Gun Works' parts and learned to shoot. That he managed to make them fit together and actually work much amused his wife. According to her it's been all downhill for the last third of a century.

Since that first rifle, he founded the Turkey Foot Longrifles in 1969, started writing for *MUZZLELOADER* in 1975 and has been one of its special features' editors since 1976. George also thinks he was the first person in the country to offer a university-level course in muzzleloading. He took up buckskinning and graduated to Revolutionary War reenacting while maintaining an avid interest in paper-punching. In addition, he considers himself an enthusiastic muzzleloading deer hunter (although a lousy deer finder), confesses a clandestine affection for black powder cartridge guns and has committed other similar acts for which he will surely be called to account at that great Final Muster.

Glenn is a member of the NMLRA, the IBHA, the SSRA and the NRA, as well as a charter member of the Iowa Black Powder Federation. He serves as the commander of the Sixth Virginia Regiment of Foot, Continental Line, in the North West Territory Alliance. This chapter marks his sixth appearance in *The Book of Buckskinning Series*.

It was a hot July day in Manheim, New York, in 1814, but it was cool in the Pig 'n Whistle, where the innkeeper, Job Evans, presided. Evans mopped the bar and cast a sidelong look at the lone customer slouched over his third mug of applejack brandy at the end of the bar. He was fairly sure he recognized the man as Nathaniel "Bloody Nat" Foster. Foster ostensibly made his living supplying venison for the down-state markets of Schenectady, Troy and Albany, but there were rumors that he also was not above murdering trappers for their furs. It was more than rumor that he was an Indian-killer. It was also more than rumor that he was accounted as the best marksman with the longrifle in the mountains.

Bloody Nat was tall and thin to the point of emaciation, with long black hair and small, sullen eyes. He was dressed in a homespun rifle frock, with his bullet pouch and powder horn slung over his shoulder and a long hunting knife suspended by a thong around his neck hanging in its sheath between his shoulder blades. His .40 caliber flintlock longrifle leaned against the bar beside him.

Evans was in the process of drawing another applejack for Foster when he became aware of a disturbance outside. Stepping to the open door, he looked out into the bright sunlight where a company of soldiers was marching into the village green opposite. He smiled in anticipation of good business as he plunked the mug of applejack down in front of Foster.

"Looks like the 13th New York Volunteers are on their way north to Niagara."

"A Company, if that's Captain Forsyth I recognized formin' 'em up by the flagpole," Foster replied with a grunt.

Receiving no more response from Foster, who continued to stare moodily into his drink, Evans went back to the doorway in time to see the troops stack their arms around the flagpole and dismiss. A good number of them headed straight for his tavern, and he bustled back behind the bar as the hot, thirsty young men came crowding in noisily. Soon Evans' supply of spring-cooled, hard apple cider was being rapidly depleted.

As the soldiers' thirst diminished, their spirits revived, and soon they were loudly telling each other how much mayhem they were going to inflict on the British forces at Niagara. Even the usually close-mouthed Scotsman Sergeant Robinson found his tongue loosened by the hard cider and began bragging about his skill as a marksman with the .54 Harper's Ferry rifle.

Foster had been ignoring the bragging soldiers, although more than one of them had glanced over at the unkempt rifleman at the end of the bar as if wondering why he wasn't also in the army and on his way to fight the British. It was Sergeant Robinson's boasts about his shooting that finally got Foster's attention, and he began muttering obscenities to himself as Robinson continued to describe his skill.

Suddenly, slamming his cup of brandy down on the bar, Foster strode over to the rambunctious group of soldiers and singling Robinson out of the crowd, growled, "You there with the big mouth! Do you do all your shooting in taverns, maybe?"

Outraged, the sergeant roared back, "Not I, ye ill-mannered scut! I'd like nawthin' better than to put a bullet between those pig eyes of yours!"

"And swing for murder!" snarled Foster. "Nay, Scotty, I have a better notion. By your big talk, I gather that you are the champion marksman of your company—nay, of your whole regiment. Well, by God, Nat Foster is the best shot in all these mountains—yes, the best shot in all of York State! Now, Mister Sergeant, either shoot a match with me for fifty dollars hard money or drink your boy's drink in respectful silence when a real rifleman stands nearby drinking a man's drink!"

Evans fumbled below the bar for his blunderbuss as Sergeant Robinson roared and made a rush towards Foster, but fortunately Sergeant Jones and young Corporal Adams managed to keep the two apart and get Robinson cooled down enough to marked out two six-inch circles in the center of the remaining blazes for the speed shoot. Pine blocks split to about six inches square were prepared for the block shoot with one side charred to face the shooters. Finally, the short, chubby Evans puffed and sweated as he paced out the distances, stretching his stride to make sure that he was getting a yard a step.

A Company gathered around their champion as Robinson and Foster came together at the firing line. Evans, mopping his brow with a huge polka-dotted handkerchief, flipped a coin to determine who would fire first. Bloody Nat won the toss and declared that he would lead off with the 100-yard block shoot.

Experienced shooters and hunters among the soldiers noticed uncomfortably the ease and familiarity with which Nat handled and loaded his rifle, which seemed an extension of his body. He wasted no time in pouring his powder charge down the barrel, positioning a greased linen patch over the muzzle, centering the ball and ramming all of it home with a single, smooth stroke of his ramrod. A quick dash of priming powder in his pan and he raised the rifle to his shoulder. Scarcely had the rifle reached his shoulder when Nat fired, and the first block spun off the top rail of the split rail fence 100 yards away.

As Sergeant Robinson prepared his Harper's Ferry, his fellow sergeant, Jones, could be heard whispering to young Corporal Adams:

"See there, Johnny. That's the way an old hunter shoots who's used to having to take snap-shots in the woods. And notice the front sight on his rifle—it's silver, to show up better in the woods."

Jones fell silent as Robinson stepped to the line, raised his piece and took careful aim. His rifle cracked and a second block leaped off the fence rail. The cheer that rose from the soldiers' throats set the village dogs to barking, but Bloody Nat was undisturbed as he stepped forward again. His second shot, as quick as the first, knocked his second block off the fence. Robinson matched him with his second shot, which he continued to do until four shots had been fired by each man. On the fifth shot Foster missed, and all the soldiers held their breath as Robinson stepped to the line, raised his rifle and took his time aiming—too much time as it turned out, for he too missed the fifth shot.

The host of the Pig 'n Whistle waddled down to the fence with a small rule, gathered up the blocks and began measuring to see which of the two shooters had shot closest to the centers of the individual blocks. Evans took his time measuring and finally stood up, waved his arms and shouted, "The winner of the block shoot is...Robinson!" The cheer that had greeted Robby's first shot was nothing to the racket the company raised on this announcement.

Ignoring the celebrating soldiers, Foster made his preparations for the next event, the 50-yard speed shoot at the six-inch bull's eye. In this match each shooter was to shoot five shots as rapidly and accurately as possible, and Foster had made some preparations in advance. He had shaved down five rifle balls with his knife so that they would be considerably under bore size, and he popped them into his mouth as he waited for the match to begin. The match was to start with unloaded rifles, and Corporal Adams watched Bloody Nat's technique in this novelty match. As soon as Evans gave the command to shoot, Foster poured an unmeasured charge of powder straight from his big horn into the barrel, spat a rifle ball into the muzzle of the rifle, slapped the stock of the rifle to settle the charge and force some of the powder into the pan as priming, raised his rifle and fired before Robinson was even

accept Foster's challenge. After some spirited discussion, it was decided that the match would take place the next day, it now being too late to start a shooting match. Captain Forsyth put up the fifty dollars while the rest of the men did a brisk business that evening betting all their money with the villagers on their sergeant, Robby.

Since Robinson was the challenged shooter, he had first choice of the matches to be shot and elected to shoot a 5-shot match at wooden blocks at 100 yards. Foster then selected a 5-round speed shoot at 50 yards, while it was agreed that the third match would be a 5-shot peg shoot at 75 yards. All three matches were to be shot off-hand. Innkeeper Evans was picked to referee the matches.

The shooting was to begin at noon, and Evans was busy all morning getting the matches ready. For the peg shoot and the speed shoot, trees were blazed with axes at a height of five feet; the blazes were smoothed with a knife. For the peg shoot, Evans mixed up a gunpowder paste with which he marked two six-inch crosses in the center of the blazes. He carefully

half-way through loading his first round. It was evident that Robinson was no match for the experienced Indian killer and market hunter at this fast, short-range trick shooting. Indeed Foster hit his mark for the fifth straight time while Robinson was getting ready to fire his third shot. With the matches tied at one each, everything was now up to the peg shoot.

"I heard that Dan'l Boone once scored a string of only five inches," Sergeant Jones muttered to young Adams. "I wonder if Foster can match that."

Robinson fired first in this match, and it didn't take long for both men to fire their requisite five shots at the black crosses 75 yards away. Tension was high as innkeeper Job Evans waddled down to the target trees to take his measurements. He inserted whittled pegs into each of the contestant's bullet holes and then tightly stretched a string around the outside of the pegs. The shortest string would be the winner. Evans measured Robinson's group first. It made an excellent string of 8-3/8 inches. But Foster's string measured only 6-1/2 inches, and for the first time since the soldiers had laid eyes on him, Foster bared his yellow, snaggled teeth in a victory grin.

Having reloaded his rifle, Foster turned to Captain Forsyth to collect his hundred dollars. Forsyth was so impressed with Foster's shooting that he offered him a job as civilian scout at thirty dollars hard money a month.

But Foster was not the type to give up the freedom of the woods for military discipline. "No, sir, Captain, I don't approve of white men fightin' each other like a passel of heathen redskins. You can just keep your thirty dollars a month—Nat Foster don't need your money."

With that Sergeant Robinson, outraged that Foster wouldn't fight for his country, grabbed him by the collar of his rifle shirt and yelled for somebody to bring a rope to hang the cowardly traitor. Bloody Nat twisted away from Robinson's grip, drew the long knife that hung at his back and thrust at Robinson with it before any of the others could make a move to intervene. Wounded in the arm, Robinson backed off and Foster retrieved his fallen rifle, cocked it and held it on Captain Forsyth as he slowly backed away into the woods. As he reached the shelter of the trees, he suddenly whirled and vanished like a shadow.

(Adapted from Norman B. Wiltsey, "A Backwoods Shooting Match," American Gun Magazine *1.2, 1961.)*

The story of the shooting match between Bloody Nat Foster and Sergeant Robinson is fairly typical, at least in terms of its description of the various kinds of matches enjoyed on the frontier. Today we would describe these as "primitive" matches as opposed to more organized shooting on official paper targets, derided as mere "paper-punching" by many buckskinners. But whether informal or formal, the goal of all shooting matches is the same—to see which rifle and which shooter is, on that given day, the best. In this chapter we'll take

a look at a wide variety of shooting matches over the years. For the most part, we'll concentrate on muzzleloading rifle matches, since mastery of the rifle as a part of our historical tradition has long been the epitome of modern muzzleloading. We'll look at both formal and informal matches and in the process get an idea of where our modern matches come from and maybe get some inspiration for future matches at rendezvous and shoots.

Marksmanship per se, including the spur-of-the-moment challenge, has probably been around since the time the first humans began throwing rocks. For many thousands of years, the bow was of course the weapon of choice for shooting contests, and when firearms had developed sufficiently to permit any kind of accuracy, many of the conditions of archery contests were appropriated for the gun. During the 15th and 16th centuries, the formation of shooting guilds in Europe and particularly in Switzerland was encouraged by the authorities to ensure a reservoir of trained marksmen for the many wars of the period. At first these guilds were for bowmen, particularly men using the crossbow, but it wasn't long before firearms were introduced.

The first guild specifically for firearms seems to have been established in Lucerne in 1466 (Trench 105). The authorities provided powder and shot, although each competitor provided his own firearm. These would have probably been the

An event that was a carryover from crossbow days was shooting at the popinjay— a stuffed bird on top of a long pole. Spectator and shooter safety was apparently not a major concern (Trench 125).

The great Shooting Tournement held in Zurich, Switzerland, in 1504. The shooters (or the spectators) are protected by enclosed firing points (Trench 156).

smoothbore matchlock arquebus (heavy musket) or caliver (lighter musket). Shooting was held on Sundays at a range of about 110 yards. In comparison crossbow matches were shot at a range of 140 yards.

The usual target seems to have been a round wooden one about a yard in diameter with a center round bull painted on it. Beside the target was a small hut for the target marker, who would signal hits with a small disc on a rod. The winner of a Sunday event would serve as target marker for the next Sunday's shooting, while the second-place shooter would have the job of tending the shooters' slow matches (Trench 107-108).

Firing for the King's Prize, August 29, 1717 (Trench 124).

The rifle made its appearance in the 15th century and its impact could be seen in the increasing ranges at which matches were shot. In 1472, matches were shot at Zurich at 230 paces and in 1487 at 245 paces at Eichstadt. By the 16th century, distances of 250 to 300 yards were not uncommon (Trench 108-109).

The rifle was not a widely used arm, partially because of the complications of loading: in the days before the undersized ball and the patch, the bore-sized ball (.80-.85 caliber) was hammered down the barrel with ramrod and mallet, a time-consuming process. But 200 yards seems to have been pretty much the limit of effective accuracy.

The rifle was still more accurate than the smoothbore, and to take maximum advantage of its capabilities, improved sighting systems were devised fairly early. The usual rear sight was a V-sight, sometimes with two or three separate leaves for different ranges. Tube sights were fairly common, and a book published in Nuremberg in 1702 mentions an effective telescopic sight (Trench 193).

It was with the development of the American longrifle from German/Swiss rifles that the rifle and advances in marksmanship came into their own. The story of the longrifle has been told many times, so there's no need to go into detail here. The main advantages of the longrifle over previous rifles were its reduced bore size (about .50) with a corresponding reduction in powder charges, the utilization of the smaller than bore-size ball wrapped in a greased patch and the length of the barrel, all of which made for a flat trajectory and greater accuracy. The longrifle shot pretty much "dead on" at ranges up to 100-150 yards in the hands of an experienced rifleman; at longer ranges the shooter applied a little "hold over" to be fairly confident of hitting game or enemies at ranges of 300-plus yards.

The skill of the American rifleman became legendary in the latter half of the 18th century, although the rifle was far from being a universal weapon. It was still a novelty to many inhabitants of the urban areas of the East Coast, but stories about its accuracy became fairly widespread during the Revolution. Colonel George Hanger's famous story illustrates the potential of the longrifle as a long-range weapon:

Colonel, now General, Tarleton, and myself, were standing a few yards out of a wood, observing the situation of a part of the enemy which we intended to attack. There was a rivulet in

134

the enemy's front, and a mill on it, to which we stood directly with horses' heads fronting, observing their motions. It was absolutely a plain field between us and the mill; not so much as a single bush on it. Our orderly-bugler stood behind us about three yards, but with his horse's side to our horses' tails. A rifleman passed over the milldam, evidently observing two officers, and laid himself down on his belly; for in such positions they always lie, to take a good shot at a long distance. He took a deliberate and cool shot at my friend, at me, and at the bugle-horn man. Now observe how well this fellow shot. It was in the month of August, and not a breath of wind was stirring. Colonel Tarleton's horse and mine, I am certain, were not anything like two feet apart; for we were in close consultation, how we should attack with our troops which laid 300 yards in the wood, and could not be perceived by the enemy. A rifle-ball passed between him and me; looking directly to the mill I evidently observed the flash of the powder. I directly said to my friend, "I think we had better move, or we shall have two or three of these gentlemen shortly amusing themselves at our expense." The words were hardly out of my mouth when the bugle-horn man behind me, and directly central, jumped off his horse and said, "Sir, my horse is shot." The horse staggered, fell down, and died....Now speaking of this rifleman's shooting, nothing could be better....I have passed several times over this ground and ever observed it with the greatest attention; and I can positively assert that the distance he fired from at us was full 400 yards....I have many times asked the American backwoodsman what was the most their best marksmen could do; they have constantly told me that an expert rifleman, provided he can draw good and true sight, can hit the head of a man at 200 yards. I am certain that provided an American rifleman was to get a perfect aim at 300 yards at me standing still, he would undoubtedly hit me, unless it was a very windy day. (qtd. in LaCrosse 76)

Americans were also impressed by the abilities of the frontier rifleman. An account of Captain Michael Cresap's company of riflemen as printed in the *Pennsylvania Packet*, August 1775, attests to the shooting abilities, if not the judgment, of Colonial riflemen:

With their rifles in their hands they assume a kind of omnipotence over their enemies. You will not much wonder at this when I mention a fact, which can be fully attested by several of the reputable inhabitants of this place, who were eyewitnesses of it. Two brothers in the company took a piece of board, five inches broad, and seven inches long, with a bit of white paper, about the size of a dollar, nailed in the center, and while one of them supported this board perpendicularly between his knees, the other at the distance of upwards of sixty yards, and without any kind of rest, shot eight bullets successively through the board, and spared a brother's thighs.

Another of the company held a barrel stave perpendicularly in his hand, with one hedge close to his side, while one of his comrades at the same distance [60 yards]....shot several bullets through it, without any apprehension of danger on either side. The spectators, appearing to be amazed at these feats, were told that there were upwards of fifty persons in the company who could do the same thing; that there was not one who could not plug 19 bullets out of 20 (as they termed it) within an inch of the head of a ten-penny nail [distance not specified]. (La Crosse 76-77)

This story of shooting at a board held by another person crops up again in reference to Cresap's men and is repeated about the "inhabitants of Red Bank" in 1796 by General Vistor Callot (La Crosse 77).

Innumerable references exist about riflemen consistently being able to hit a man's head at a distance of 200 yards—enough of them that the accuracy of the rifles and the ability of the riflemen to hold a six- to eight-inch group at 200 yards must be believed, although I am tempted to dismiss as propaganda Richard Henry Lee's claim (1775) that there "is not one of these Men who wish a distance less than 200 yards *or a larger object than an Orange* [emphasis mine]" (La Crosse 80).

Two things conspire to make these tales of shooting ability credible: one is the ability of the riflemen themselves. Numerous accounts emphasize that these individuals were accustomed to being armed with the rifle for virtually their entire lives, and thus the effective use of the rifle must have become instinctual

Target shooting at Zurich, Switzerland, in 1532. Note the arrangement of the firing line, target and scorer's hut. The relative accuracy of the weapons is indicated by the great number of bullet holes on the wall behind the target (Trench 108-109).

with them. Second, the weapons themselves were accurate. Most of us are aware of the excellent shooting that can be performed with good, modern reproductions, but the originals were at least as good. Dillin, in *The Kentucky Rifle*, presents examples of actual targets shot by the old rifles, giving groups of an inch or so at 100 yards, and he himself supervised the shooting of an original 18th century rifle that turned in two-inch groups (Trench 207).

The British of course had their riflemen too, the most famous of whom was Captain Patrick Ferguson and his breech-loading flintlock rifle. The Ferguson rifle was loaded by rotating the trigger guard that dropped the breech plug so that a ball could be inserted into the breech to be followed by a charge of powder. Raising the plug cuts off the excess powder. The weapon was primed in the usual manner and it was ready to fire. A contemporary account of a demonstration at Woolwich, England, on June 1, 1776, attests to the rifle's effectiveness:

Notwithstanding a heavy rain and the high wind, [Ferguson] fired during the space of four or five minutes at the rate of four shots per minute, at a target two hundred yards distance. He next fired six shots in one minute, and also fired (while advancing at the rate of four miles an hour) four times in a minute....Lastly, he hit the bull's eye lying on his back on the ground, incredible as it may seem to many, considering the variations of the wind and the wetness of the weather. He only missed the target three times during the whole course of the experiments. (qtd. in Peterson 219)

Although Ferguson and his riflemen didn't survive the Battle of King's Mountain, in 1800 the British Army did form an experimental rifle corps armed with a rifle developed by a Whitechapel gunmaker, Ezekiel Baker. The Baker rifle was .615 caliber, with a very slow rifling twist of one turn in 120 inches. It was not usually renowned for its accuracy and in fact was sighted in for 100 yards although it had a folding 200-yard leaf. Official tests were conducted in 1800 and 1803. With the rifle embedded in mortar, twelve shots were fired at a nine-foot diameter target at 300 yards. The result was a 4-foot-10-inch group, hardly remarkable. Baker then fired off-hand at a seven-foot diameter target at 100 yards and only scored fifteen hits out of eighteen shots, a 3-foot-6-inch group (Trench 206-207).

Considering these rather dismal official results, there are accounts of some excellent shooting with the Baker rifle. Trench recounts a story that he "treats with some incredulity," but "which nevertheless seems to be authentic":

It concerns the 2nd Battalion, Rifle Brigade, whose commanding officer in 1805 was Lieutenant-Colonel Wade, an excellent rifle shot. He and two private soldiers named Smeaton and Spurry used to hold targets for each other up to 150 and even 200 yards. When the Earl of Chatham, inspecting the battalion, remarked on the danger of this practice, Wade protested that there was no danger, and bidding a rifleman hold a target for him, aimed and hit it. Lord Chatham was horrified, but Wade nonchalantly informed him, "Oh, we all do it." He then held a target for the rifleman's fire. The story reflects high credit not only on the Rifle Brigade's marksmanship, but on the relations between officers and men: it cannot have been a regiment where discipline was maintained by the lash. (207)

The United States' first official rifle was the Model 1803, better known as the Harper's Ferry Rifle. It was .54 caliber to take a half-ounce patched .525 ball. The 33-inch barrel was half-round half-octagon and was rifled with seven grooves. It was capable of good accuracy; Surgeon John Gale reported in 1819 an event during the "Yellowstone Expedition":

The Troops were classed [on May 6] and commenced shooting at targets with ball cartridges at which they continued intill [sic] the 22nd daily practicing. Those who hit a circul [sic] of three inches diameter off hand fifty yards three times in six were raised from the awkward squad to the 2nd class. Those who can hit the same mark one hundred yards three times in six are raised to the first Class. They make rapid improvement. There are but few who are not in the first class. (qtd. in Garavaglia and Worman 13)

Such a report certainly gives credence to Sergeant Robinson's reported performance in 1814.

Stories of relatively formal shooting matches become more frequent in the early 19th century, although in the United

States they seem to be still pretty much a frontier or backwoods phenomenon. In England, however, there was no frontier; shooting was a village pastime. A certain E.B. Cayley reported that:

[D]uring the great French war almost every village hereabouts had its prizes for shooting at a mark with ball, and the most popular pastime of the day it was. "Where did you get that fine copper kettle of yours!" I said the other day to a tenant of mine. "Oh, I won it; a prize at target practice in our village near 50 years ago [1809]. (Times [London] 25 Apr. 1859: 11)

Baker's 100-yard, man-sized target. The first two shots at the top of the head were probably sighting shots. One would still expect better accuracy from a rifle at 100 yards (Trench 260).

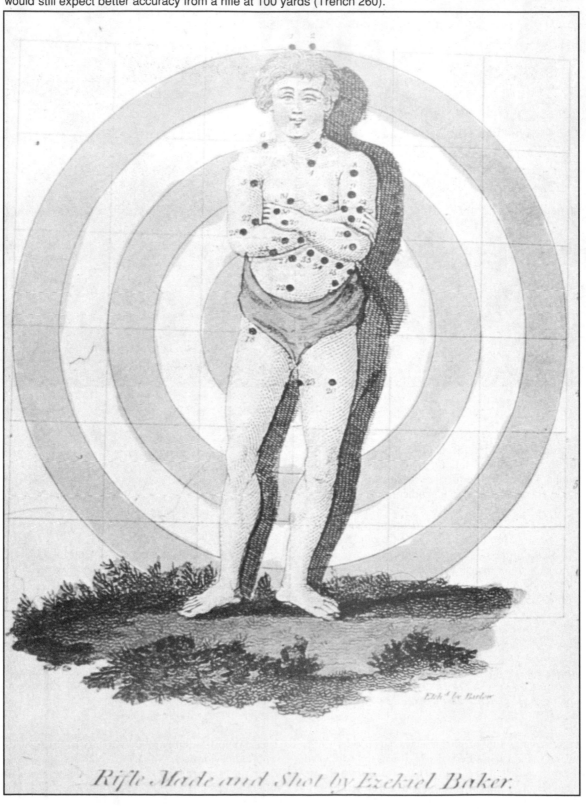

Rifle Made and Shot by Ezekiel Baker.

It is not certain that at this early date the contestants were shooting rifles. Certainly the winner of another match scored very poorly if the contest was with rifles:

Wednesday, after two days contest in shooting at a target at the distance of 100 yards, by 250 subscribers, at half a guinea each, at Kentish town, for a Leicester ox, supposed to be the largest in England, Mr. Barrow, of Mary-le-bonne-street, cheesemonger, was the successful candidate. He hit the target within four inches of the bulls' eye. (*Times* [London] 5 Sept. 1801: 2)

Even with smoothbores this is somewhat poor shooting. It would seem that the law of averages would dictate that in two days of shooting by 250 people, somebody would hit closer to the center of the bull than four inches.

Shooting for a beef was, of course, not a purely English phenomenon. It was a favorite contest throughout the United States well into the 20th century. A typical contest was shot in 1834 in Tennessee:

In the latter part of summer our cattle get very fat, as the range is remarkably fine; and some one, desirous of raising money on one of his cattle, advertises that on a particular day, and at a given place, a first-rate beef will be shot for.

When the day comes, every marksman in the neighborhood will meet at the appointed place, with his gun. After the company is assembled, a subscription paper is handed round, with the following heading:

"A.B. offers a beef worth twenty dollars, to be shot for, at twenty-five cents a shot." Then the names are put down by each person thus:

D.C. puts in four shots, ...$1.00
E.F. " eight " ... 2.00
G.H. " two " ... 0.50
And thus it goes round, until the price is made up.

Two persons are then selected, who have not entered for shots, to act as judges of the match. Every shooter gets a board and makes a cross in the centre of his target. The shot that drives the centre or comes nearest to it, gets the hide and tallow, which is considered the first choice. The nearest gets his choice of the hind quarters; the third gets the other hind quarter; the fourth takes choice of the fore quarters; the fifth the remaining quarter; and the sixth gets the lead in the tree against which we shoot..

The judges stand near the tree, and when a man fires they cry out, "Who shot?" and the shooter gives in his name; and so on, till all have shot. The judges then take all the boards and go off by themselves, and decide what quarter each man has won. Sometimes one will get nearly all. (Crockett 150-151)

The distance of such a shoot isn't indicated, nor the shooting position, but both might be inferred from another Crockett anecdote stemming from about the same period (1834):

I now started to Jersey City, where I found a great many gentlemen shooting rifles, at the distance of one hundred yards with a rest. One gentleman gave me his gun, and asked me to shoot. I raised up, off-hand, and cut within about two inches of the centre. I told him my distance was forty yards, off-hand. He loaded his gun, and we walked down to within forty yards, when I fired, and was deep in the paper. I shot a second time, and did the same. Colonel Mapes then put up a quarter of a dollar in the middle of a black spot, and asked me to shoot at it. I told him he had better mark the size of it and put his money in his pocket. He said "fire away." I did so, and made sleight-of-hand work with his quarter. (Crockett 123)

"Sleight-of-hand" may also explain the amazing effectiveness of some of the early shooters. For example this story as told by Randolph B. Marcy in *Thirty Years of Army Life on the Border*:

[Captain Martin Scott] *proposed to me, upon one occasion, that we should take an old-fashioned United States yager [Mississippi Rifle] that he had, and determine which could load and fire three shots in the shortest space of time, and make the best target. Accordingly, a playing-card, with a spot or bull's-eye in the centre about the size of a dime, was attached to a log of wood, and placed at seventy-five yards from where we proposed to stand. Captain Scott then took the rifle uncharged, and with the powder flask at hand, and the balls and patches in his mouth, and he made the three shots "off-hand" in one minute and twenty seconds. I then myself went to the target, and found one round hole directly through the centre of the bull's-eye. I was surprised at the precision of the shot, but observed to the captain that the other two had entirely missed the target. He shook his head and called for an axe, when we split the log, and found the three balls in one mass, all having passed through the same round aperture directly in the centre of the card.* (Garavaglia and Worman 53-54)

A three-shot one-hole group off-hand at 75 yards seems unbelievable, but a similar story might explain it. When Davy Crockett was visiting Little Rock, Arkansas, he writes:

[I]*t was proposed that we should go beyond the village, and shoot at a mark, for they had heard I was a first-rate shot, and they wanted to see for themselves....Well, I shouldered my Betsey, and she is just about as beautiful a piece as ever came out of Philadelphia, and I went out to the shooting ground, followed by all the leading men in Little Rock, and that was a clear majority of the town, for it is remarkable, that there are always more leading men in small villages than there are followers.*

I was in prime order. My eye was as keen as a lizard, and my nerves were as steady and unshaken as the political course of Henry Clay; so at it we went, the distance, one hundred yards. The principal marksmen, and such as had never been beat, led the way, and there was some pretty fair shooting, I tell you. At length it came to my turn. I squared myself, raised my beautiful Betsey to my shoulder, took deliberate aim, and smack I sent the bullet right into the centre of the bull's eye. "There's no mistake in Betsey," said I, in a sort of careless way, as they were all looking at the target, sort of amazed, and not at all over pleased.

"That's a chance shot, Colonel," said one who had the reputation of being the best marksman in those parts.

"Not as much chance as there was," said I,..."I can do it five times out of six any day in the week."

...They now proposed that we should have a second trial; but knowing that I had nothing to gain and everything to lose, I was for backing out and fighting shy; but there was no let-off,...so to it again we went. They were now put upon their mettle, and they fired much better than the first time; and it was what may be called pretty sharp shooting. When it came to my turn, I squared myself, and turning to the prime shot, I gave him

a knowing nod, by way of showing my confidence; and says I, "Look out for the bull's eye, stranger." I blazed away, and I wish I may be shot if I didn't miss the target. They examined it all over, and could find neither hair nor hide of my bullet, and pronounced it a dead miss; when says I, "Stand aside and let me look, and I warrant you I get on the right trail of the critter." They stood aside, and I examined the bull's eye pretty particular, and at length cried out, "Here it is; there is no snakes if it ha'n't followed the very track of the other." They said it was utterly impossible, but I insisted on their searching the hole, and I agreed to be stuck up as a mark myself, if they did not find two bullets there. They searched for my satisfaction, and sure enough it all come out just as I had told them; for I had picked up a bullet that had been fired, and stuck it deep in the hole, without anyone perceiving it. (Crockett 171-172)

Davy Crockett was moving west with the frontier, and as the explorers and fur trappers moved west, so did their shooting contests. The shooting continued to be at "targets of opportunity": a blaze on a tree, a chunk of wood, a piece of paper tacked to a charred shingle or barrel stave, a candle flame (as reported by Audubon in *Delineations of American Scenery and Character*), the head of a nail. Driving in a nail with a rifle bullet was a very popular frontier match and was mentioned as a favorite competition of Cresap's riflemen, although it is physically impossible to see a nail head at some of the distances claimed in the various stories. I have reasonably good distance vision (20:15) and I can't pick up the head of a 16 penny nail at more than 25-30 yards depending on the light, and at that I can't be sure that I'm really seeing it or just remembering where it was. Maybe they used bigger nails.

Audubon left an account of driving the nail at forty paces:

A shot which comes very close to the nail is considered as that of an indifferent marksman; the bending of the nail is, of course, somewhat better; but nothing less than hitting it right on the head is satisfactory. Well, kind reader, one out of three shots generally hits the nail, and should the shooters amount to half a dozen, two nails are frequently needed before each can have a shot. (qtd. in Burrell 2:11)

A similar account by a Robert Wilson is a little more believable:

It is almost incredible what marksmen those riflemen are. I once saw two of them, for a wager, shoot at a pin's head: they placed a piece of paper, about an inch square, against a post, in the center of which they stuck a pin, and fired at a distance, as near as I could guess, of ten yards. They fired a single ball. The first man who shot, struck the head of the pin and drove it into the post, the other did the same. They fired again; when the first man grazed the head of the pin, but did not drive it into the post as before; his antagonist's shot was doubtful; some said it hit the pin's head, others thought not. (qtd. in Burrell 2:11)

Another interesting contest dates from 1826, as reported in the *American Turf Register and Sporting News* for 1831. In this backwoods match, the contestants, shooting rifles of about .36 caliber, fired five shots into the muzzle of a musket barrel 30 yards away. Reportedly most of them got between two to four balls into the muzzle of the musket barrel (Garavaglia and Worman 33-34).

In Cresap's day riflemen astounded onlookers by holding boards or barrel staves to be shot at by their comrades. By the 1830s, this stunt was still being performed, but the target of choice was now a whiskey-filled tin cup either held on the outstretched hand or positioned William Tell-style on the head. (This kind of shooting has always seemed to be a terrible waste of good whiskey, not to mention what it does to the tin cup.) The character with whom this stunt is most often identified is the legendary Mike Fink, described in an 1829 article, "The Last of the Boatmen" by Morgan Neville that was published in *The Western Souvenir*:

He was leaning carelessly against a large beech; and...his left arm negligently pressed a rifle to his side....His stature was upwards of six feet, his proportions perfectly symmetrical, and exhibiting the evidence of Herculean powers....Long exposure to the sun and weather on the lower Ohio and Mississippi had

changed his skin....Although at least fifty years of age, his hair was as black as the wing of a raven. Next to his skin he wore a red flannel shirt, covered by a blue capot, ornamented with white fringe. On his feet were moccasins, and a broad leathern belt, from which hung, suspended in a sheath, a large knife, encircled his waist.

As soon as the steam boat became stationary, the cabin passengers jumped on shore. On ascending the bank, the figure I have just described advanced to offer me his hand.

"How are you, Mike?" said I.

"How goes it?" replied the boatman—grasping my hand with a squeeze, that I can compare to nothing but that of a blacksmith's vice.

"I am glad to see you, Mannee!"—continued he in his abrupt manner. "I am going to shoot at the tin cup for a quart—off hand—and you must be judge."

I understood Mike at once, and on any other occasion, should have remonstrated, and prevented the daring trial of skill. But I was accompanied by a couple of English tourists [and] a few bloods from Philadelphia and Baltimore..., and I resolved to give them an opportunity of seeing a Western Lion—for such Mike undoubtedly was—in all his glory....

Mike, followed by several of his crew, led the way to a beech grove, some little distance from the landing. I invited my fellow passengers to witness the scene.—On arriving at the spot, a stout, bull-headed boatman, dressed in a hunting shirt..—in whom I recognized a younger brother of Mike, drew a line with his toe; and stepping off thirty yards—turned around fronting his brother—took a tin cup, which hung from his belt, and placed it on his head....

"Blaze away, Mike! and let's have the quart."

...Mike, throwing back his left leg, levelled his rifle at the head of his brother. In this horizontal position the weapon remained for some seconds as immovable, as if the arm which held it, was affected by no pulsation.

"Elevate your piece a little lower, Mike! or you will pay the corn," cried the imperturbable brother.

I know not if the advice was obeyed or not; but the sharp crack of the rifle immediately followed, and the cup flew off thirty or forty yards—rendered unfit for further service. There was a cry of admiration from the strangers, who pressed forward to see if the foolhardy boatman was really safe. He remained as immovable, as if he had been a figure hewn out of stone. He had not even winked, when the ball struck the cup within two inches of his skull.

"Mike has won!" I exclaimed; and my decision was the signal which, according to the rules, permitted him of the target to move from his position. No more sensation was exhibited among the boatmen, than if a common wager had been won. (qtd. in Botkin 30-32)

The tin cup match was, of course, Fink's downfall, as has

been related in numerous variations. The gist of them all is that in 1822, when Fink was with Ashley on the Upper Yellowstone, Fink had a misunderstanding with a young companion, one Carpenter. During a wild drinking spree Fink proposed, as a demonstration of confidence, that they shoot tin cups off each other's heads at 60 yards. According to one account, just before he fired Fink called "Hold your noddle steady, Carpenter, and don't spill the whisky, as I shall want some presently." Fink then fired, shooting Carpenter in the center of his forehead. "Carpenter," he then said, "you've spilled the whiskey" (Monaghan 51).

In another account, from the St. Louis *Reveille* of October 21, 1844, Carpenter took the first shot at 40 yards and creased Fink's scalp. "Carpenter, my son," said Fink, "I taught you to shoot differently from that last shot! You've missed once, but you won't again!" Whereupon he raised his rifle and shot Carpenter through the head (Botkin 47-50).

As a result of the shooting, which Fink claimed was accidental, Fink was shot and killed by a gunsmith, Talbot(t), who either snatched up a pistol and shot Fink on the spot (Monaghan) or waited some months before he confronted Fink and shot him with a pistol (Botkin).

Times were changing in the 1830s and 40s, and

A NEW ERA BEGINS

---

developments were on the horizon that would forever alter the conditions of formal, and informal, shooting matches. Many of the traditional frontier or backwoods matches continued in one form or another well into the 20th century. Then, of course, they were rediscovered by the modern muzzleloader or buckskinner. But while these traditional matches continued, beginning in the 1840s other traditions were being created in the more urban areas. Both in Europe and America, rifle associations and shooting clubs were founded and formal, organized matches became popular. New technology and new weapons combined to create new matches, new targets and methods of scoring, new shooting organizations and, after the Civil War, an explosion of popular interest in rifle marksmanship.

In 1854, the Hebretian Rifle Club of New York sponsored its second annual Swiss-style rifle festival. All matches were shot off-hand at the distance of 535 feet (178 yards) and "without the aid of any spy-glasses or telescopes" (*Spirit* 14 Oct. 1854: 1). The targets were a "sliding" target (whatever that is) with a 3-1/2-inch diameter bull's eye and the "Hebretia Target of Honor" with a 10-inch diameter bull's eye:

Out of 12,880 shots on the sliding targets, 829 bullseyes were made in a centre of 3 1/2 inch diameter, and out of 185 on the target of "honor," 78 10 inch diameter bullseyes.

The 40 finest shots on the sliding targets...were all within 3 1/2 eights [sic] of an inch from the centre of the bullseye to the centre of the passage of the ball. These all hit in the space which a 3 cent piece would cover in the centre of the targets....One of the amateur Riflemen counted among his shots 110 bullseyes, while two other members each made 90....On the target of "Honor," where but five chances are allowed, one person made the five bullseyes in succession, and three others made each four out of their five chances. (Spirit 14 Oct. 1854: 1)

In 1861, a "National Convention of German Riflemen" was held in Gotha, Germany. This four-day festival was a combination of shooting matches with a state fair-like atmosphere, with side shows, parades, beer tents ("beside a single one of these I counted, at eleven o'clock in the morning, thirteen empty beer-barrels!" [Cornhill 494]), dances and so on. The occasion was a celebration of one of those many attempts to unify Germany. The shooting was done by 1,300 riflemen, each one representing a different German state (except Austria), province or city:

The distance was four hundred feet [133 yards] for ten of the targets, and two hundred and fifty feet [83 yards] for the [remaining twenty targets]. The manner of shooting was divided into three classes, so arranged that each class should apply to both distances: 1st, shooting with "free hand," without rest or aid of any kind; 2nd, with the use of the diopter, or sight-gauge; and 3rd, with rests, and all other appliances, at will. Thus, the rifleman who combined the first-class with the greatest distance, and hit the centre oftenest in proportion to the number of shots, would be entitled to the highest prizes....

We were interested in noticing the arrangement of the targets. Each was double, turning on a pivot midway between the two, so that when one was up the other was down, and concealed from sight in a pit, in which the attendant sat. His duty was, whenever a shot was fired, to turn the axle, bringing the target down to note the shot with the same movement which elevated the other for a fresh one. The shots were carefully registered, and the record sent back to the pavilion from time to time, in a bag attached to a travelling rope. It is a lucky circumstance that none of the attendants were wounded during the festival. Once, indeed, there was a slight alarm. One of the targets having failed to revolve, the firing was suspended and the pit examined, when the man was found lying sound asleep at the bottom, with an empty beer-mug beside him! It is no less an illustration of the care and method native to the German character that, although 35,000 shots, in all, were fired, no accident of any kind occurred. (Cornhill 492-493)

Unfortunately no indication of scores or accuracy was noted by the commentator, but the relatively short distances involved indicate that the elongated bullet had not yet been adopted in German Schutzenfests.

New technology and weapons allowed more accurate shooting at greatly increased ranges. We have already observed that the longrifle was extremely effective up to 200 yards and good shots could be made up to 400 yards, but 400 yards was (is) probably the outside limit of effectiveness with the longrifle. Even the Western successor to the longrifle, the half-stocked, heavy-barrelled, larger caliber plains rifle, wasn't capable of extending that effective range much farther. The necessary slow rifling twists and the patched round ball, effective as that

Shooting offhand with a telescopic sight, circa 1848 (Trench 295).

combination is, just wasn't capable of accurate, ultra-long range shooting.

A couple of stories from England illustrate some of the changes that were in the offing. In 1834, a relatively traditional match was shot at Purdey's shooting grounds, Notting-hill, between a Captain Ross, M.P., and Count D'Orsay, for a stake of 50 pounds:

The distance was 150 yards from the shoulder to the target; 50 shots. The match was won by Captain Ross, whose balls, on measurement, proved in the aggregate, including the distance of each ball, 398 inches from the bull's eye, some having struck the eye; while Count D'Orsay's balls, by similar measurement, proved to be 699 inches from the bull's eye. Captain Ross shot with Mr. Purdey's rifle, and the Count with Mr. John Manton's. (Times [London] 9 June, 1834: 3)

We'd be better able to judge these strings, which were apparently measured as we now do it (rather than as in the peg

shoot), if we knew the size of the bull's eye and the caliber of each rifle, since it appears as if the measurements were made from the outside of the bullet hole. If we assume that the string was taken from the center of the target, then Ross shot a group about eight inches in diameter at 150 yards off-hand while the Count's group was about 14 inches in diameter. That's not bad off-hand shooting.

Fifteen years later some changes were evident:

The firing at the butt in the Royal Arsenal by Colonel Dundas, C.B., and Mr. Minesinger, is still carried on, and the range has been extended to 300 yards. Previous to concluding the firing at 200 yards' range, Colonel Dundas made a number of excellent shots, striking the target every time, with balls of the sugar-loaf pattern, submitted by Mr. Lancaster, jun. These balls were fired from a beautiful rifle, of French pattern; and by a very simple appliance are made to fit quite tight in the rifle without wadding. A small groove is cut round the sugar-loaf shaped ball near the base, and two or three worsted threads

tied round and raised beyond the diameter of the base, to the extent required. The long barrelled gun used by Mr. Minesinger contains a space for a chamber at the breech end of the barrel, and he loads his chambers before he commences firing and fires five rounds before he again charges the five chambers he carries in his pocket. The gun, consequently, requires no ramrod; a small piece of wood and a stone from the ground being sufficient for driving home the powder and balls in the chamber—which is only three inches in length. Each chamber has a projecting nipple on which the percussion nipple [sic] is placed, and is held securely to the stock by a sliding hinge, and is capable of firing 20 rounds per minute. (*Times* [London] 23 Mar. 1849: 7)

Although the results of the scoring are not given, there are two significant facts about this story that point the way to new shooting techniques: the introduction of the elongated bullet, ballistically superior to the round ball; and breech loading, the end of the predominance of muzzleloading after 500 some odd years of success.

To begin with the elongated bullet made the greatest impact on muzzleloading, although Lancaster's idea of taking up windage with worsted thread wrapped around the bullet wouldn't catch on. The ballistic advantages of elongated bullets and fast-gain, twist rifling were well-known: the problem was to load the bullet from the muzzle so that it was exactly parallel with the bore. Minie and his followers solved the problem one way for military rifles, but it was Alvan Clark who

solved it for sporting rifles.

In 1840, Alvan Clark patented his "loading muzzle," what we today call a "false muzzle." As Clark explained it:

...I have fixed upon and patented the [detachable loading muzzle. This muzzle] *is enlarged at the entrance...and may in a moment be taken off and replaced....In using the gun, the operations of wiping and loading are performed through it, in which case it shields from wear that part of the gun which must give direction to the ball....After loading, the muzzle is removed, and in discharging, a very uniform delivery is effected, even when a force of powder is used sufficient to destroy all regularity in a common rifle.* (Garavaglia and Worman 47-48)

Working together, Clark and gunmaker Edwin Wesson produced a rifle that in 1841, when fired "at the distance of 36 rods, or 198 yards, twenty successive shots were placed within a parallelogram eight inches only in length and five in breadth. This was done with a long and pointed slug...about 70 [to the pound or .40 caliber]" (Garavaglia and Worman 48).

In 1854, Sir Joseph Whitworth was given a grant by the British government to make improvements to the new Enfield military rifle. Whitworth reduced the bore from .577 to .45 and gave it a longer bullet although of the same weight as the government Minie. Whitworth's real innovation, however, was to give the bullet spiral grooves to precisely fit the lands of the rifle. The Whitworth rifle turned out to be very accurate; there are official records of it making 20-shot groups of 6-1/2 inches at 500 yards and 21 inches at 1000 yards. "In 1865 Victorian marksmen competed even at 2,000 yards: the target was a large one, 12 x 24 feet, and at this range fourteen hits out of twenty-five shots was thought a good score, and a century later 2,000 yards was still a very long shot" (Trench 286).

As I write this, the latest *Guns & Ammo* (September 1991) has an article by Ross Seyfried detailing his creation of a $3,000, .30-416, 18-pound ultra-light rifle especially for long-range shooting. With the loan of a $1,300 Leupold Mark 4 Ultra 16-power scope, the purchase of an army surplus artillery range-finder, and a sophisticated ballistics program for his computer, Seyfried shot a 3.9-inch group at 805 yards and a 9-inch group at a mile (1,760 yards). The bullet had a muzzle velocity of about 1,500 fps. Can't help but wonder what the 10-pound muzzleloading Whitworth could do with those optics and some computer help at 1.14 miles or 2,000 yards, can you?

The Whitworth was the primary weapon of the British National Rifle Association (founded in 1859) in its early years of long-range competition (800, 900 and 1,000 yards) at a 36-inch bull. It out-shot the Rigby, which was its primary competitor. "The new rifle raised what might be called an average winning score from about 50 per cent with the Enfield in 1861-2, to about 84 per cent with the Whitworth in 1862-63" (Trench 286).

Similar improvements were being made in firearms in the United States, although here, as technology-minded as we were even then, the trend was away from muzzleloaders and toward breechloaders. The Civil War and the period immediately following marked the high point in participation and public interest in long-range precision shooting. Prior to the Civil War, references in the press to formal (or informal) shooting matches are hard to find: after the Civil War, hardly a week goes by without the mention in any major metropolitan newspaper of a shooting match held by one or another amateur rifle association. Talk about the "good, old days!" How long has it been since the New York *Times* has devoted two entire front-page columns to a favorable shot-by-shot analysis of a shooting match?

The Civil War was a stimulus to improved rifles and marksmanship. It was probably the first breech-loading war, but there was also a place for the super-accurate, long-range target, or sniping rifle, and Colonel Hiram Berdan was one of the first to exploit the new technology with the formation of his Sharpshooter corps. Berdan gave a demonstration of his and his rifle's capabilities in August 1861:

The "man target," christened Jeff Davis was set up at a distance of a little more than 200 yards. Colonel Berdan inaugurated the firing. In an easy, business-like way, he loaded his rifle, an ordinary target piece with a telescope sight, and approached the "rest." (Harper's 24 August 1861)

Shooting from a variety of positions Berdan "called" his shots and hit the Jeff Davis figure wherever the crowd indicated: "between the eyes," "in the end of the nose," and so on (*Harper's* 23 August 1861).

Berdan admitted no one to his regiment who could not fire

British Volunteers firing what are probably supposed to be Whitworth rifles from two rest positions, 1861 (Trench 294).

THE MARKER & THE TARGET.

TARGET FIRING - DISTANCE 35 RODS.

Colonel Berdan's shooting exhibition at Weehawken, New Jersey, August 7, 1861. Also illustrated is Berdan's back-action lock rifle with telescopic sight and false muzzle (Harper's, August 24, 1861).

a ten-shot, five-inch group at 200 yards. Berdan himself fired a 1-1/10 inch group at that distance, with, one assumes, a telescopic sight. A variety of weapons were possible for the regiment:

They will be armed with the most improved Springfield rifle, with a plain silver pin sight at the muzzle, and a notched sight, or the globe sight at the breech for long range shooting. It was first intended to arm them with the Northern target rifle, but it was found that there were not enough in the country. Each man may take his own rifle if he wishes. Colonel Berdan has invented a ball which is superior to the old Springfield rifle ball [the Minie], *and will carry with great accuracy a distance of 3000 feet. It is a grooved and conical ball, and is almost certain for a horse at the distance of three-fifths of a mile.* (Harper's 24 August 1861)

Interest in shooting, as was natural, continued through the

Civil War and became a popular spectator sport after the war. The number of shooting associations increased as did the number of people involved in the sport.

Ironically, the high point of the super-accurate, long-range muzzleloading rifle also marked the point of the ascendancy of the breechloader over the muzzleloader, although it would be some years before muzzleloaders were retired from national and international competition. This high point, of course, was the first Creedmoor match outside of New York in September 1874. The New York *Herald* headlined it as "The Battle of the Rifles—Muzzle-Loaders vs. Breech-Loaders" (28 Sept. 1874: 3).

It all started when the Irish rifle team, which had won the national matches at Wimbledon (England), issued an open challenge to an American team, not knowing that there was by this time an American National Rifle Association. The NRA did not respond to the challenge, but the "up-start" Amateur Rifle Association did and spent the spring and summer of 1874 practicing and selecting team members at the new Creedmoor 1,000-yard rifle range. The Irish team was to come here to shoot at Creedmoor. The American team needed to practice: the club had only held five matches before 1874, had only seventy-odd members and no member of the club had ever fired a shot at more than 500 yards (Roberts 129).

In addition to the Amateur Rifle Association's lack of experience, there was a lack of money and a lack of appropriate weapons. E. Remington and Sons and the Sharps Rifle Company came to the rescue, donating the necessary funds and producing the necessary match-grade breechloading rifles (Roberts 131).

Berdan's Sharpshooters practicing in 1861 (*Leslie's*, October 5, 1861).

The Irish, who included John Rigby on their team, shot exclusively with Rigby muzzleloading rifles. The American team, on the other hand, were about evenly divided in their use of Sharps and Remington breechloaders. Lieutenant H. Fulton, Colonel J. Bodine, L.L. Hepburn and General T. S. Dakin shot Remington Sporting Rifles, while G.W. Yale and Colonel H.A. Gildersleeve shot Sharps Sporting Rifles (New York *Times* 27 Sept. 1874: 1). Both were .44 caliber and shot a 550-grain bullet, but the Remington shot 90 grains to the Sharps' 95 grains (New York *Times* 4 Oct. 1874: 9). Granulation was not specified, but it was probably Ffg.

Other than the method of loading the rifles used by the two teams, they were remarkably similar. They were half-stocked rifles weighing no more than ten pounds, with a trigger pull of no less than three pounds. They were equipped with long-range, Vernier tang rear sights (adjustable for elevation) and globe or hooded bead or aperture front sights, with a spirit level and adjustable for windage (New York *Times* 4 Oct. 1874: 9). The Rigby rifles, of course, had false muzzles.

The New York *Herald* recorded this about the targets:

[A]ll are of heavy boiler iron, and the various portions on them are indicated by white and black paint. They are all placed on a line, and in front of them is a deep trench in which the markers are stationed. They are protected from all danger by a heavy mound of earth in front and a flange of sheet iron at the bottom of the target....Up to 300 yards the target is six feet in height by four feet in width, the bull's eye eight inches square and the centre two feet square. When the range of from 300 to 600 yards the target used is exactly six feet square, the bull's eye is two feet square and the centre four feet square. When the range is over 600 and up to 1,000 yards...the target used is six feet high by twelve wide, the bull's eye is three feet square and the centre six feet square. No provision is made for outers on top or bottom of this target....The bull's eye was painted black and hitting it counted four on the score....The centre was white and was separated from the outer by heavy black lines, which were distinguishable even at the distance of 1,000 yards. A hit in the centre counted three in the score. The outer included three feet on either end of the target, was also

The Irish team at Creedmore, 1874: (left to right) Dr. J.B. Hamilton, Major Arthur B. Leech, Captain P. Walker, J.K. Milner, J. Rigby, Edmund Johnson, and James Wilson. Some details of the Rigby rifle can be seen. Note the tang sight in the standard position on Hamilton's rifle and the position of the sight near the butt on Milner's rifle. Also notice the globe front sights and the false muzzles (*Harper's*, October 10, 1874).

A sketch of the firing range at Creedmore during a practice session. Judging from the descriptions of shooting positions, the first individual lying on his back is the Irishman Milner while the next one is American shooter Fulton (*Harpers*, October 10, 1874).

white, and a hit within its limits counted two in the score. A bull's eye shot was signalled by a white disk placed over the black part of the target, a centre shot by a red disk and an outer shot by a black disk. Thus every shot could be read and the score kept by every person on the field. (27 Sept. 1874: 7)

I'm still not sure how the markers or scorers could keep track of the hits, since three shooters shared a target and shot in rotation; that is, there were two targets for each six-man team, and each shooter fired 15 shots at each of the three distances (800, 900, 1,000 yards). They must have re-painted the targets at intervals, but there's no mention of how they managed it in any of the accounts I have seen.

A "possible" composite score for all three distances would have been 180 points for an individual or 1,080 for a team. Lieut. Henry Fulton of the American team shot a 171, which was the highest score ever shot in this kind of competition.[3] Of course Fulton "fudged" a little, although shooting a Remington breechloader, he loaded from the muzzle.

The shooting was from any position but with no artificial rest allowed and the positions were varied. The majority of the shooters assumed the standard prone position but some shot from their backs or sides. It is the unusual positions we associate with Creedmoor. J. K. Milner and E. Johnson (Irish) adopted a "peculiar" shooting position. Describing Milner the *Herald* said:

He lies on his back, with the butt of his rifle resting on the hollow of his shoulder while the barrel rests on his toe. In order for him to take aim the back sight of the rifle is placed near the heel plate. The position is neither very graceful nor does it appear very solid. It posses the disadvantage that the rifleman can only see one object, and in target shooting it exposes him

to the danger of shooting at the wrong target. (28 Sept. 1874: 3)

Lieut. Fulton (American) shot thus:

[L]ying down on his back and crossing his legs, [he] *turns slightly to the right, placing the butt of his rifle over the right shoulder, resting against his cheek. The barrel rests in the V formed by his crossed legs, finding a remarkably solid support. The left hand is passed behind the neck, grasping the heel of the butt holding it firmly against the cheek. In this way the rifle is held as in a vice, and the marksman proceeds to take aim coolly and with the greatest deliberation. When the aim is complete the trigger is pulled by the right hand, kept free for the purpose, and five times out of six the white disk* [signifying a bull's eye] *comes up in response.* (New York *Herald* 28 Sept. 1874: 3)

G. W. Yale (American), "a dark, robust looking man with plenty of grit in his composition," shoots by lying down "slightly turned to the right, and supports his rifle over the left knee" (New York *Herald* 28 Sept. 1874: 3). The rest of the shooters, Irish and American, shot "face downwards, grasping the rifle firmly in [their] left hand[s]" (New York *Herald* 28 Sept. 1874: 3).

The inexperienced American team's victory over the Irish was as unprecedented as was the American hockey team's victory over the Russians in the Olympics a few years ago and generated as much excitement from the public and the press. It was a motley group. Fulton was a "tall, spare man, clad in blue flannel." John Bodine was "an old man who must be closing rapidly toward the sixties. He wears blue spectacles while firing and when cleaning and examining his gun is obliged to use additional glasses owing to his near-sightedness. He is over six feet in height and stands erect as a poplar tree." T.S. Hepburn, foreman of the Remington mechanical department, was "well advanced in life, but not old, cool and imperturbable in temperament." Gildersleeve was a young man "in the prime of life..., of medium height, but a powerful frame." Dakin was a "hearty, well-preserved man of some fifty summers" (New York *Herald* 28 Sept. 1874: 3).

In some ways the shooting conditions were good; and in some, bad. The weather was unseasonably warm, and the Irish

---

[3] The other American scores were: Yale, 162; John Bodine, 158; Gildersleeve, 155; Hepburn, 149; Dakin, 139. The Irish scored: Rigby, 163; Dr. J. B. Hamilton, 160; Captain Walker, 144; James Wilson, 160; J. K. Milner, 154; Edmund Johnson, 150.

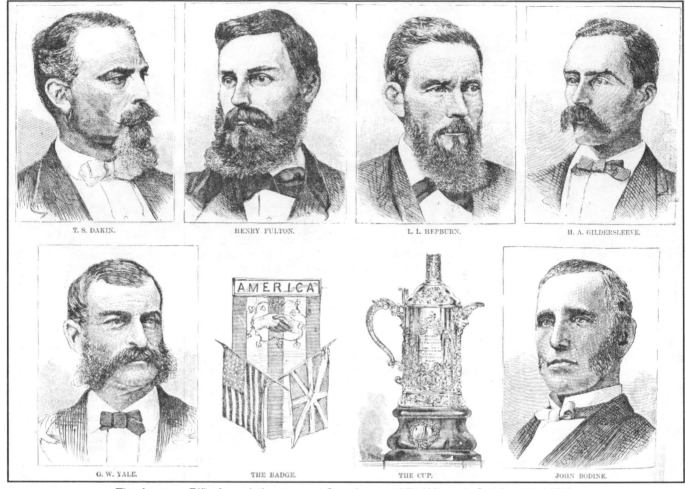

The Amateur Rifle Association team at Creedmore, 1874 (*Harper's* October 10, 1874).

T. S. DAKIN. HENRY FULTON. L. L. HEPBURN. H. A. GILDERSLEEVE.

G. W. YALE. THE BADGE. THE CUP. JOHN BODINE.

AMERICA 1874

team suffered from the heat, even though they had maneuvered their firing positions to take advantage of afternoon shade from a large tree. What wind there was blew toward the targets, but mirage was a real problem. One member of the Irish team was ill.

The scoring was very close. The Irish shot faster than the Americans because they didn't wipe between shots; they all shot the whole course of fire without cleaning their muzzleloaders. The Americans, on the other hand, had to clean their breechloaders after every shot, even Fulton who was loading from the muzzle. The Americans used a system of continuous coaching; they had spotters who kept close watch over changing mirage and wind conditions, and they talked continuously among themselves (New York *Times* 4 Oct. 1874: 9). They also were careful about the shooting order, saving their steadiest shooters for the last. The Irish, on the other hand, used very little coaching and talked little among themselves:

Whatever points were to be communicated were whispered in a few words, and the marksmen lay down, fired, rose, loaded and prepared to fire as though they were unconscious of the thousands who watched these cool, resolute figures as they did their work with a quick intelligence and quiet pluck that eventually lifted them out of the rut into which they had fallen and brought them to the very threshold of victory. (New York

Herald 28 Sept. 1874: 3)

The American team took a good lead at the 800-yard range, helped by the Irishman Milner's firing a bull's eye on the wrong target and thus losing four points automatically. As it turned out, the Irish, although they out-scored the Americans at 900 and 1,000 yards, were never able to take the overall lead. It all came down to the last shot. The Irish had completed their 1,000-yard targets while the Americans were still shooting with Henry Fulton and John Bodine at the line. The aggregate score was 913 for the Americans and 931 for the Irish, with six shots left:

Word was sent out to the American targets not to lose a point—that the issue was remarkably doubtful. Lieutenant Fulton had three shots to fire, as had Colonel Bodine. The unexpected news so threw the lieutenant off his balance that he finished up with three centres [6 points]. The fate of the contest hung on the result of Colonel Bodine's last shot [for the first two of his last three shots he had shot a 3 and a 4: at his last shot the score stood at 930-931]. If he should miss, the victory remained with the Irish. A moment before this the old marksman had cut his hand with a broken bottle. Having stanced [sic] the blood he lay down to take the decisive shot. The state of the case had already been whispered about, and the people crowded in to watch the effect of the last shot. There was an ominous

150

silence among the crowd gazing at the old marksman lying motionless on the ground. At length a white puff of smoke, followed by the sharp ring of the explosion, told that the leaden messenger had sped on its way. Had her missed? "It is on!" broke from a hundred throats, and as the white disk came up telling it was a bull's-eye, the people set up a hearty cheer for the victor, and seizing the lucky rifleman, chaired him as some acknowledgement of the service he had rendered. (New York *Herald* 28 Sept. 1874: 3)

Ironically, the Irish would have won by one point had Milner not fired on the wrong target.

So which won, muzzleloader or breechloader? The Americans felt that their faith in the new breechloaders was vindicated, while the Irish saw no advantage to breechloaders. Of course the Irish were the last of a dying breed, at least so far as international competition was concerned, although they didn't know it. Both teams felt good about their performances and the outcome couldn't have been better for international relations; neither team "blew away" the other. As an interesting postscript to the match, Walker, captain of the Irish team, challenged the Americans to another match, 25 shots each at 1,000 yards, to be fired without cleaning between shots. The Irish won by a margin of 321-201 (Roberts 139).

After 1874, international and national "big time" shooting moved inexorably away from the muzzleloader; the introduction of smokeless powders hammered the last nail in the coffin. Muzzleloading was relegated to the backwoods as an arcane, outmoded curiosity, until the founding of the National Muzzle Loading Rifle Association in the 30s. Of course muzzleloading is still arcane and outmoded to the majority of the population, and much as we may wish otherwise, the breechloader is here to stay.

But we know that we are keeping the traditions alive. The majority of us shoot the same kind of rifles in the same kinds of matches as our grandfathers and great-great-great grandfathers. We've given up holding barrel staves and tin cups for others to shoot at (or I hope we have), but we still shoot at Xs, blocks (or their equivalent), candle flames and so forth. Some of us are still trying to put five shots into one caliber-sized hole in a piece of paper at impossible distances. And I sometimes feel that looking over my shoulder and encouraging me are the spirits of Robinson, Crockett, Fulton and the thousands of others who have passed their traditions and way of life on to us.

APPENDIX A: WORKS CITED

Botkin, B.A. *A Treasury of American Folklore.* New York: Crown Publishers, 1944.

Burrell, Wesley R. "James Fenimore Cooper and the Long Rifle." *Muzzle Blasts* Nov. (1960): 5-6, 20-21: Dec. (1960): 10-11.

"The First German Shooting Match." *Cornhill Magazine* October (1861): 488-496.

Crockett, David. *The Life of Davy Crockett, by Himself.* New York: Signet, 1955.

Frank Leslie's Illustrated Newspaper. 5 Oct. 1861.

Garavaglia, Louis A., and Charles G. Worman. *Firearms of the American West, 1803-1865.* Albuquerque: University of New Mexico Press, 1984.

Harper's Weekly. 24 Aug. 1861.

La Crosse, Richard B., Jr. *The Frontier Rifleman: His Arms, Clothing, and Equipment During the Era of the American Revolution, 1760-1800.* Union City, TN: Pioneer Press, 1989.

Monaghan, Jay, ed. *The Book of the American West.* New York: Julian Messner, 1963.

New York Herald 27 Sept. 1874: 7; 28 Sept. 1874: 3.

New York Times 27 Sept. 1874: 1; 4 Oct. 1874: 9.

Peterson, Harold L. *Arms and Armour in Colonial America, 1526-1783.* New York: Bramhall House, 1956.

Roberts, Ned H. *The Muzzle-Loading Cap Lock Rifle.* New York: Bonanza Books, 1952.

Spirit of the Times 14 Oct. 1854: 1.

Times [London] 5 September 1801: 2; 9 June 1834: 3; 23 Mar. 1849: 7; 25 April 1859: 11.

Trench, Charles Chenevix. *A History of Marksmanship.* Chicago: Follett, 1972.

Wiltsey, Norman B. "Backwoods Shooting Match." *American Gun Magazine* 1.2 (1961).

APPENDIX B: WORKS CONSULTED

New York Times 1859-1876.
Times [London] 1801-1874.

Period Trekking

by Mark A. Baker

The flash and crack of a flintlock long rifle have long held great fascination for Mark Baker. Ever since Fess Parker and Gary Cooper first captured Mark's imagination, he has wanted to learn and experience as much as he could about the use and history of such an enchanting firearm. In the summer of 1977, his cousin Glenn Fortney taught him the art of loading and shooting a graceful long rifle. The smoke, the sound, the feel of a fine-tuned flintlock started Mark on a journey that has continued him in the sport of muzzleloading for the last 15 years. Since then, the author has followed the lure of muzzleloading down trails that first led to organized shoots, then to rendezvous, and on to different avenues of living history. Mark has found lasting satisfaction in the research format typically called "experimental archaeology." Since September 1986 Mark has written over 40 articles reflecting on his experiences, and the bulk of his work has appeared in the magazine *MUZZLELOADER* in the column titled "A Pilgrim's Journey." Mark has also written three chapters on his own brand of experimental archaeology for Jay Anderson's *A Living History Reader: Volume Two* published in 1992 by the American Association for State and Local History. During the summer of 1991, Mark served as a historical consultant in the filming of "The Last of the Mohicans" by Twentieth Century-Fox. One of the most rewarding "jobs" on the movie set for Mark was working with Daniel Day Lewis ("Hawkeye") in shooting and reloading in a traditional manner. Mark and his wife, Marlys, along with their children, Clint, Carrie and Clayton, make their home in Logan, Utah, where Mark works as the associate director of writing in the English Department at Utah State University.

I awoke to the gentle but constant thumping of rain on my blanket. How long the storm had pelted the forest floor I did not know. But from inside the relative comfort of my wool covering I could smell the heavy dampness and hear the hardwood coals sputter and sizzle as the cold rain intermittently hit the small fire pit. Since just after dark, I had enjoyed the peace of a sound sleep while wrapped warmly in a single wool blanket. I had drifted into slumber under a brilliant canopy of an autumn sky peppered with a myriad of stars. I did not stir until the dull pattern of the rain beating on the top of my blanket interrupted my rest.

Out of habit I quickly checked all of my accoutrements. My longrifle still rested inside the blanket folds by my side, with the muzzle pointing well above my head. I gently thumbed the plug of my powder horn, making sure that it remained snugly in its rightful place. Although I was still wearing both powder horn and bag, I felt no discomfort because of their form. Along my woolen sash, I scooted my belt knife around to the front of my waist and found that my belt axe remained hanging under my right shoulder. I then made sure that my extra moccasins and my bag of tinder still rested behind my hips and against the inside folds of the blanket. I peeked out from under my woolen cocoon and made sure that the bottom edge of my blanket was still folded back and over my lower legs. Without disturbing the collected warmth of my wrappings, I placed a fresh section of seasoned maple on the glowing coals of the fire. While enjoying the shifting colors and the dancing flames beginning to surround the fresh wood, I rearranged my homemade wool cap and brushed the hair away from my face. Until the rain discovered my face, I continued to enjoy the peaceful sights and sounds of the early morning darkness. After blinking from the rain drops one too many times, I once again resigned myself to bury completely under the shelter of my brown blanket.

Although I had previously dug a slight depression in the ground, I felt an annoying ache in my hips. But the slight movement quickly relieved the pressure, and I snuggled deeper into the folds of my woodland bed and drifted back into a sound sleep. The gentle thump, thump, thump of the nighttime serenade was good company.

In the darkness of that late autumn night, I was far from the security of my own house and the warmth of my customary linen and wool-covered bed. But that stormy night did not find me playing the part of a stranger. I found the woods to be a temporary home and the leaves of the hardwood forest to offer my tired body a certain level of comfort. I accepted the wet weather and cold wind and did not fight the turn of events. Because I was prepared to do just that, I spent the night in relative comfort.

The preparation needed to endure or even sleep soundly through such a night did not begin with the first raindrop. The training began with previous treks and continued throughout a variety of experiences, coming from a collection of instructors or mentors. As I rediscover habits long forgotten by this modern society, my understanding of the challenges encountered by an 18th century frontier traveler continually matures.

Since I started period trekking, my perceptions of a Colonial woodsman's life have become much more realistic and my persona has therefore become more believable. I am no longer satisfied with just looking or acting like the hero who can be found in various novels and silver screen interpretations and is even personified by certain primitive, black powder participants. Period trekking involves a search for a clearer understanding of what life was like for the original woodsmen, soldiers and voyageurs, life styles long since vanished from the

families who hunted and killed for the survival of all in which they believed? What did they use to load, maintain and shoot so accurately? Such questions can go on and on for the black powder buff who has just been smitten with the fever to carry an old-time gun. The yearning to drink as much knowledge about the period in which a favorite black powder gun was used can be a constant thirst.

Efforts to satisfy such cravings often guide a pilgrim to books or movies about famous frontiersmen such as Daniel Boone and Jeremiah Johnson. But oftentimes these works are rooted in romantic and often stereotypical notions about early American history, and using such sources to guide one's search for a better understanding of a particular era usually results in false and naive conclusions. However, period trekking, in itself a form of historical investigation, can offer the participant a brand new, endless menu of experiences to help satisfy the desire to know more and more. Professional living historians often refer to this investigation and resulting experimentation as "experimental archaeology." Jay Anderson, in his book *Time Machines: The World of Living History,* explains this concept in detail and his ideas concerning experimental archaeology have proven a great benefit in molding my methods of both researching and doing. "Living" our nation's past is enjoyable and will undoubtedly remove the unrealistic notions of the forever tall, athletic, honorable and able frontiersman roaming free in an 18th century Garden of Eden.

I first discovered period trekking by savoring articles in the various black powder publications about certain individuals going out in the woods and living "like a mountain man." Such an adventure sounded very intriguing. Looking through magazines like *MUZZLELOADER* or through publications like *The Book of Buckskinning Series* is a sound start. Such texts can also be a valuable check as one's skill and persona improve. Reviewing them can fill hours upon hours with inspiration, but getting acquainted with the appropriate magazines and books is the easy part. Finding someone to interact with personally can frequently be a challenge.

Any would-be trekker can benefit greatly by finding an individual or a group who emulates the degree of authenticity that the newcomer wishes to obtain. But not just any buckskinner will do as a tutor. When attending various black powder events, I would mingle through the crowds looking for anybody who appeared to be doing something right. Their clothing usually attracted me first, then their accoutrements and their long gun, and finally their mannerisms. Those leaders, as I saw them, displayed a high level of both research and historically-based experience. The way the clothing draped their bodies, the way the stains had developed on their leggings and hunting shirts, and the way they hung their powder horn, shooting bag and knife all reflected their experience. As I began to spot such reenactors, I realized that combining research with experience greatly accelerates any efforts to emulate properly a particular historical character.

Then when I heard Jeff Hengesbaugh spin his Rocky Mountain horse-trekking tales I sat spellbound. Here was a

American scene. It is experimenting with what I know in order to learn even more, and it's also just plain fun. This process of "living it" is the new romance I have with the original Cumberland woodsmen.

For folks who own muzzleloaders, curiosity about the history surrounding these old weapons seems to be a natural progression. Who were the soldiers, settlers, explorers and

After four long days of horseback trekking, Mark Baker and Jim Briggs have settled into a routine of daily camp chores. Mark is filing out a rough spot on the blade of his belt axe while Jim casts round balls. Each woodsman's rifle, powder horn and shooting bag are within arm's reach and the rest of the gear remains packed and neatly stowed away.

man who was doing what I had always yearned to do, venturing into the wilderness and experiencing a vanished life style. I couldn't get enough of his stories or his insights, but the only catch for me was finding someone who was emulating the Eastern long hunter. I finally stumbled across an article in *MUZZLELOADER* about David Wright and some of his Tennessee trekking experiences. Like Jeff's horse-trekking stories, the images of those boys in Tennessee proved enticing. During one spring rendezvous in the New Mexico mountains, I met another pilgrim who also yearned to emulate the long hunter experience. He too had looked to the same buckskinning personalities as leaders in the trekking game. From that rendezvous on, Jim Briggs and I spent several treks and rendezvous together realizing our misconceptions and honing our craft.

I needed the inspiration, company and leadership of those three period trekkers in order to get started right. After encountering their expertise, I eventually stopped looking like a 1970s rendezvouser and started resembling a mid-18th century Cumberland woodsman.

Although my research has centered on developing a better representation of a Cumberland drainage long hunter, the methods I will share in the following passages have parallels in the life styles of Western fur trappers, wilderness soldiers, French voyageurs and others. The various Europeans who migrated into and eventually subdued the North American wilderness all practiced the same basic skills. Their secrets of managing the challenges of our land came from the worlds of both the Indian and the European, and my insights for period trekking reflect those same influences. However, I sincerely hope that the influence of a third culture, my own late 20th century environment, is almost nonexistent in the following discussion.

DRESSING FOR A PERIOD TREK

The first big step toward looking like a woodsman is assembling an appropriate outfit. By examining primary sources, that is eyewitness accounts of the time period, I gradually pieced together a general image of what a trans-Allegheny woodsman probably looked like. Perhaps the most widely quoted description of an Eastern backwoodsman comes from Joseph Doddridge, who spent his youth along the then-disputed western borders of Pennsylvania and Virginia. For anyone interested in emulating the Ohio river country woodsman, Doddridge's description is a valuable resource. I have found his careful details a great help in refining my own historical look. But as both a researcher and a doer, I have also come to realize that one primary source is not always enough and may not always be right. Therefore, in my efforts to understand better what a woodsman looked like in the last half of the 18th century, I have tried whenever possible to compare Doddridge's words with other eyewitness accounts.

In the *Journal of Nicholas Cresswell 1774-1777*, Cresswell offers a different perspective of what a back-country woodsman looked like in the Ohio region during the months just before the Revolution. Cresswell, a loyalist fresh from England and bulging with island-bred snobbery saw the frontiersmen as a rather rough breed. But he did appreciate many of their skills and held a reserved respect for those in his company. Although Cresswell does not elaborate on the woodsmen's dress, his intermittent comments offer a valuable viewpoint that Doddridge never acknowledges.

Cresswell acknowledges that the locals in his Kentucky river hunting party "behave very kind to me, I believe that there is but two pair of breeches in the company" with the remainder

Trekking brings out the good points in your outfit and gear. It also shows you what needs fixing. Through repeated excursions into the deep woods, the author has learned to do without fringe, keep his hunting shirts knee length, tie his sash in back and carry no more "possibles" than what can be carried in his knapsack.

During a cold December trek, the author is wearing a wool cap, a linen scarf, three linen hunting shirts, a wool-ticking waistcoat, linen breech clout, brain-tanned deerskin leggings and wool-lined center-seam moccasins. A breech clout and leggings allow freedom of movement for forest traveling.

wearing "breechclouts, leggings and hunting shirts, which have never been washed only by the rain since they were made" (83-84). The Englishman explains that the breeches were worn by himself and Mr. Tiling, another newcomer to the frontier culture. The rest of the hunting party, seven woodsmen of various experience, were wearing what Doddridge refers to as "Indian dress."

Concerning his own hunting shirt, leggings and moccasins,

For most short-term walking treks, Baker packs only his hand-woven blanket for making an "open" camp. Packed inside the bedroll is some jerky, dried corn and a small tin pot. The secret to carrying such a load comfortably is to use a wide leather strap that holds the bedroll snugly against one's back and above the waist.

work that may not be well-known is *Reminiscences of the French War*, edited by Luther Roby, which reveals the French and Indian War through the words of Robert Rogers and General John Stark. And finally, the Forces of Montcalm and Wolf publishes a journal for members that offers information on the uniforms, accoutrements, weapons and rations of the various soldiers who fought in North America during the mid-18th century.

Despite the efforts of Doddridge and Cresswell, as well as these others, their words leave me with a multitude of questions. Why did Doddridge remember the woodsmen buckling or tying their waist belts in the back? How did woodsmen stuff a variety of items inside the fold of their hunting shirts and still work, hunt, run and bend over? How exactly did the woodsmen tie their moccasins up and around their ankles? Why was the "Indian dress," the breech clout and leggings, so popular in Cresswell's party, and are the dimensions of Doddridge's breech clout large enough for the 20th century reenactor? Period trekking allows you to experiment with the possible answers to these questions.

Carrying the powder horn so that it rides in the hollow of one's ribs and hanging the bag just below the horn keeps them out of the way. They ride comfortably for long durations and stay out of the way when walking, climbing, running or stalking.

Cresswell makes one important comment while he is preparing to enter the upper Ohio river country with an Indian trader, John Anderson. While trying to draw on his letters of credit at Fort Pitt, Cresswell referred to his own hunting clothes as "ragged dress" and blamed his attire for none of the frontier merchants lending him any currency (101). A few days later, when preparing to leave Fort Pitt with Anderson, the trader instructs Cresswell to change out of his hunting shirt, for "the Indians are not well pleased at anyone going into their country dressed in a hunting shirt" (103). According to Cresswell after a season of hunting in "Kan-tuck," his hunting attire reflected his then-present working class situation, which was held in varying degrees of contempt by both the Fort Pitt merchants and the Ohio Indians.

To supplement the information of Doddridge and Cresswell, Appendix B at the end of this chapter contains a list of works offering more information on various time periods and personas. Many of these titles are probably familiar to the reader, but one that may be new is *Up Country: Voices from the Great Lakes Wilderness*, which was edited and compiled by William Joseph Seno. This book is a collection of French colonial writings that have been translated into English. Another

During warm weather the author wears two deerskin moccasins on each foot. Each of those on the left are really two moccasins in one—a pucker-toe on the outside and a center-seam shoe on the inside. Both pairs have tall flaps that wrap around the ankle. The two moccasins on the right are also each two moccasins in one, but in this case both are center-seams. All of the moccasins have extra soles sewn to the bottoms.

Perhaps the most important piece of clothing for any period trekker is footwear. Not just any footwear, but well made, properly fitting, historically correct "traveling shoes," and for me that means the best moccasins I can make. In his comments on moccasins, Doddridge says the flaps of center-seam moccasins were "left on each side to reach some distance up the legs" (141). These flaps "adapted to the ankles, and lower part of the leg by thongs of deer skin, so that no dust, gravel, or snow could get within the moccasin" (141). He also notes that such woodland footwear was much better in the forests than shoes but qualifies the advantages of wearing moccasins by declaring that their upkeep was "the labor of almost every evening," and in "wet weather it was usually said that wearing them was "a decent way of going barefooted' " (141). Doddridge further acknowledges that:

the greater number of our hunters and warriors were afflicted with the rheumatism in their limbs....[and as a result most] slept with their feet to the fire to prevent or cure it as well as they could. This practice unquestionably had a very salutary effect, and prevented many of them from becoming confirmed cripples in early life. (142)

I prefer two styles of moccasins: the center-seam, and the pucker-toe. I mastered both styles by learning firsthand from one of my mentors. In my opinion such one-on-one teaching is the best way to make moccasins for the first couple of times. But if that is not possible, I recommend the book *Craft Manual of North American Indian Footwear* by George M. White. In

this manual of native footwear, the directions are easy to follow and the patterns are simple. With this book even the novice can make usable moccasins. They might even look like a pair.

Looking good is nice, but making moccasins that are comfortable, hold up on the trail and do not rub raw spots on one's feet are the prime concerns. Through my experiences I have found that with proper upkeep moccasins which fit correctly can serve me through several period treks. As a result I no longer have to make new moccasins with every upcoming event or even with every new season of the year. Instead, I spend my time caring for my footwear.

Routinely greasing my moccasins is perhaps the most common ritual in trying to make those woodland shoes last. During the warmer months of the year, when I wear a pair of center-seam moccasins inside an outer pair of pucker-toe moccasins, I only grease the outer pair. Since I usually do not wear knee socks, the inside center-seams act as my stockings. (In fact, I have not had any blisters from long treks since I gave up wool socks and instead used these leather substitutes.) Therefore, it is much more comfortable if the inner moccasins remain soft and breathable.

Shown here is Baker's cold weather footwear. The center-seam pair on the left is composed of sheepskin inner moccasins and greased, deerskin outers. The "shoe-pack" pair on the right is made from oil-tanned cowhide lined with wool blanketing. The wool blanket liners are a single thickness on the sides and double on the bottom.

If my moccasins are dry after the day's walk, then I like to make moccasin greasing an evening chore. After I have completed my fireside meal and before darkness settles over the forest floor, I place my lard tin along the edge of the fire, allowing the heat to soften the grease. In the meantime I remove my outer moccasins, brush them off and turn the shoes inside out. Once the white lard has softened, I remove it from the heat and rub the grease into both moccasins, starting along the seams and taking extra care that the grease is worked through the puckered stitching. I then coat the bottoms, the sides, the top and even up the flaps of both moccasins. When I have rubbed as much grease into each area as possible, I hold the moccasin over the fire to allow the grease to soak further into the grain of the leather. If any area appears to dry up, I rub another coat of lard into that section and heat the shoe again. Once the inside of the moccasins will take no more grease, I turn them right side out and repeat the process. This whole procedure requires patience and should not be rushed by the threat of darkness or a foreboding storm.

When my moccasins are wet at the end of the day, I must wait until they dry before I can grease them again. I like to carry an extra pair of moccasins wrapped up tightly in my blanket roll and wear the fresh pair while the wet ones dry slowly. To dry my wet moccasins, I prop them bottom side up along the edge of the fire pit, but when that will not work, I have often hung them on sticks over the edge of the fire. If the rain is heavy and constant and I have no other shelter than my blanket, I have taken my wet moccasins to bed and slept with them between

my thighs, allowing my body heat to dry them somewhat by morning. Drying moccasins requires patience, for setting them too close to the heat will cause them to draw up, crack or become unmanageable. If they begin to steam, then they are getting too hot.

When done faithfully the greasing routine has kept my feet dry through small creek crossings, canoe handling, dew, light rain, even after a day's worth of snowshoeing in spring snow. But I know that the waterproofing serves me well only when I make it a routine labor. And greasing is not a sure thing, for no period moccasin with 18th century waterproofing will remain watertight indefinitely.

While I am preparing to grease my moccasins, I check the linen thread stitching and the soles. If the threads have pulled free or worn through or if there are holes in the bottoms, I spend a few minutes before greasing and make repairs to the damaged area. I try to pack in my knapsack a strip of elk, moose or deer leather for such impromptu patching. With the extra leather, my awl, some deer sinew and a needle, I can repair the hole permanently in a matter of minutes. I say permanently, because upon occasion I have found the deer sinew still attached to the sole of my moccasin long after the patch has worn through.

Part of this moccasin upkeep also includes periodically attaching an extra sole to my moccasins. This was a common practice by wilderness travelers, and sewing an additional layer of leather to the bottom of a center-seam moccasin is much faster than manufacturing a brand new shoe. When sewing an extra sole to my moccasins, I like to use the thickest leather I can find. I prefer brain-tanned moose hide, but I have to settle for oil-tanned cowhide most of the time. That is okay, however, because oil-tanned leather was the material commonly used for saddles, saddle bags, portmanteaus, boots, shoes, harness leather and strapping. I always place the leather hair side down and cut the soles wider and longer than the bottom of my foot. Then I pull up the extra leather and whipstitch the edges of the sole to the sides of my moccasin. If I take my time, sewing on an extra sole gives me additional mileage to the original pair. I prefer to do such labor at home, but I have sewn extra soles to my moccasins at a period camp. Unfortunately, the process takes most of a morning. I have lately gotten in the habit of sewing an additional sole to each new pair of otherwise-soft-soled moccasins I make. That extra step has made most of my cross-country walking a pleasure.

Doddridge mentions his woodsmen wearing moccasins with extra long flaps that reached up the leg. These flaps were subsequently wrapped tightly and tied with thongs to keep out debris. I usually make my moccasin flaps long enough to extend up my leg to the bottom of my calf muscle. The flaps are attached to the sides of my moccasin in the traditional center-seam or pucker-toe fashion, but as they extend upward, they become gradually wider so that they will completely cover my ankle and lower leg. I have also attached a tongue to the front of each moccasin, which I tuck under the flaps. I then wrap several times around the extended flaps with leather thongs and tie them off with a square knot.

With both an inner and outer pair of moccasins thus wrapped and tied tightly about my lower legs, I have sturdy support for my ankles. That is a comfort when walking over uneven terrain and carrying a load. I usually put my moccasin flaps under my leggings and, once my moccasins are thus secured, tie down the bottom edge of my leggings to the outside of my moccasins. Placing a long leather thong under the arch of one foot, I pull it up and around to the front of my ankle, twist the two lengths together, pull the ends around behind my ankle

It is a good idea to carry a bundle of oil-tanned leather for moccasin repairs. Leather thongs always come in handy, as do an antler whistle, two smooth stones for sharpening cutting edges, and a tin of lard for greasing moccasins and sealing your gun's frizzen.

and tie off with a square knot.

For the colder months of the year, I have a pair of center-seam deerskin moccasins lined with 1/4-inch sheepskin nap supported by extra oil-tanned soles. I have worn this pair of moccasins in the autumn and early spring for at least eight years and have replaced the soles three times. My second pair of "wintering" moccasins is much heavier. I like to wear these shoe packs in the coldest months of the year. They are made from oil-tanned cowhide and lined with inner, wool-blanket shoe packs. Both the outer and inner shoe packs were constructed along the moccasin pattern included on page 25 of Robert Klinger's *Sketch Book 76*. The wool inner shoes were sewn with linen thread and have a single blanket layer on the sides and tops and a double thickness for the soles. The soles of the outer shoe packs are laced to the sides with a leather thong (like the original specimen from Fort Ligonier), but the heel and top of the foot are sewn with linen thread. I have worn this heavier pair of winter moccasins when it was only five degrees above zero and remained comfortable throughout the day.

On my lower body, I prefer to wear side-seam leggings made of brain-tanned deerskin and a linen breech clout. In his *Notes on the Settlement and Indian Wars of the Western Parts of Virginia and Pennsylvania from 1763 to 1783*, Doddridge introduces his discussion on the woodsmen of his youth by commenting that their dress was "partly Indian, and partly that of civilized nations" (140). He recalls that during his time on the frontier "a pair of drawers or breeches and leggins, were the dress of the thighs and legs" (141). But according to Doddridge, as the "Indian Wars" progressed along the Ohio river frontier, the "young men became more enamored of the Indian dress" and took to wearing Indian-style leggings and a breech clout made of "linen or cloth nearly a yard long, and eight or nine inches broad...[with the] flaps sometimes ornamented with some coarse kind of embroidery work" (142). Much to the dismay of the one-time preacher, the men even wore such attire to "places of public worship,...[which] did not add much to the devotion of the young ladies" (142).

My brain-tanned leggings fit tightly and reach to mid thigh. Sometime in the past I cut the side flaps off of each legging. A 1/4-inch strip of the same deerskin is attached to the outside of each legging and tied to a leather thong around my waist that supports my linen breech clout. I wrap a leather thong several times around my leg just below each knee and tie it off with a square knot on the outside of my leg. If the weather is extremely cold, I may opt to wear a wool breech clout, but I do not like the bulkiness of the wool as compared to linen. Regardless of the material, I have come to appreciate a breech clout a little bigger than what Doddridge remembers his neighborhood woodsmen wearing. I cut mine 11 inches by 72 inches. The length of six feet may seem long, but when worn in the traditional manner, the two ends of my clout barely reach my mid thigh. Perhaps Doddridge got his measurements wrong or perhaps I am either a little taller and thicker than Doddridge's woodsmen or a little more modest.

After making several long treks in linen breeches and leggings, I have come to fully agree with the Frenchmen whom Peter Kalm encountered when traveling through southern Canada in 1749. The Swedish botanist pointed out in his memoir, entitled *Peter Kalm's Travels in North America*, that when "the French are traveling about in this country, they are generally dressed like the natives; they wear no trousers" (560). As the Indians had adopted the Frenchmen's "jacket and vest,...[and] red cap or hat," the French civilians had learned to appreciate the Indians' leggings and breech clouts. The Canadian Indians refused to wear trousers, for "they thought that these were a great hindrance in walking" (Kalm 560). I agree. Since I have begun to wear a breech clout, I have enjoyed a greater freedom of movement and have eliminated the rub spots formerly caused by my waist thong bearing down on my linen breeches.

To cover my upper body, I dress much the same as Kalm's Frenchmen and Indians or as Doddridge's frontiersmen. Doddridge describes his woodsmen as "universally" wearing the "hunting shirt" (140). His detailed discourse reflects the classic shirt so often associated with Revolutionary War-era riflemen and backwoodsmen:

This was a kind of loose frock, reaching half way down the thighs, with large sleeves, open before, and so wide as to lap over a foot or more when belted. The cape was large, and sometimes handsomely fringed with a ravelled piece of cloth of a different color from that of the hunting shirt itself. The bosom of this dress served as a wallet to hold a chunk of bread, cakes, jerk, tow for wiping the barrel of the rifle, or any other necessary for the hunter or warrior. (140-141)

Doddridge later noted that the hunting shirt was generally constructed of "linsey, sometimes of coarse linen, and a few of dressed deer skins" and declared that the deerskin hunting shirts were "very cold and uncomfortable in wet weather" (141). According to his memory, the "hunter or warrior" of Ohio also wore underneath the hunting shirt a "shirt and jacket" of the "common fashion" (141).

There is plenty of discussion presently floating around the reenactment circles on exactly what the term "hunting shirt" meant to George Washington in 1757, to Cresswell in 1775 or to the graying, older Doddridge, who tried to recall in 1823 the events of his youth. Basically, the argument centers on the question of when the fringed, open front, wrap-around hunting shirt of Doddridge's classic description came into common fashion along the middle colony frontier. At this time clear, documentable clues have eluded both the static and living historian alike. We know that the term "hunting shirt" was used from the days of the French and Indian War to well after the American Revolution. But clearly written descriptions or artist's descriptions similar to Doddridge's do not abound until America's fight for independence and what the words meant in 1775 may not have carried the same meaning twenty years earlier.

Since so little is known about the earliest days of the wrap-around hunting shirt, I understand the historical risk of wearing one if I am to emulate the Cumberland long hunter. Woodsmen commonly market-hunted in the Kentucky and Tennessee areas between the close of the French and Indian War and the opening of the American Revolution. The heyday of their roaming occurred in the late 1760s. Since I am striving to be common, then I need to dress appropriately, and at this time I understand the common hunting shirt to be simply a pullover

A hand-woven, wool sash keeps Baker's belt knife snugly at his side. The knife, made by George Ainslie, was crafted along the same lines as an original French trade knife pictured in Madison Grant's book *The Knife in Homespun America*.

linen or linsey woolsey garment cut in the typical shirt pattern of the period. So to be safe in my interpretation of the common look, I wear only pullover hunting shirts.

I also follow the same garment cleaning practices as did Cresswell's Ohio country woodsmen and do not wash my hunting shirt or shirts unless it rains. That doesn't mean they stink. An occasional airing out can get rid of the stench. But by not washing my hunting shirts, the garments begin to reflect my experience. As the grease, the black powder residue, the dirt and the wear marks accumulate, I begin to come a little closer to the look of Cresswell's guides.

All of my hunting shirts are made of 100 percent linen. That was one of the most common materials woven along the frontier and I have found the fabric suitable for my purposes. My linen hunting shirts have taken plenty of abuse yet have remained soft and comfortable. I wear only one hunting shirt in the hot months then begin putting on two, three or even four as the weather turns colder and colder. All of my hunting shirts are large, reaching down to my knees, and do not have capes. All but one have a loose hem along the bottom, allowing time to transform the edge into fringe. Most have the side seams split about nine inches up the sides. The sleeves sport a single pewter or bone button and the collars are of the common 18th century style. These hunting shirts are plain but well-made; functional, but not flashy. And each one has spent time soaking in a bubbling batch of black walnut hull dye.

As Doddridge suggested, I sometimes don a weskit and/or sleeved weskit over my one or more hunting shirts. Like the shirts, these over-garments were comfortable and loose-fitting and could have belonged to someone else. Around my neck I sport a checked, linen scarf that is tied according to the weather. Around my waist I tie a hand-woven wool sash. As with all of the linen I wear, each has soaked up time and tint in a hot batch of walnut dye.

In his comments on clothing, Doddridge says that a woodsman's "belt was always tied behind" and provided the hunter with a convenient place to stash "mittens, and sometimes the bullet-bag" (141). The retired Presbyterian minister then commented that "a tomahawk" hung on the right side of the woodsman's belt while on the left side was suspended a "scalping knife in its leathern sheath" (141). After covering countless miles when walking in period gear, I have come to understand some of the reasons why his frontiersmen might have done as he recalled. Whether wearing a belt or a sash, I don't have a buckle or a knot to interfere with my movements when bending over or fighting a bucking horse. With the buckle in back, I never hear the annoying "clang, clang, clang" of a powder measure or powder horn knocking against it, and I have the entire front and sides of my belt or sash to store mittens, bullet bags and priming horns. Through historical investigation I have grown to appreciate the hints concerning a waist belt offered by Doddridge. The knot in the back is just one example of that learning by doing.

On my belt or sash I carry my belt knife. The blade is a hand-forged reproduction of an 18th century, French trade knife. This everyday tool is carried in a leather sheath and kept snug inside my sash. My "Kentucky pattern" belt axe hangs by

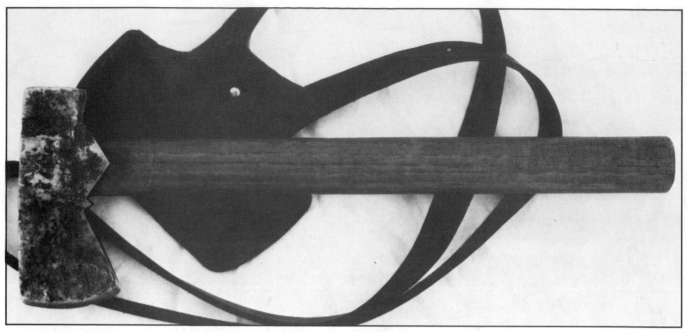

Trekking demonstrates the value of a polled belt axe over a tomahawkl for the many chores of a period adventure.

a shoulder strap and pouch on the opposite side of my belt knife. When considering the belt axe, I cannot help but also consider my knife. Besides working well together, these two cutting tools carry best when hanging opposite each other. In his description Doddridge hinted at this, and through experience I have come to agree. When packing my knife and axe on opposite sides, I do not feel the weight of either tool. Since I am left-handed, my knife rides on my right side and my axe hangs even with my waist on the left. I like the knife to stay put, but I prefer my axe to hang free under normal conditions, so that when I lay down, sit up or even run the belt axe naturally moves out of the way. The pouch keeps the axe head in place with a copper ball-shaped stud, yet the sheath can be opened quickly for easy retrieval. If I am going to climb, portage or travel risky country, I simply slide the axe handle through the sash in back, where it is then kept motionless.

Headgear was probably the most individual garment worn along the frontier. This is much the same today with reenactors. A modern woodsman often becomes identifiable by the shape of his slouch hat, his tricorn or his wool bonnet. In addition, the more one wears a hat, the more comfortable it becomes. So when the perfectly seasoned hat is lost in the rapids of a spring-flooded creek, it is understandably cause for lamenting. The hat will truly be missed.

In that sense the headgear of the woodsman is individual. But because the head fashions of the frontier were comparatively few, the headgear available to the period trekker lacks a great deal of variety. The same limited styles were commonly seen throughout the 18th century frontier. Typical head coverings of the Colonial frontier included: the silk or linen scarf; the flat-brimmed, round-crowned felt hat; an occasional tricorn; and a homemade wool, linen or fur cap.

I have probably been through more hats than anything else and have eventually come to the conclusion that no style or material is perfect. When period trekking I have endured all sorts of weather, all sorts of terrain, and no single hat proved to be perfect for all conditions. Many of my trekking partners, though, feel differently about their headgear. Some prefer a tricorn with the three sides held up with a pin of sorts, so that one or more sides may be let down, depending upon the conditions. Others prefer a silk scarf, perhaps even two, wrapped in some fashion around their heads. Some like a slouch hat with the brim cut down to two inches all the way around the crown, and a few prefer a homemade four-piece fur cap to keep the cold and rain off a balding head.

Whenever possible I prefer to wear no hat at all. If I am moving, paddling or portaging, a felt or fur hat is usually too hot for me. When in the woods I like to see all around me without a brim to impair my vision. If the sun gets too hot, then a linen or silk scarf tied about my head does just fine, and if the weather turns cold or rainy, then I like to pack a four-piece wool cap. It is cut along the same pattern as a Canadian fur cap but without the fur around the edge. The turned up edge can be pulled down over my neck and ears for ample protection in most conditions.

During most treks I try to do without a coat. Come nightfall or while enduring a piercing rain, I sometimes miss the comfort of being wrapped in my civilian wool justacorps. But when traveling light and on foot, a wool coat is bulky and very heavy. If I can use my brown wool blanket as my coat, then that means one less item I have to pack, and if that means less sweating during the traveling times, then that also means I will run a better chance of not having damp clothes come nightfall. If all of that comes true, I will be more comfortable while using less through the cold of the night. Of course, all of this theory depends upon the period trek planned, the method of travel, the time of the year and the objectives of the event.

If the weather is very severe, then I like to wrap a rectangular-shaped piece of thick, hand-woven wool around my neck, ears and chin. My wool justacorps then wraps around and over the scarf, sealing my body heat within. Two hand-knitted mittens on each hand provide ample protection for my fingers in sub-freezing weather. If the weather is particularly cold and the ground covered in snow, then I can wrap strips of old wool blanketing around my lower legs.

No matter the type or amount of clothing I decide to wear or pack on a period trek, I always have the same goals in mind. I am constantly trying to dress common, dress wise and dress comfortably. Understanding the best combination of linen, leather and wool for each experience is an on-going process of experimentation.

SHOOTING ACCOUTREMENTS

Like woodsmen's clothing the shooting accoutrements were all basically the same for the Colonial hunter. Yet each set of shooting tools carried the unique "mark" of the hunter. Very seldom did two horns or shooting bags look exactly alike nor were the accoutrements within two different bags entirely the same. Since the shooting routine was taken for granted, they did not think to record the details of their everyday shooting business. The common things of a hunter's life were seldom written down as news for relatives and business partners back home. As a result rarely does any information remain in existing primary sources concerning the typical shooting routine or the customary ingredients of a hunter's shooting bag.

What information does exist concerning the shooting and reloading habits of the Colonial woodsmen is in the form of traders' business ledgers, a brief comment in a letter or folk stories perpetuated after a good fight. Some such clues are offered through the revolving account of the Illinois hunter Lewis Viviate, who worked for the Kaskaskia trader George Morgan. Lewis Viviate was most likely an Illinois Frenchman who, like many other Illinois-born hunters, was hired by Morgan to market hunt for the Englishman's trading firm. Morgan sent his men up the Cumberland river for "Buffalo beef" in the winter and the "Virginia Red Deer" in the summer. On October 20, 1767, Viviate withdrew from Morgan's store six pounds of powder and 12 pounds of lead (Beyer). Through extensive research of Morgan's business accounts, I have found that this ratio of twice as much lead to powder withdrawn from the Illinois trading post is repeated by several other hunters during this same time period. But as of this writing, I

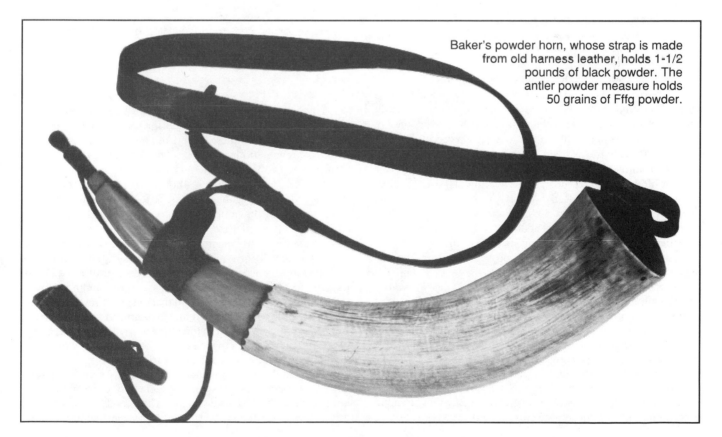

Baker's powder horn, whose strap is made from old harness leather, holds 1-1/2 pounds of black powder. The antler powder measure holds 50 grains of Fffg powder.

can find no clues in Morgan's correspondence explaining how Viviate packed and eventually used his powder and lead. Clear explanations of such a common routine are unfortunately absent.

Filling in the gaps is where experimental archaeology really pays off. Through historical investigation, I can begin to create a probable picture of Lewis Viviate's hunting and packing practices. As an example if my horn carries one pound of powder, then I would be safe to carry two pounds of lead. With a little mathematical figuring, I can estimate how many shots and the amount of individual charges Lewis Viviate might have enjoyed in packing away such a large quantity of powder and lead.

But the best clue of all that Viviate's account offers is much more practical for the period trekker. By the repeated purchase of lead and powder in such a fashion, I can surmise that Morgan's hunters ran their own round ball. For my personal interpretation of a woodsman on a cross-country trek, such an insight is important. If my portrayal is to be complete and if I am going to understand the challenges of such a life style, then I must try to emulate the common practice of Viviate and his fellow hunters and so carry lead, a mold and occasionally run my own bullets. The practice should come as second nature and should be a typical chore during a period event.

Since so much helpful information is absent from primary sources, investigation and educated guessing is the best way to fill the shooting bag with loading accoutrements. My bag and powder horn are the result of such experimenting, and my trekking partners fill their hunting bags in much the same manner. We carry the same basic implements, but how we do it and how we use them are often quite different. Since my shooting accoutrements are the result of such experimentation, in the future these items may change and the way I carry my powder horn and shooting bag will undoubtedly evolve with each mile I cover in the hardwoods. What I carry and use is, to the best of my judgment, most likely the same accoutrements that Lewis Viviate packed and used during his time in the woods. But although they are basically the same as Viviate's, my shooting equipment is my own, individually marked with my experience and by the hands who originally made the them.

Like my other period gear, my powder horn and bag are simple in looks but well-made in their construction. My powder horn is relatively plain, that is, it is void of any engraving on the body, although "MB" is carved on the butt plug. The horn measures 15-1/2 inches along the outside of the curve and holds about 1-1/2 pounds of powder. The powder horn shoulder strap is sewed to a hand-forged, U-shaped staple at the plug end and is fastened tightly around the neck of the horn. The strap is made of two sections of worn harness leather, with two very old copper rivets connecting the two lengths on the backside. I can adjust the hanging of my horn by changing the tie near its neck. I hang an antler powder measure from the neck of the horn by a leather thong just to the rear of where the shoulder strap wraps around the horn. When I carry my horn and bag under my left shoulder, the powder measure rides inside my shooting bag.

In an effort to emulate a 1760s woodsman-turned-long hunter, I have opted to carry the powder horn and shooting bag on separate straps. Since contemporary art work of the American Revolution commonly depicts riflemen with their powder horns and shooting bags hanging off a single shoulder strap and French and Indian War paintings show separate straps for the implements, I have chosen the earlier carrying style.

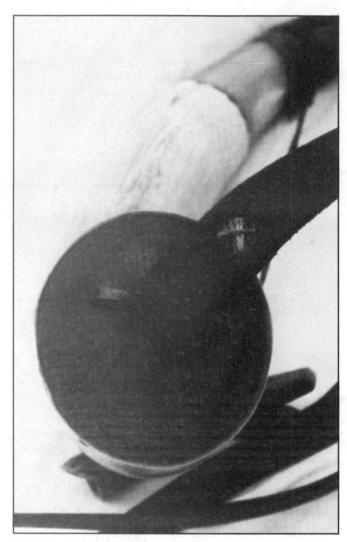

In striving for the "common look," the only markings on the author's powder horn are his initials, crudely carved into the butt of the horn.

Since there is also much conjecture concerning the styles of shooting bags typically in use during the 1760s, I have once again opted for the simplest and most common pattern associated with the French and Indian War. And for woods running and hunting, the D-shaped single pouch has been a perfect choice for me. This deep bag keeps all of my accoutrements in one compact spot, making them less prone to bounce out of the bag when I run, fall down or crawl through the brush, and I can easily find any needed items by feel.

The strap of my pouch is an old, much-worn leather belt that has a hand-forged buckle on the back side. By examining 18th century art work, photographs of the "old timers" who frequented Friendship in the early days and through my own trekking experience, I have found that the shooting bag carries best in the hollow of my ribs. I like to be able to tuck my elbow and run, giving no regard to the items in my shooting bag. An adjustable strap allows me to keep my bag in the same place no matter how much clothing I am wearing.

I have only two items that hang from my shoulder strap. One is my loading block, which is made from curly maple and holds seven patched round balls. This handy 18th century device hangs by a thong at the center of my chest with very little

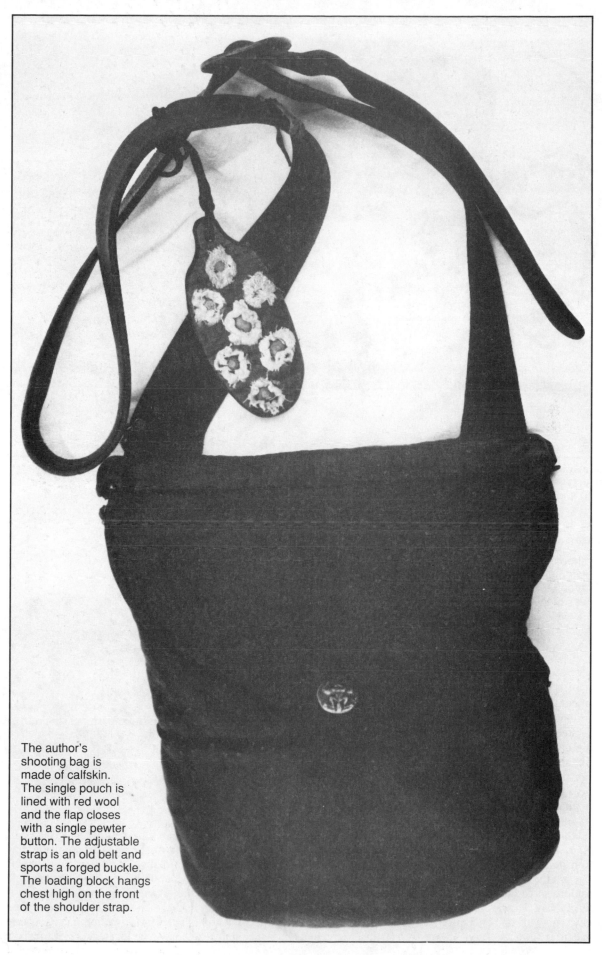

The author's
shooting bag is
made of calfskin.
The single pouch is
lined with red wool
and the flap closes
with a single pewter
button. The adjustable
strap is an old belt and
sports a forged buckle.
The loading block hangs
chest high on the front
of the shoulder strap.

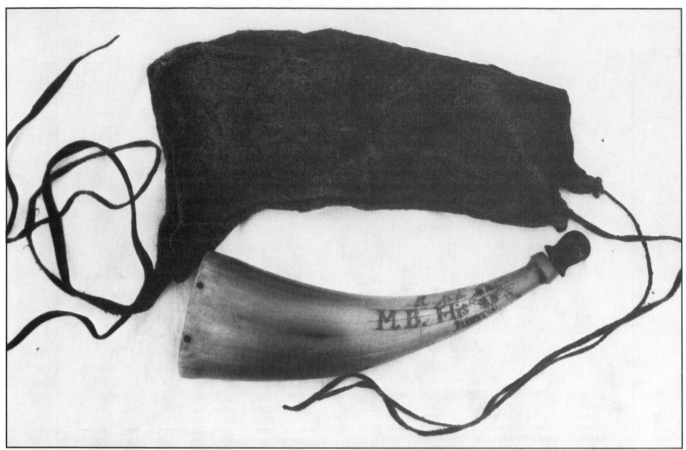

Shown above is a cow's knee made from brain-tanned deerskin that has been well-greased. The flat priming horn is about five inches long and sports some simple engraving.

Inside his shooting bag, Baker packs one of his most cherished gifts — a hand-made copy of an original French and Indian War-era compass. The compass was crafted by Oliver Frank Twist of New York State.

free movement. The loading block allows me to reload my rifle quickly without going inside my shooting bag and that makes the entire system so much smoother and quieter than fumbling around in the covered pouch. I hang my vent pick and pan brush by a hand-made wire chain attached near the bottom of the front side of the shoulder strap, making their quick retrieval and storage within the pouch a simple practice.

The pouch itself is made of calfskin lined with red wool and sports a single pewter button to hold the flap secure. I have found through years of trekking that nothing beats a button to hold the flap shut. I used to believe the folk story that the powder horn held the flap closed, but through experience I found that when the horn hangs low enough to keep it closed, the horn seldom stayed in place.

Inside my bag I carry only what I need to shoot and maintain my rifle with one exception, a hand-crafted copy of a mid-18th century compass given to me by a special friend in

this sport. I store the compass in the pouch for quick access when trekking or hunting. Besides the compass I have packed away a flat priming horn that sports a small amount of primitive engraving. Three separate brain-tanned deerskin pouches of various sizes contain a fist full of tow for cleaning my rifle, a ball screw, which I have been known to need upon occasion, and a collection of rifle flints. I prefer to use separate pouches for such items because I can locate them by touch very easily

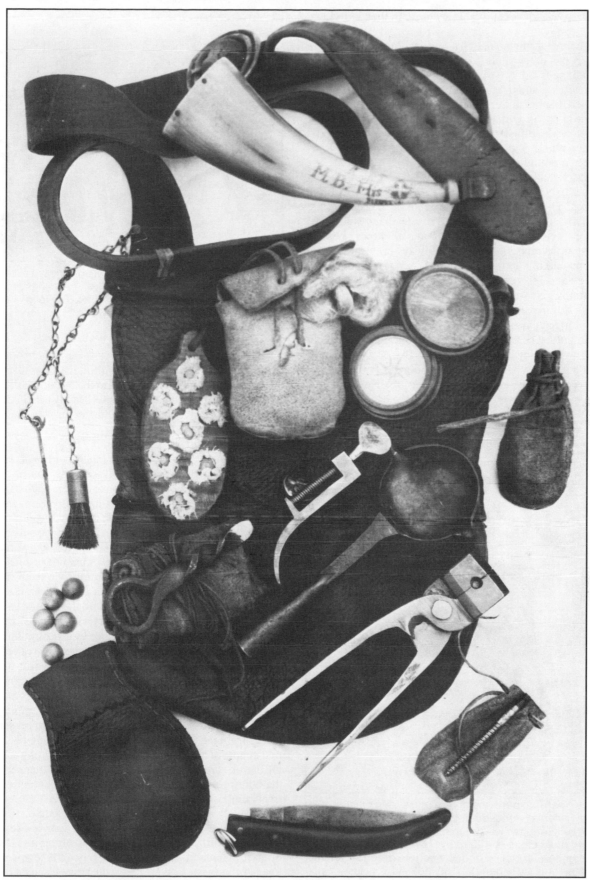

One's shooting bag and its accoutrements are perhaps the best examples of the rewards of experimental archaeology. The accoutrements shown are: a flat priming horn, a compass, a pouch filled with tow, a cow's knee, a screwdriver, a bullet mold, a ladle, a mainspring vise, a bag of flints, a ball puller, a folding knife, and a bullet bag. The vent pick and brush are attached to the shoulder strap and carried inside the pouch.

and the otherwise loose items ride securely in their individual bags.

I also carry within the pouch a few pre-cut patches, a strip of patching or some patches cut out in paper doll fashion. Patching changes all the time for me, depending upon the material available and the time I have to prepare it. I also have an oil-tanned, leather bullet bag that I can retrieve by touch and drop out a single ball with just one hand. This bag has come in handy when my loading block is empty and I am watching a red squirrel run along a distant hickory limb. The bag holds comfortably a pound of .490 round balls.

A greased leather cow's knee is always a standard item in my shooting bag. This is a leather covering made to fit around my rifle lock. The cow's knee comes out of the bag every time rain threatens and has kept my load dry in many situations. However, experience has taught me that sometimes even the best of intentions on my part will not always protect my main charge from soaking up the humidity. When it rains hard and long enough and I have nowhere to hide completely, my rifle load eventually gets wet. But that, too, is the romance of trying to do as the original woodsmen did.

I have long ago made it a habit to pack a hand-forged copy of an 18th century screwdriver in my shooting bag. This tool weighs almost nothing and is unique enough in shape that I can quickly find it even when buried in the bottom of my shooting bag. I also carry in the pouch a folding knife. The blade lies

Inside his shooting bag, the author carries a brain-tanned deerskin pouch stuffed with tow for cleaning his rifle and another pouch with a dozen or so flints. The long, slender ball puller is kept in its own pouch as well.

lengthwise in the bottom of the bag and is always there if I need an extra cutting edge. Also found in the bottom of my pouch is a hand-forged bullet mold made specifically for my rifle, along with a small lead ladle and an 18th century style mainspring vise.

I line the wooden patchbox of my rifle with a few greased patches, then store on top of the patches a few trimmed bird feathers. I cut off most of the shaft and vane from each one, for I am only concerned with the quill end of the feather. When my rifle is not in use, a quill inserted snugly into the touch hole will help greatly in keeping the main charge dry and likewise signal to all in the trekking party that my rifle is loaded but not primed. The last thing to fit into the patchbox is a tow worm, along with a small hank of tow. The tow hank, about the size of a pencil, is twisted lengthwise and then fed into the teeth of the tow worm. When shooting or hunting, it is then a simple matter to retrieve the tow and worm, attach it to the ramrod and quickly wipe the bore a few times. The dry tow "scrubs" the rifling, allowing me to keep shooting as accurately as possible under such period conditions. Most of the time the original hank of tow can be used throughout a morning's worth of squirrel hunting or a day's worth of target practice. When on a period trek, the tow kept within my shooting bag allows me to clean my rifle thoroughly during the time spent in camp.

To clean my rifle when in camp, I pull several pencil-size pieces from the tow bundle kept in my shooting bag. I dip the first couple of hanks into warm water and, starting at the top of the barrel, scrub up and down in a deliberate manner, clearing the bore of the residue. I repeat the slow descent until I can freely run a wet hank all the way down against the breech. Then I repeatedly run a wet hank the entire length of the bore, periodically re-dipping the tow into warm water and re-threading it into the worm. Once it comes out free of fouling, I run hanks of dry tow up and down the bore. When the tow is dry to the touch, I slide a fresh hank against the muzzle and then stand my rifle upside down, allowing any remaining moisture to run away from the breech. After a short time, I remove the tow and reload my rifle. I tie the used tow to the strap of my shooting bag where it hangs until dry and then put it in my fire-starting

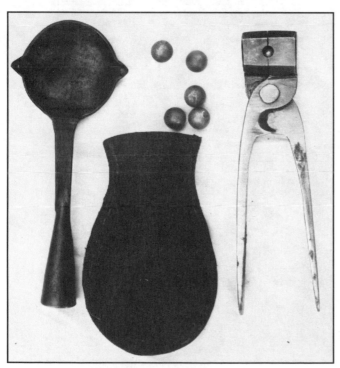

In striving to learn, experience and practice the common skills of the Colonial woodsman, Baker casts all of his rifle balls from the items packed within his shooting bag. The hand-forged mold casts a .490 round ball, and the handle of the ladle is hollow, enabling one to wedge a green stick into the hole for a temperate handle. The ladle itself holds a half pound of melted lead.

kit for extra tinder.

My powder horn and shooting bag, even when packed with the maximum amount of powder and round ball, will ride comfortably and practically upon my right shoulder all day long and through the night. The wide strapping helps to dissipate the weight. The location of the horn and bag keeps both of them out of the way so they do not interfere with my daytime movements. I very seldom lose any of the small items, and because experience has taught me the best way to wear and use such essential "tools of the trade," I usually sleep comfortably the whole night with the horn and bag still on my person.

My historical investigation has helped me to rid myself of anything that is questionable historically or unneeded for my style of loading. I still wish to shoot straight. I still like to win a shooting contest every now and then. But now I concentrate on loading smoothly, quickly, quietly and strive constantly to load by touch even after a hard day of trekking.

ACCOUTREMENTS AND FOODSTUFFS

Figuring out what to carry on a period trek and how best to pack it are questions that will perhaps never be fully answered. After most treks at least one person in the party, sometimes myself, usually makes the comment, "Well, I carried way too much stuff." The continuing challenge to pack both a bedroll and a kit of personal accoutrements in the best period fashion is also the most individualistic aspect of period trekking, because each trek brings different learning experiences and most period trekkers do not spend enough time in the woods for the 18th century packing routine to become second nature.

The lack of clear information on this topic also complicates the problem of how and what to pack. Just like shooting bag

The hand-made tin pot contains a cloth sack filled with white corn flour, plus a small salt horn, a wedge of maple sugar and a horn container filled with cayenne pepper and other favorite spices of the Colonial woodsman.

accoutrements, the contents of the haversack or knapsack are largely hidden through more than 250 years of history. When itemized lists are found in primary sources, the inventories are usually those of the French or English regular forces and the supplies mentioned are usually those of the officers. The common man's way of packing his goods, especially those of the lower class hunters, were neglected by the historians of the period.

Fortunately, every now and then a list of supplies packed by the common soldier turns up in a primary source, allowing the reenactor to draw parallels between the soldier and the probable practices of a civilian from the same area and time period. The journal of Louis Antoine de Bougainville, *Adventure in the Wilderness: The American Journals of Louis Antoine de Bougainville 1756-1760*, is a prime example. On February 17-28, 1757, the French officer mentions in his journal the clothing, food and accoutrements rationed to the soldiers who were leaving presently on a winter expedition. For a period trekker who wishes to emulate a French civilian, Bougainville's list is doubly good, for the officer mentions that the rations were the same for both soldier and militiaman alike, except that the soldiers wore "breeches and drawers instead of a breechclout" (87).

Bougainville's inventory of food, clothing and accoutrements for the men venturing into the winter wilderness includes the following items, with the prices of some:

One overcoat	25 livres
One blanket	9 "
One wool cap	3 "
Two cotton shirts	16 "
One pair of mitasses[1]	5 "
One breechclout	2 livres, 10 sous
Two hanks of thread	One waistcoat
Six needles	One awl
Two pair of deerskin shoes	One tinderbox
One dressed deer skin	One drag rope
Two portage collars	One comb
One butcher's knife	One worm
One pair of snowshoes	One bearskin
One tarpaulin per officer, one	One tomahawk
large one to every four men	Two pair of stockings
Two siamese [?] knives	One pair of mittens. (87)

[1]Edward P. Hamilton, editor of Bougainville's journal, explains that mitasses were "loose leggings made of coarse, heavy cloth, fastened with garters at ankle and knee" (87).

Bougainville also mentions that each man received 12 days of rations, which included "bread, salt, pork, peas on the basis of field ration" (87). The Frenchman's thorough note-taking is of great value for the period trekker. In fact, such "finds" do not get any better than this entry in Bougainville's journal, especially for those emulating the French during the French and Indian War. But since much of what the French officer mentions was available along most of the North American frontier, any 18th century period trekker can glean valuable information from Bougainville's thoughtful entries.

George Morgan's October 1767 series of entries for the hunter Lewis Viviate is a perfect example of the type of clues that may be uncovered through careful investigation. When trying to figure out the best personal supplies and the least amount to pack on a period trek, the list of goods and services charged to Viviate offers some solid help. The goods ordered from Morgan's Fort Pitt warehouse and shipped to Kaskaskia for Lewis Viviate included:

One Bateau	75"	0"	0"
One Kettle	1"	15"	0"
Two Knives	"	8"	0"
Salt	"	7"	6"
200 lbs. Flour	4"	0"	0"
Barrel for Flour	"	10"	0"
1 Axe	"	10"	0"
5 lbs. Chocolate	1"	5"	0"
14 lbs. Loafe Sugar	2"	16"	0"
1 Small Kettle	"	15"	0"
6 lbs. Powder	2"	5"	0"
5 Beaver Skins	3"	0"	0"
1 Rifle Gun	6"	0"	0"
12 Flints	"	2"	0"
12 lbs. Lead	"	15"	0"

(Beyer)

[The items charged against Lewis Viviate were listed in pounds, shillings and pence, according to their appraised worth in Pennsylvania currency. During Morgan's day 12 pence made a shilling and 20 shillings equaled a pound. As an example one kettle cost 35 shillings but was listed for the clerk's ease at 1 pound, 15 shillings or 1" 15" 0".]

Apparently, not every hunter owned a horse, for Viviate also hired a horse for 40 shillings and had to pay for "a boy to take the horse back" (Beyer). The return service cost the hunter an additional one pound, 10 shillings. Also during October George Morgan charged Viviate for the transport of a "fuzee from Philadelphia," along with two pairs of shoes, two more pounds of sugar, one silk handkerchief, "one breeches and coat" for Viviate's hired man John Street, three powder horns, an additional kettle, a charge for "mending Street's gun," plus a canoe and "three oars for paddles" (Beyer).

As I compare the detailed ration list of Bougainville's enlisted men with Viviate's account, I can see that similar needs are manifest in both accounts. Each list included a variety of knives, axes or tomahawks and overcoats. But I can also spot some differences between the needs or wants of the French soldiers and those of Viviate and his hired hunter John Street, especially when it comes to the staple foods used. The French took with them bread, salt, pork and peas. Viviate also

took salt, but apparently he counted on making his own bread, for he took 200 pounds of flour, plus chocolate and sugar to drink his "boiled chocolate." Yet in Canada, chocolate was, according to Bougainville, a treat that only the French officers enjoyed (87).

As an experimental archaeologist trying to figure out the most practical personal items to carry and how to pack them, both of these lists offer me an education in Colonial habits. And since I am emulating a Cumberland hunter, I give Viviate's choice of food staples greater weight than the Frenchman's peas, pork and bread. But for a French trekker, the choices might very well be the other way around.

With my ongoing historical investigation, I have gradually whittled my personal accoutrements down to a manageable level. My pack usually weighs no more than 11 or 12 pounds. That includes my blanket and food, plus the maintenance accoutrements necessary for living 18th century-style in the woods. In the warmer months, when I trek during a long weekend, I prefer to go as light as possible. For those leisurely scouts through the woods, I like to wrap my personal rations inside my blanket, forming a tight bedroll that I carry using a tumpline. As a consequence I have no haversack, no knapsack, just my blanket rolled up and carried across my back. Inside the blanket might be a section of slab bacon, a cloth bag filled with cornmeal, a folding skillet, a fire-starting kit, a sewing kit and a tin boiler holding a brain-tanned deerskin pouch of chocolate

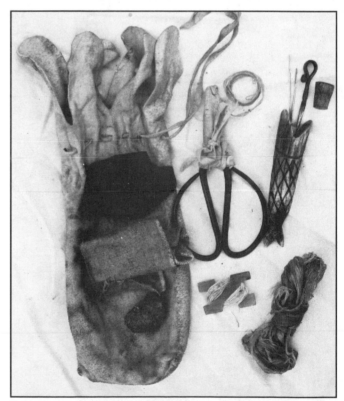

Baker's sewing kit includes: a hollow antler tip concealing sewing needles and a small awl, a horn bobbin holding a length of waxed linen thread, a bundle of dried deer sinew, scissors in a leather "boot," a chunk of beeswax, a strip of linen, and a small square of greased leather. The various accoutrement pouches have different openings, helping one to identify quickly the contents by touch or sight.

Here the author is holding up his blanket roll and knapsack, which contains everything that is necessary for the trail. The blanket is tied to the bottom of the shoulder straps. The total weight of the knapsack and bedroll is 11 pounds.

and muscavado sugar. I could go a pound or so lighter by substituting jerky and dried corn for bacon and cornmeal. Such rations, as far as I can presently determine, were the common foodstuffs carried under similar conditions by a typical backwoodsman of the middle Colonies.

If I am trekking by canoe or hunting in the woods for several days at a time, then my "needs" list tends to get longer. Then I like to carry both a knapsack and a blanket roll. I use a hand-loomed, brown wool blanket that is a little larger than a 4-point. The color blends in well with the woods during all seasons of the year, and I am no longer bothered by flies and bugs that were naturally attracted to my white Whitney blanket. I fold the blanket in half lengthwise then place a cloth sack of tinder and tow, plus an extra pair of moccasins, at one end of the blanket. Before rolling up the blanket, I fold in the two sides, making a long strip equal to the width of my shoulders. Then starting at the end with the tinder and moccasins, I roll it up as tightly as possible and tie it off with three leather straps.

KNAPSACK CONTENTS

- Tin pot containing a sack of white cornmeal, a chunk of brown sugar and two small horns filled with salt and cayenne pepper.
- Oil-tanned leather pouch holding a sewing kit, which consists of a horn bobbin of linen thread, scissors, dried deer or elk sinew, beeswax, an antler "fish" hollowed out to hold an assortment of needles and a few patches of linen and leather.
- Horn comb and a horn, boar-bristle toothbrush contained in a linen pouch.
- Folding skillet with a cloth sack containing slab bacon wedged inside the dish of the pan.
- Chunks of chocolate and muscavado sugar within a brain-tanned deerskin pouch.
- Wool pouch holding a few pieces of castile soap.
- Dried corn within a linen pouch. (Two pounds of fresh whole corn dries to 1/4-pound.)
- Cloth sack of dried meat, commonly called "jerk" in the 18th century.
- Oil-tanned leather pouch containing a fishing kit, which includes: a small, brain-tanned deerskin pouch holding several fishing hooks; a handful of split sinkers made from .32 caliber balls; two H-shaped horn bobbins filled with silk fishing line (surgical silk suture thread); a couple of small sticks wrapped in linen fishing line; a deer sinew leader tied to a hook; and a leather thong tied to a two-inch willow branch used as a stringer.
- Oil-tanned pouch filled with tow for cleaning one's rifle, starting fires in a pinch, scrubbing a frying pan or plugging a bad wound.
- Well-worn silver spoon.
- Fire-starting kit in a greased goatskin pouch. The kit includes: flint and steel, a "bird's nest" of dried cottonwood bark, a tin of charred cloth, two short beeswax candles, a bundle of candle wick that has been dipped in hot beeswax, and a few pieces of pitch pine.
- Tin of lard, grease, beeswax or any combination of the three for greasing moccasins, rubbing the stock of one's rifle and dressing the lock.
- Two flat creek stones for sharpening knives and one's belt axe.
- Antler whistle on a leather thong.
- New Testament.
- Coil of leather thongs for spare strapping and a bundle of elk skin for moccasin patching.

My knapsack is made from linen that is reinforced with oil-tanned leather along the bottom and inside the top of the flap. The straps are made from old harness leather. I attach my blanket roll to the bottom of my knapsack using the two outside straps that secure the blanket roll. Within the knapsack I use wool, linen and leather pouches to carry my goods. Wool sacks absorb moisture and linen pouches allow air circulation. The items carried within my knapsack, which are listed in the adjacent table, and bedroll are the result of lessons learned from each period trek and notions gleaned from research. Each accoutrement, though, is often used for more than one purpose. Experience, watching others and asking questions have taught me that advantage, and I carry these same items with me whether I go on a long walk through the woods, float a slow river in a canoe or ride a horse to a rendezvous. I pack the same way when I walk a short distance to a black powder shoot, a fort encampment or a living history trade fair. I am the same woodsman wherever I go, whatever activity I attend. These are the accoutrements that make me an individual, yet they also speak of the common experience of all woodsmen who have shared similar trails before me.

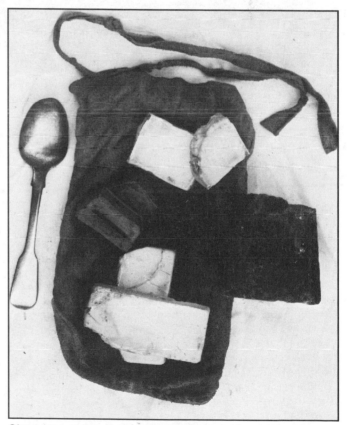

Facing page: Ready for a trek of several days, the author is packing his knapsack and blanket roll. Like the single blanket roll and tumpline, the secret for comfort and durability is to keep the knapsack and blanket roll tight against the back.

Chocolate apparently was the most popular hot drink of Joseph Hollingshead's long hunters. The lighter blocks are maple sugar, the dark wedges are chocolate and the cylinder is a chunk of muscavado sugar—the by-product of making molasses from sugar cane. Such ingredients make a zippy hot chocolate that offers quick energy and a pleasant taste for any trekker. Next to the deerskin pouch is a silver spoon.

Here are three of the canteens used by the author on various treks. The two outside canteens are leather, crafted by John Busch of Wisconsin. The middle canteen is made of copper, holds over a quart and was fashioned by Tom Brown of Westminster Forge.

CONCLUSION

For anyone interested in taking that first step toward truly understanding the life style of a favorite pre-1840 character, I would like to make a few recommendations. If I had followed all of these suggestions, I would have saved myself much time, expense and frustration. First, the attitude of the new trekker is the most important characteristic he can bring to a company of trekkers. A new member willing to think like an original woodsman is much more likely to be taken in by a group of reenactors that is normally very careful about inducting new members. It's not that new faces are a bad thing or that the party is necessarily elitist, but rather that they have been disappointed so much in the past. Relatively few "buckskinners" are ever willing to journey away from the spotlight of a rendezvous and get wet and dirty and perhaps go hungry.

Doddridge recalls that his woodsmen neighbors were "afflicted with the rheumatism in their limbs" (142). Peter Kalm notes that the Canadian Indians "lay in this manner during cold and rainy nights in the damp and wet forests without having any other clothes [shirt, breechclout, leggings, moccasins] to put under or on top of themselves at night than those they wore during the day" (561). The skills of the original

woodsmen emulated the best of both the European world and that of the woodland Indian. But as demonstrated by these two primary sources the opportunity to be miserable was common, and not many folks are willing to experience the possibility of such hardships. After all, it's supposed to be fun.

But bringing the right attitude, that is, demonstrating the willingness to endure the good and bad experiences with the same charm, will make a new member of a period trekking group very welcome indeed. And if a new member keeps feeding this drive to understand through doing, then that attitude will affect the veterans of the company. The want to understand through historical investigation will thus perpetuate itself through the trekking party.

First-time period trekkers should also start out with simple, short routes, and it helps if one has someplace to go, a reward of sorts. On the first trek that I feel was worthy enough to be considered somewhat authentic, I only traveled about three miles in two days and ended up at a rendezvous near Mt. Taylor, New Mexico. I slept on the ground and carried everything I needed with me for the entire weekend. My shoulders hurt, my heels were bruised, but I gained a little of the skill for which I was searching and had tasted the romance without trying my temper, knowledge or stamina. Although I had only walked that short distance, I felt as if I had traveled clear to St. Louis. I privately swelled with pride for trekking into the rendezvous, even though I experienced only a tiny fraction of the independence that those original woodsmen surely felt.

Period trekkers new to the game should also plan some activities along the way. Not too many and not too fast. Just something to occupy the daylight hours. Small game hunting seasons are excellent times to trek into the woods. A roasted squirrel can fill the belly and ease a set of sore shoulders. Trekkers can soak up a wealth of information after a weekend spent trapping beaver and fleshing the hides in base camp, and fishing season offers an activity that is not usually associated with the primitive black powder sport. Trekking into a secluded hollow and spending the weekend building a half-faced shelter can also be a rewarding weekend.

Both fresh and seasoned period trekkers find pre-determined ground rules a great help in planning an activity within the context of a particular time period. A clear perception of the time period and personas involved, a solid purpose for the trek, an understanding of the physical and mental effort anticipated and an explanation of exactly what each member is expected to contribute all help participants to comprehend the hopes and expectations of the planners. Once the scenario is explained and the rules established, then anyone wishing to participate has the responsibility either to go along with them or remain at home. A period trekker should never accept an offer and then try to change the established understanding after the party is deep into the woods. Complaining about sudden changes in the weather or the effort involved never help the atmosphere of a trek.

If a group invites an outsider on an upcoming trek, then the prospective member should be willing to meet their prescribed level of authenticity, whether the group's demands are unusually stringent or more relaxed. Simply put, a trekker new to any party should investigate, understand and ultimately accept the association's level of authenticity, and understanding what a particular living history group means by "authentic" is the key to understanding what they expect on a period trek. The best thing a new trekker can do is to find a small party of kindred spirits who seem to have an understanding and expectation of what is authentic that is similar to his own. Some groups merely debate the word "authentic" while others compose and continually improve bylaws concerning their level of authenticity. Some parties take newcomers into their fold who have the right attitude but perhaps lack the complete run of accepted clothing and equipment. Other organizations will accept fresh participants if they have the proper clothing and the attitude. A few living history clubs inspect each other's equipment before every trek begins, and if anything is questionable, then it must be discarded. Other parties review one another's accoutrements at the close of a trek, agreeing on what is acceptable or forbidden on any future gathering. Fewer still won't accept synthetic fabrics, chemically-tanned leather or 20th century underwear, toilet paper, eye glasses or medicines on any trek. Finding a group that holds similar values and goals is the trick to enjoying and seeing fruitful results through period trekking.

But no matter how hard one strives "to step back in time," reenactors will always face one dilemma that can never be entirely overcome. Regardless of the preparation, all period trekkers have to deal with trekking out of context. Most living history events happen on weekends or around holidays, times between the responsibilities we face every day. To combat the

Depending upon the circumstances, Baker carries these two pouches either inside his knapsack or within the folds of the blanket roll. The linen sack holds over a pound of dried whole corn, and the oil-tanned goatskin pouch holds about a pound of extra tow.

Trekking doesn't have to be just laborious walking. Checking out fresh game tracks, stalking and even hunting are possible when the knapsack, blanket roll, the powder horn and shooting bag are carried snugly and high.

limited time factor, most reenactors plan carefully each trek they take. But at one time or another, nature's temperament, accidents or sickness will interrupt the plan. Having to deal with work on Monday morning, getting back home for a family commitment or having to travel from point A to point B by Sunday evening all interfere with the goals of any period trek. A hunting party in the 18th century normally waited out a snow or rainstorm, made camp while a partner took sick or changed

course when situations dictated. The ticking of a clock did not generally matter on a day-to-day basis to backwoodsmen of the 18th century. But unfortunately, such a curse is part of every modern woodsman's life, and periodically, often unexpectedly, it will get in the way of the best-prepared, most knowledgeable trekker.

Even though I have periodically been frustrated by conflicts between my two worlds, my treks have continued to extend my knowledge, stretch my endurance and refine my outfit and gear. I have learned because I have continued to *do*. I keep repeating the same skills, the same trekking experiences over and over again.

A trekker should never be content with saying, "I have done a winter trek. I know I can do it. There is no need to do it again." Period trekking teaches *every* time, even if the season and method of travel is repeated. It builds character in a reenactor's outfit, underscores what a researcher already knows and verifies what one thinks is true. It teaches secrets that only historical experimentation can whisper in the period trekker's heart.

APPENDIX A: WORKS CITED

Anderson, Jay. *Time Machines: The World of Living History.* Nashville: American Association for State and Local History, 1984.

Beyer, George R., ed. *Baynton, Wharton, and Morgan Papers.* Manuscript group 19. Harrisburg: Pennsylvania Historical and Museum Commission, 1967.

Bougainville, Louis Antoine de. *Adventure in the Wilderness: The American Journals of Louis Antoine de Bougainville 1756-1760.* Trans. and ed. Edward P. Hamilton. Norman: University of Oklahoma Press, 1964.

Cresswell, Nicholas. *The Journal of Nicholas Cresswell: 1774-1777.* London: Jonathan Cape, 1925.

Doddridge, Joseph. *Notes on the Settlement and Indian Wars of the Western Parts of Virginia and Pennsylvania From 1763 to 1782.* Albany, Joel Munsell, 1876.

Kalm, Peter. *Peter Kalm's Travels In North America: The English Version of 1770.* Ed. Adolph B. Benson. New York: Dover Publications, 1937.

Klinger, Robert Lee, and Richard A. Wilder. *Sketch Book 76: The American Soldier 1775-1781.* Union City, TN: Pioneer Press, 1967.

White, George M. *Craft Manual of North American Indian Footwear.* Ronan, MT: Ronan Pioneer Print, 1969.

APPENDIX B: RECOMMENDED READING

French and Indian War Era:

Bougainville, Louis Antoine de. *Adventure in the Wilderness: The American Journals of Louis Antoine de Bougainville 1756-1760.* Trans. and ed. Edward P. Hamilton. Norman: University of Oklahoma Press, 1964.

Kalm, Peter. *Peter Kalm's Travels in North America: The English Version of 1770.* Ed. Adolph B. Benson. New York: Dover Publications, 1937.

Knox, John. *An Historical Journal of the Campaigns in North America for the Years 1757, 1758, 1759, and 1760.* 3 vols. Ed. Arthur G. Doughty. Freeport, NY: Books for Library Press, 1970.

Papp, Mary M., ed. *Journal of the Forces of Montcalm and Wolfe.* Grand Rapids, MI.

Roby, Luther, ed. *Reminiscences of the French War.* 1831. Freedom, NH: Freedom Historical Society, 1988.

Western Fur Trade Era:

Berry, Don. *A Majority of Scoundrels.* Sausalito, CA: Comstock Editions, 1971.

Blevins, Winfred. *Give Your Heart to the Hawks.* Los Angeles: Nash Publishing, 1973.

Hanson, James Austin, and Kathryn J. Wilson. *The Mountain Man's Sketch Book.* 2 vols. Chadron, NE: Fur Press, 1976.

Russell, Osborne. *Journal of a Trapper.* Ed. Aubrey L. Haines. 1955. Lincoln: University of Nebraska Press, 1986.

Voyageurs and Frenchmen:

Ekberg, Carl J. *Colonial Ste. Genevieve: An Adventure on the Mississippi Frontier.* Gerald, MO: Patrice Press, 1985.

Hanson, James A. *Voyager's Sketch Book.* Chadron, NE: Fur Press, 1981.

Johnson, Mary Moyars, et al. *Historic Colonial French Dress.* West Lafayette, IN: Ouabache Press, 1982.

Nute, Grace Lee. *The Voyageur.* 1931. St. Paul: Minnesota Historical Society Press, 1987.

Seno, William Joseph, ed. and comp. *Up Country: Voices from the Great Lakes Wilderness.* Minocqua, WI: Heartland Press, 1985.

Revolutionary War Era:

Klinger, Robert Lee, and Richard A. Wilder. *Sketch Book 76: The American Soldier 1775-1781.* Union City, TN: Pioneer Press, 1967.

Martin, Joseph Plumb. *Private Yankee Doodle.* 1830. Boston: Little, Brown, 1961.

Neumann, George C., and Frank J. Kravic. *Collector's Illustrated Encyclopedia of the American Revolution.* 1975. Texarkana, TX: Rebel Publishing, 1989.

Finger Weaving

by Tim Connin

At an early age, Tim Connin was a "runner of the woods" in his native Ohio. He cannot remember a time when he did not love the woods and history in general, and he grew up on a diet of *The Frontiersman* and other historical influences. As a boy Tim remembers seeing Friendship, Indiana, home of the National Muzzle Loading Rifle Association, featured on *Wide World of Sports* on TV. He first visited Friendship in 1974.

Connin evolved through several areas and eras of interest after the Friendship experience, from mountain man to plains Indian to coureur de bois. His main interest in history is now the French and Indian War and the fur trade in the Great Lakes area. The Great Lakes Indians are currently his main course of study. Another love is pilgrim century furniture.

Tim's interest in weaving began from a desire to own a finger-woven sash and not having the funds to buy one. He spent two years researching finger weaving and how it was done before he ever picked up a thread.

Not surprisingly, museum research and traveling to historic sites throughout the U.S. are two more of Tim's pastimes. Being a twin helps in this area as he and his brother, Tom, share their "finds" of information and their skills. Connin is a member of The Forces of Montcalm and Wolfe and has been a member of the NMLRA since 1974.

Tim is a devoted father and husband and resides with his wife, Angie, and their two daughters, Carrie and Abbey, in Continental, Ohio. He has dedicated this chapter to the memory of Loren Herrington, who was the first to tell him, "Just do it."

A thorough study of finger weaving has never really been attempted to my knowledge. One can find vague references in early writings and archaeological evidence if you really dig for it, but there is really very little information on the subject of finger weaving. What we do know about finger weaving is mainly gleaned from the artifacts themselves and from period paintings. Therefore, some of the information in this article is my own opinion formed on the subject after viewing old pieces in museums and private collections, after reading everything I can find on finger weaving and from discussions with other weavers. Please understand that all the information isn't in and our knowledge is always evolving.

There are many weaving techniques used to achieve the different designs on sashes, garters, bags and straps that we see at historical events and rendezvous. In this chapter I want to deal mainly with a technique of finger weaving that I know as the "oblique weave," also called the plain weave, the open face weave and the basket weave. Webster describes the term "oblique" as slanting or inclined and that is just how this weave looks. Each strand goes over or under the next thread slanting either left or right, making small gaps between the threads for all those little white beads. This technique of weaving was used on the majority of the 18th century pieces that I have observed in museum collections. Artifacts woven in the oblique technique were usually of a solid color, sometimes having a different color selvage. White beads were then added to make the overall design, rather than different colored yarns forming the design.

Textiles in the ground decay rapidly, so examples of any woven material that pre-date European contact are few. The oblique weave has shown up occasionally at pre-contact sites with one possible example of a chevron weave. In some areas of the country where there are dry environments more artifacts have survived. In the state of Missouri, pieces of the oblique weave have been found in dry rock shelters. Dates on these pieces aren't really known, but they certainly pre-date the European contact period. The woven artifacts that remain are too small actually to tell what they were or what they were used for, but some appear to be belts or straps. The artifacts were woven out of bast fiber, which is the inner bark of trees and/or various plants.

One thing I found intriguing in this information on pre-contact pieces was a complete bast fiber bag, which was found in one of the rock shelters in Missouri. This type of bag was mostly used for storage and does not usually have a strap on it. But this particular bag has a carrying strap—a must for a pocketless society. The storage-type bag stayed the same for thousands of years. Usually these bags are woven in a finger-weaving technique called twining where the threads are twisted together. Using this technique and incorporating contrasting colored fibers, patterns such as stylized animals and bold geometrics could be produced. The similarity of this bag and an 18th century bag in the Pitt Rivers Museum in Oxford, England, are very interesting. Two design elements are similar on both the bags, one being the strap; the other, the method used in constructing the mouth openings of the bags. The two bodies were woven using different techniques; the older bag was done in the twined technique, while the Pitt Rivers bag was made in the oblique weave.

Another interesting twined bag done in the storage bag style that also has a carrying strap is shown in the book *A Basketful of Indian Culture Change* by Ted Brasser (79). Unlike the previous twined bag, this bag, which is dated 1730, is fully decorated with moose-hair embroidery and quill-wrapped warp threads at the opening of the bag.

The similarities and differences of these bags makes me

Bison hair bag with beaded human figures on one side and zigzags on the other. This 18th century brown bag is from the Northeast woodlands, possibly Illinois. There is only one other bag of this description known and it's in the British Museum. The treatment of the top is similar to twined utilitarian bags.

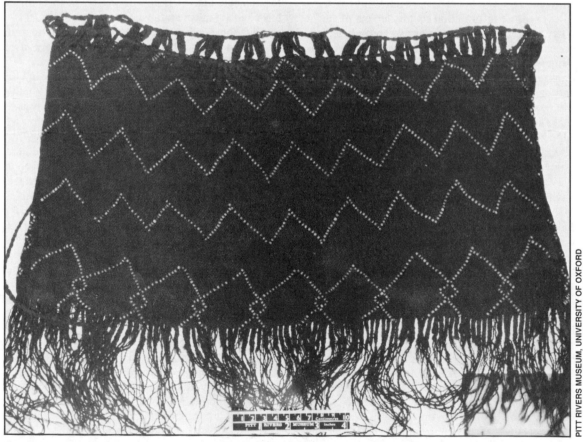

Winnebago twined medicine bag with a black design on beige backgound.

wonder about the evolution of these bag types. Even though the dates of the bags cover a wide range of years, the techniques employed in them are similar. Some decorative styles and material variations may have been regional or fashionable or served some function besides mere adornment, such as religious purposes. The availability of design elements during each time period is another thing to consider in the matter of their evolution.

All of the bags we have just considered are important examples because they show how the bag styles were already developed at an early time and were definitely carried over to later periods. I believe it is possible that all the finger weaving techniques used by weavers today were developed during the European pre-contact period, rather than when new materials (that is, different colored wool yarns) were introduced to the indigenous peoples by white traders. Actually, the old pieces aren't there to prove this theory, but the remaining woven artifacts display a seemingly endless variety of complex techniques.

Looking for material on older pieces of finger weaving, I went to several books that deal with historical grave sites. Of all the material that has survived the grave, textiles have fared the worst, and the fragments that have turned up are very small.

At the Angel Site, which is a prehistoric mound, there was discovered an intrusive burial of the historic period around 1800. The grave included all types of trade goods of the late 18th century and early 19th century.

Among the trade goods discovered were two small pieces of a finger-woven item that had some of its beaded pattern still visible. This piece could have been a bag because of the large amount of artifacts gathered in the general area of the piece, or it could have been a sash judging from the number of beads left behind, which numbered 3,942. That may sound like a large quantity of beads, but my own sash's beaded design is not very complex and it has over 2,000 beads in it. The pattern of beads that can be discerned from the Angel Site fragments is a chevron design of four parallel rows. The beaded design is on the selvage of the piece, and according to Glen Black in *The Angel Site*, there may have been more of a beaded pattern than what survived. He mentions trying to make out a pattern during

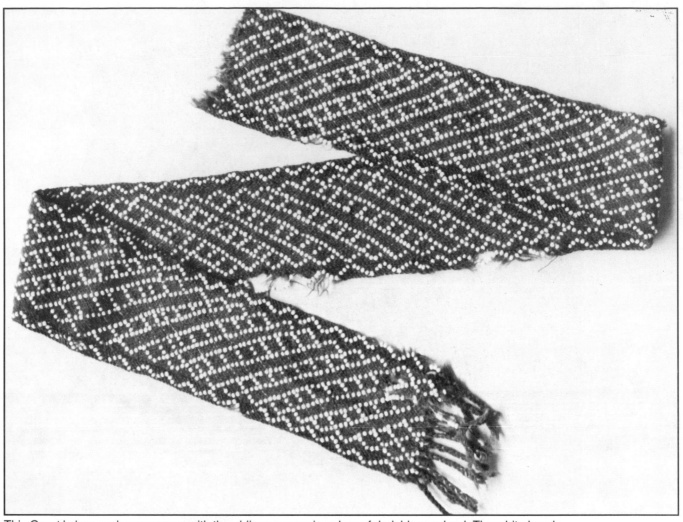

This Great Lakes sash was woven with the oblique weave in colors of dark blue and red. The white beads were applied with tan cotton thread. This sash is in a private collection and no historical data is available.

the excavation of the grave. Black spent four days using a dissection needle, working without gloves in near zero weather trying to save the design. Obviously, it didn't work because the book didn't describe any other pattern (Black 251-256).

Another fragment of finger-woven textile to survive time and the elements was found at Rock Island, one of the islands at the mouth of Green Bay, Wisconsin. This fragment, found in burial number five, is even smaller than the pieces found at the Angel Site. Once again there is no way to tell what its function was, because it had deteriorated so badly. Found in the same area were 250 white beads and 119 blue seed beads. Ronald J. Mason, author of the book on the Rock Island site, suggests that it may have been a bundle or a bag because of the small area it covered, which was 2" x 4 1/2". In the same area as the beads were larger glass trade beads, reel shaped catlinite beads, remnants of fur and cloth and five Jesuit rings. Whether the surviving piece was from inside the bag or part of the container itself is not clear. The grave site was dated 1760-1770. There were other beaded textile pieces recovered from this site, but they all appeared to be of European or Caucasian manufacture. The beads on these items were tubular-shaped beads, much like native wampum (Mason 137-138).

Journals of travelers are another source of information concerning finger weaving. The early French accounts dealing

Facing page: (left) Iroquois or Seneca sash of red wool with white beads woven using the oblique weave, (middle) Iroquois or Seneca sash of red wool with white beads woven in a lozenge design, (right) Huron sash of red wool with a pale and dark green selvage and white beads woven with the oblique weave.

with the Great Lakes have been my main area of study, so there may be more information in English journals of which I am unaware. Given that, the first mention of weaving that I have come across is by Peter Espirt Radisson around 1658. Radisson was in the Great Lakes region from 1652 to 1684 and left a very interesting account of his extensive travels. While in the upper Great Lakes region, he observed, "The Hurons and Ottawas would go to the farthest part of Green Bay to trade for light earthenware pots, small sea shells, and woven girdles" (Kinietz 245). The information is vague and raises a host of questions, but at least it is an eyewitness account of woven belts. It is frustrating not to know a little more, such as the material used and the colors, but at this early time period, I'm sure the belts would have been natural cordage.

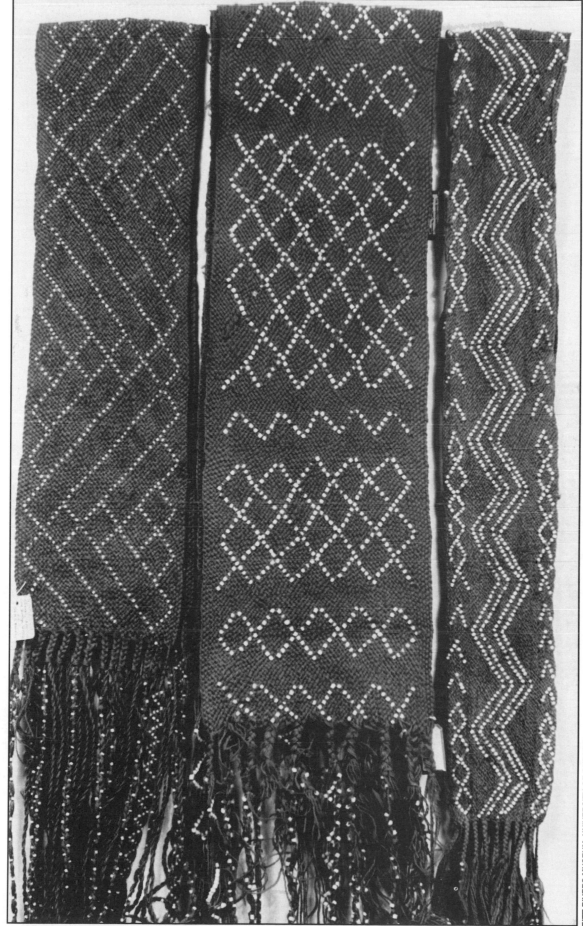

Kickapoo sash, circa 1880, with black, red and navy blue stripes outlined in ochre. White beads outline the zigzag stripes superimposed on the wider stripes. The colors continue to the long fringed ends, which are also partially beaded. The beads are strung on bast fiber. The overall length of this sash is seven feet three inches, and the woven portion measures 33 inches.

This next mention of weaving is somewhat better, in that the author mentions what material was used and the color of it. This quote is taken from the book *Indians of the Western Great Lakes* by W. Vernon Kinietz. While among the Miami Indians sometime between 1721 and 1728, Pierre Charlevoix states, "The wool of the buffalo was used to make such articles as socks, belts, garters, and scarfs" (Kinietz 177). Indeed, on this subject Charlevoix waxed enthusiastic, saying, "Their women are very neat-handed and industrious. They spin the wool of the buffalo, which they make as fine as that of the English sheep; nay sometimes it might even be mistaken for silk. Of this they manufacture stuffs which are dyed black, yellow, or a deep red" (Kinietz 177).

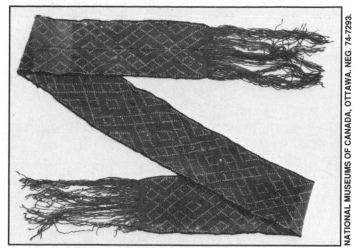

Eastern Great Lakes sash, c. 1780. Deep ochre-red with two transverse bands in yellow, produced by resist dye technique. White beads of irregular size are strung on blue cotton thread. Black selvage. A blue cotton thread is twined through the end of the sash. Fringes are of twisted double strands.

Front and back of an 18th-century Great Lakes pouch made from hard-textured yarns, tightly finger woven. Non-aniline dyes have been used. The main color is deep ochre-red, with 2 transverse bands (one front, one back) in yellow, produced by either discharge or resist dye technique. The border is brown. White beads are interwoven to produce a diamond pattern on the face and vertical zigzag lines on the reverse. The back above the pocket and the down-turned flap at the pocket top are each of tanned skin decorated with three lanes of orange, white and black porcupine quillwork in zigzag band technique. The fringe at the base is of quill-wrapped thongs, metal cones and bunches of red-dyed hair. The sewing was done with sinew and cotton thread.

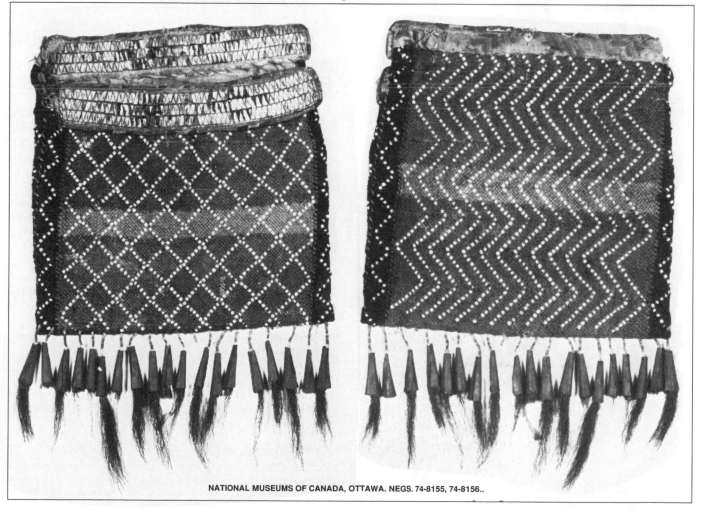

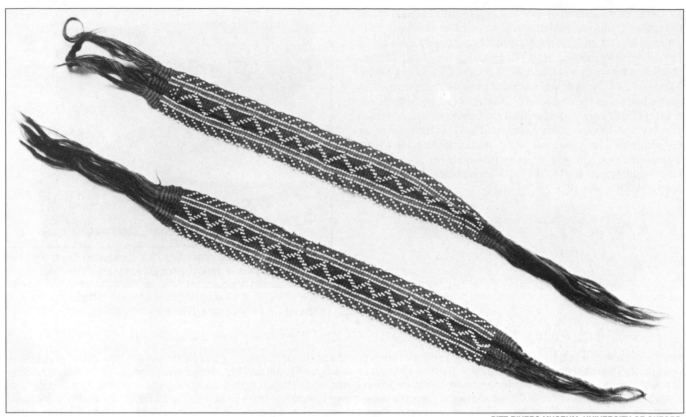

Great Lakes, heddle-loom garters in red, blue and green wool with white beads.

Late 18th century Eastern Great Lakes garter pendant. It is black with red borders and white beads in geometric motifs with white bead edging. The unfringed edge is bound with yellow silk ribbon.

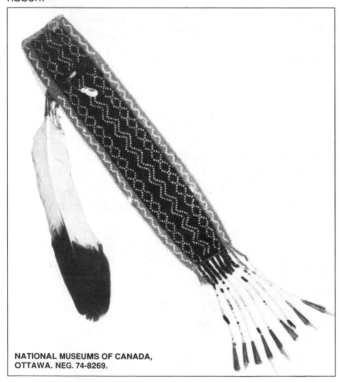

The French archives of the Quebec region yield these entries, as quoted in *Assomption Sash* by Marius Barbeau:

A.J. Pellerin's inventory in 1734 who owned 'une centure de rassade', 3 lb. [a beaded sash valued at three French pounds or louis] *and a Charles Gavel of the same district, dated 1750, owned 'duex ceintures de rassade'* [two beaded belts or sashes]. (19)

It would be interesting to know if these men were involved in the fur trade or if wearing beaded sashes was in fashion at the time. The two following quotes are found in *Peter Kalm's Travels in North America*, edited by Adolph B. Benson:

Though many nations imitate the French customs, I observed, on the contrary, that the French in Canada in many respects follow the customs of the Indians, with whom they have contact relations. They use the tobacco pipes, shoes, garters, and girdles of the Indians and many other Indian fashions. (511)

During the week the men went about in their homes dressed much like the Indians, namely, in stockings and shoes like theirs, with garters and a girdle about the waist; otherwise the clothing was like that of other Frenchmen. (558)

Peter Kalm wrote this in the year 1749 while he was in Quebec. The previous statement may explain why sometimes the French fur traders were mistaken for Indians. I would like to know if they went so far as to wear the same hair styles as the

188

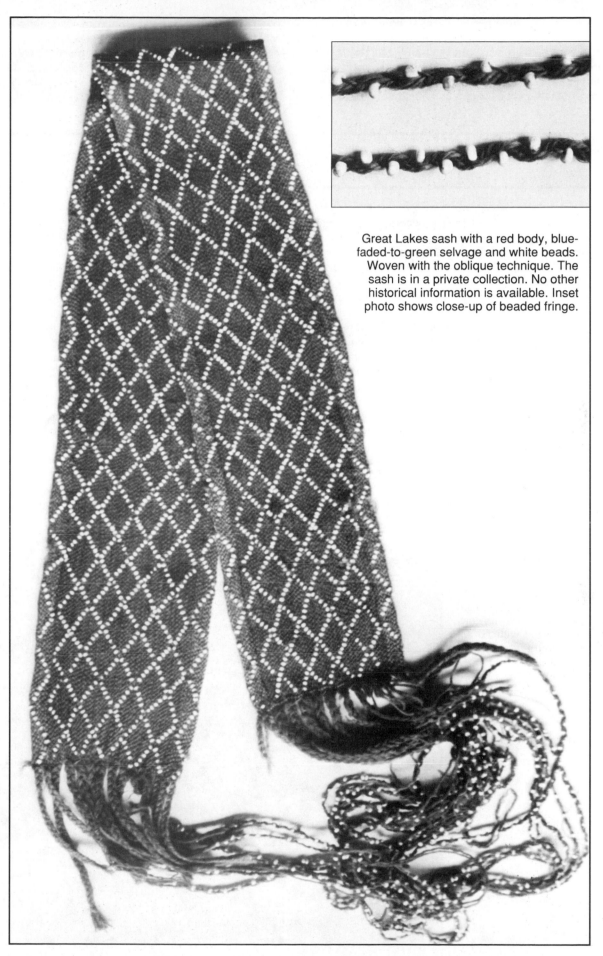

Great Lakes sash with a red body, blue-faded-to-green selvage and white beads. Woven with the oblique technique. The sash is in a private collection. No other historical information is available. Inset photo shows close-up of beaded fringe.

Indians, who, at that time period, were shaving most of the head.

James Smith, who was captured and adopted by the Delaware in 1755, described his adoption ceremony quite thoroughly. Smith states that all the hair was plucked from his head except a small spot on the crown about three or four inches square, which they dressed up in their own mode. Two locks were wrapped with a narrow beaded garter made by the Indians for that purpose, and a third lock that was plaited at full length was stuck full of silver brooches. His appearance was altered a little more by having his nose and ears bored and hung with a nose ornament and earrings (Smith 28-29).

DECORATIVE ELEMENTS

One of the more obvious forms of decoration associated with finger weaving is beading. After viewing many old pieces and being a weaver myself, I believe the beads were usually sewn in after the piece was woven. In my opinion Indian weavers would not have made the job harder than it already was, and it is much simpler to figure out the pattern and sew the beads in after the weaving has been finished. Furthermore, woven-in horizontal and vertical beaded lines are impossible to do on oblique weave pieces, because there are no horizontal or vertical woven threads. The beads must be sewn in afterward.

Another factor which leads me to believe that beads were sewn in after weaving is that I have never viewed a Great Lakes piece with the beads directly on the warp threads. The beads were always on a different type of material, such as a cotton thread usually in a different color than the piece. These differing threads could have been woven in as the piece was made but I don't think so. Another reason for my disbelief is that these threads don't run out to the selvage and turn back into the weave, which means they are changing direction somewhere in the weave. If they were being used as a regular warp thread and

the threads suddenly change direction, the weave is thrown totally off. See the drawing on the facing page.

I have seen a sash woven in a technique similar to the oblique weave that was very popular in the Southeast. The weave was tightened in some areas and relaxed in others to produce diamonds in solid colors that were outlined with beads woven directly into the body of the piece. See the photo below. However, I have not seen this technique used in the Great Lakes areas, my primary area of interest, and unless otherwise stated I am mainly referring to the Great Lakes region. Other areas of the United States have different methods and are areas I know little about. Also keep in mind that I am discussing the oblique weave and not other finger weaving techniques. There are other techniques I have seen with the beads strung right on the threads. These techniques are woven differently and produce what is called a warp face weave, which means that after it has been woven, you can only see the warp threads. These are the threads that hang down while weaving. The weft threads are the threads that move left or right under the weave. Warp face weaves are much denser than the oblique weave, and if you sew

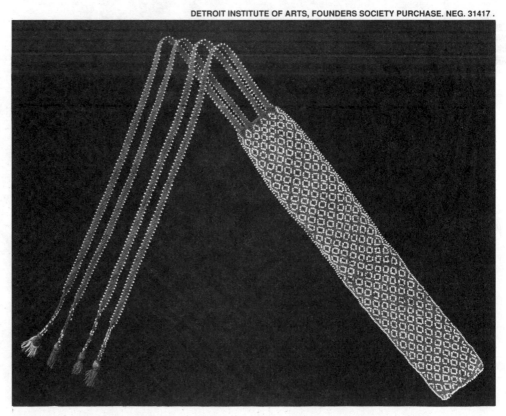

A blue and white Cherokee sash, circa 1830, with four long woven and tassled fringes at one end only. The sash is covered with an all-over lozenge pattern in white beads. The sash measures 56-3/4 inches long by 4-1/8 inches wide. The woven portion is 23-5/8 inches long.

in the beads later, they tend to ride on the surface instead of lying in the body of the weaving. The arrowhead and diamond patterns are good examples of how warp face weaves are used by artists to weave beads in while making the piece. It is not an enviable task.

Bead patterns are another aspect of decoration that should be considered. The bead patterns on items such as sashes, bags and garters cannot be pinned down as to tribal origin unless the collected piece has a known history. Stationary trading posts were gathering places for individuals from several nations, and traders collecting curios could conceivably trade with nearly every nation in the Great Lakes during one season in times of peace. Therefore, most finger-woven articles are labeled as "Great Lakes Region" instead of being attributed to a particular tribe. The congestion of nations increased during the late 18th and early 19th centuries because of the push by Colonists into the wilderness areas. This makes tribal identification more difficult, especially after the French and Indian War.

Colors on the old pieces aren't too numerous. Various shades of reds, blues and greens are most common. Other colors that are found but not in abundance include black, yellow, gold and even some shades of purple. Yarns were sometimes native dyed.

It has been said that trade cloth and blankets were taken apart and the yarn used to weave articles. This may or may not be true. If so, the colors would have been the same as those available in trade woolens. One thing lending credence to this theory is that I have been unable to find yarn in the trade lists prior to the 1800s. From the book *Assomption Sash* by Barbeau, we find listed among the Northwest Company archives white beads and worsted yarns (12). These were being sent to some of their posts during the first quarter of the 19th century. Therefore, prior to 1800 the Indians may very well have been recycling materials.

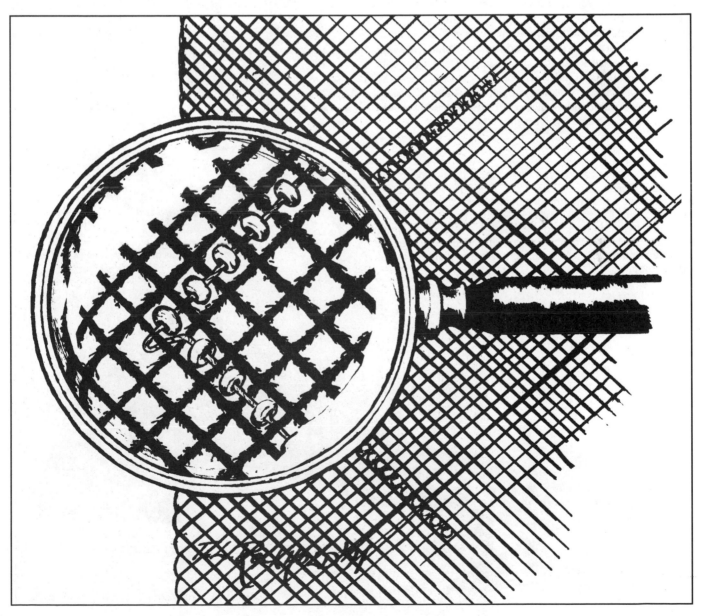

Great Lakes Algonquians sash with powder horn, circa 1774-80. The sash is tightly finger-woven of hard-textured red, black, yellow, blue and white yarns. The strands at the ends are twisted and knotted to form fringe. The sash is attached to the horn with tanned, smoked leather thongs.

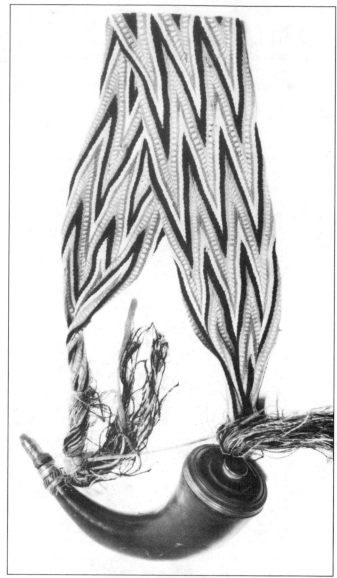

Occasionally a piece of finger weaving will have a band of resist dye decoration on it. These pieces were obviously native dyed since the artifact had to be dyed after it was woven. The Indians then added the pattern they wanted resist dyed onto the body of the weaving. In the articles I have seen, the underlying color was a pale yellow. I'm not sure if this was the actual color of the yarn or if it was caused by the resist dye method. Although to my knowledge they are rather rare, I have included several resist-dyed pieces in the photographs for this chapter. One example is shown below. On Indian weaving resist dyeing seems to be only an 18th century decorative art form.

Sashes, bags and garters have all been decorated with quillwork. The fringes of these items are at times quill-wrapped. The book *Bo'jou, Neejee!* by Ted J. Brasser shows a sash that is alternated finger weaving and quill-wrapping (151). A few garters have net-woven quillwork panels or tabs on one end, although this is not a common adornment. Many bags have quilled panels at the top of the bag. Usually there are two panels of zigzag technique. Quillwork looks great on finger-woven pieces, but it is an art form and subject all its own. I'm blessed because my brother and my wife do quillwork and I am able to trade my weaving for quillwork.

An Eastern Great Lakes-type sash that is tightly finger woven of hard-textured yarns. The main color is deep ochre-red bordered with a narrow strip of woven black wool that is braided to the body of the sash. Three yellow transverse bands were produced by either discharge or resist dye technique. Opaque white beads threaded on a single strand of ochre-red yarn are interwoven on the body to form an equidistant, repeated zigzag motif.

NATIONAL MUSEUMS OF CANADA, OTTAWA. NEG. 74-8308.

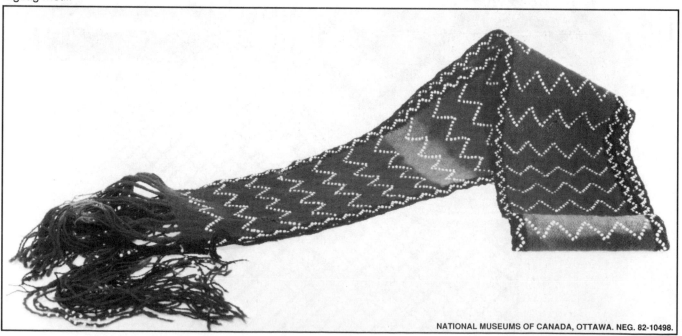

NATIONAL MUSEUMS OF CANADA, OTTAWA. NEG. 82-10498.

A Great Lakes, Central Algonquians woven bag made of wool yarn. Opaque white beads are interwoven in zigzag line patterns which differ on either side. Originally yellowish yarn had been dyed a deep ochre brown. A separately-woven band in black yarn with a vertical zigzag line in white beads has been introduced down either side of the pouch. The carrying strap is of the same ochre-brown yarn, finger woven with white beads in the pattern, and was originally edged with white beads. At the base of the bag, warp strands are braided together to form fringe. Each strand is wrapped with porcupine quills and strung with a metal cone. Around the top edge of the bag are small vertical slits.

Another decorative element is tinkling cones, which are used quite extensively on bags, garter pendants and sometimes sashes. Brass or tin is mainly used for tinkling cones. Some museums have them listed simply as metal cones. They can range from large, about an inch in length, to as small as 1/4-inch. A small amount of deer hair is usually knotted in the flared end on a leather thong on bags and right on the warp threads of garters and sashes. The hair is most often dyed orange, red or on occasion black. Red is the color most widely used.

Moosehair embroidery is to me a form of native art with no European influence. With the exception of the storage bags, all of the items discussed so far were not only twined but also employed moosehair embroidery in their construction. This is done by wrapping a dyed moosehair around the cord you are twining with, as you twine. This method creates pleasing and varied patterns. The earliest bags that we know of in museum collections, which were collected after the contact period, are done in the twined technique with the moosehair embroidery for decoration. The full embroidery technique is better described by Geoffrey Turner, author of the book *Hair Embroidery in Siberia and North America*. He states:

> *The decoration is applied as the twining proceeds: as each weft strand is brought forward (up) to cross over the warp a moose hair is wound tightly around it from four to six times. The surplus length of the hair then passes to the next emergence of the weft. As each hair is used up its tip is either concealed or, especially at the edge of a motif or where the color changes, brought out to the underside of the object and secured by the general pressure of the weaving.* (Turner, *Hair* 38)

The author has studied several pieces of moosehair embroidery in collections and has found the finest examples of this form of decoration to be amazing. The twined threads appear to be painted instead of being wrapped with hair.

193

A form of finger weaving that usually isn't considered when dealing with this subject, is what is known as twining. This is the same technique used to finish off the end of a sash or garters. Twining keeps the ends from unraveling. In the twining of bags the whole bag is done in this type of weaving. Storage bags are mostly woven using this technique. These bags are made using several different twining techniques so as to produce different patterns, such as geometrics and stylized animals. The fibers used in these bags include moosehair, Indian hemp and nettle. An example of a twined bag in Paris has a quill-decorated carrying strap. Could these bags have been in use before the yarn ones became popular? There are many examples of storage bags to be seen in books and museums. Other items that are twined, but not so numerous are tumplines, belts, garters (only one I know of), a wallet, powder horn straps and moccasin flaps.

Tumplines, or burden straps as they are called, are used to carry heavy loads. They have long thongs on them that are wrapped around the object to be carried. The strap part itself is then adjusted across the chest or forehead. Some tumplines date to the mid-17th century. The ones decorated with white beads are mostly of the 18th century. Not all straps are known as tumplines. Another type is known as a prisoner tie or halter. An example is shown on page vi of the color section. The two prisoner halters I have seen had a round halter-like thong attached to it instead of the regular flat thong of the tumplines. These were designed to hold a prisoner but not to strangle

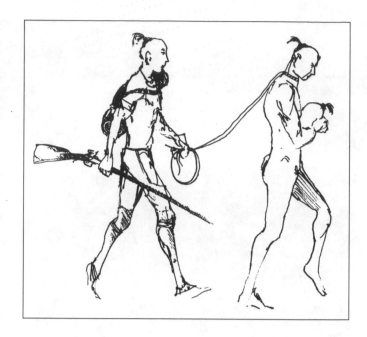

him. See drawing above.

I have only seen three twined belts. These belts may have been an earlier style before yarn sashes came into vogue. The paintings of the four Iroquois kings of 1710 by John Verelst has all of them wearing such a belt.

The author's own horn and finger-woven strap. The horn was made by Olaf Jensen.

SASHES, BAGS AND GARTERS

The majority of oblique woven sashes with beads were shades of red and green or red and blue, although black and green or gold can be found also. Lengths of sashes are a controversial subject around the campfire. In my research I have found that the earliest sashes, being of the oblique weave, solid-colored and beaded, are also the shortest. They mostly range from 44 inches to 55 inches in length. One theory of why they were so short is that the length of material available to them had an effect upon the length of the piece. One of the sashes in the Denver Art Museum (circa 18th century) is even sewn together in the middle. There are also several bag straps known to have been sewn together in this fashion. The sash was generally wrapped around the waist once, maybe twice. The extremely long and wide sashes were produced later when skeins of yarn were available through the trade.

Most solid colored and beaded sashes date to the 18th century. Some have collection dates from the early part of the 19th century. In the book *Bo'jou, Neejee!* there are two pieces done in the Chevron technique that were collected in 1780. This is the earliest collection date that I know of for this design. As stated earlier a sample of prehistoric weaving found in the West looks like it could be of this technique, but it lacks color changes to help identify it.

Sashes usually have their fringes done up in some decorative manner. The simplest means is by twisting two strands separately until the threads begin to kink. At this point tie the two threads together in a simple overhand knot. Let them go to spin back on themselves, forming a single strand from the two threads. Women are able to do the twisting on their bare thighs by placing the two threads side by side and rolling them with their open palm to twist the thread tightly. The reason I say women and not men is that it is quite painful done on a hairy leg.

Another way to finish the ends is to divide the threads into groups of four and braid them for about four inches. Finish the rest of the ends by twisting them together in the aforementioned method. A third way to finish fringes, which was common, is

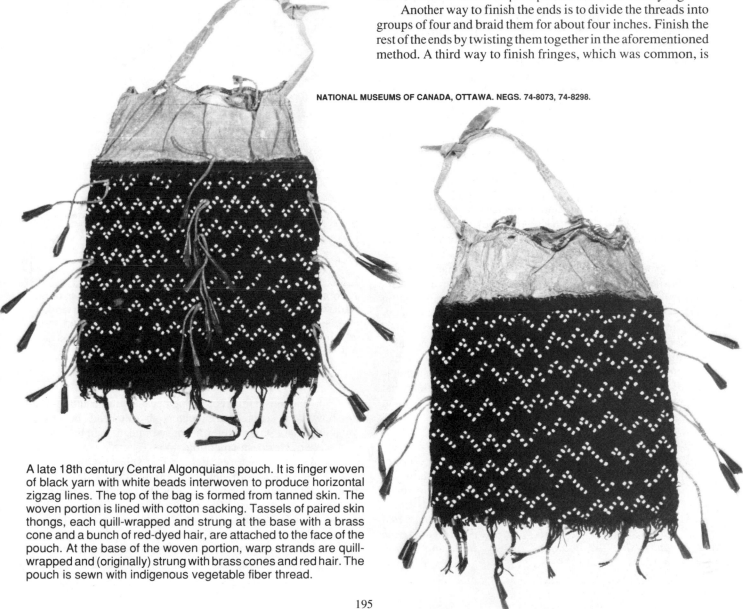

A late 18th century Central Algonquians pouch. It is finger woven of black yarn with white beads interwoven to produce horizontal zigzag lines. The top of the bag is formed from tanned skin. The woven portion is lined with cotton sacking. Tassels of paired skin thongs, each quill-wrapped and strung at the base with a brass cone and a bunch of red-dyed hair, are attached to the face of the pouch. At the base of the woven portion, warp strands are quill-wrapped and (originally) strung with brass cones and red hair. The pouch is sewn with indigenous vegetable fiber thread.

to thread the beads on cotton thread, spacing the beads 1/8-inch to 1/4-inch apart. Taking three of the wool yarn fringes, braid the strands together, adding the beaded cotton thread to one of the wool strands.

A sash was most often tied with the fringe. A good friend of mine, who knew and lived with the Indians, told me there was a language of the sash. If the sash were tied behind you, it meant that you were married or at least not available. If you tied your sash rackishly in front, you were said to be "looking." I'm not sure if this was just for social events or for everyday. I do know that when you go into the woods, if don't wish to get caught on every bramble, branch or burdock, you should wrap your sash around you as much as possible, tieing the fringes together and up out of the way. A lot of the old sashes have most of their fringes pulled off, a good indication that sashes were tied with the fringe.

Sashes were not only used to tie about the waist. A great many Indians wrapped them around the head, turban-like. Charles Bird King painted a number of Indians in this manner. A hair roach was usually worn with a turban for a very dramatic effect. Examples of how turbans were worn can be found in *The McKenney-Hall Portrait Gallery of American Indians* by James D. Horan. In the *Handbook of the North American Indian, Northeast*, there is a painting dated 1858 with Indians wearing sashes for turbans (Trigger 712). Although all of these examples are late (usually mid-1800s), I believe turbans were also worn earlier.

Two period paintings with sashes are pictured in *Bo'jou, Neejee!* by Ted J. Brasser: *The Presentation of a Newly Elected Chief of the Huron Tribe, 1841*, after H.D. Thielcke, page 193; and *Nicholas Virent Isawanhoni, a Huron Chief Holding a Wampum Belt, 1825*, after Edward Chatfield, page 184. Somewhere in France are two collections of sashes that were collected between 1740 and 1780. I have tried to find their present location but have had no luck. These sashes are good examples of the type of sash being worn during the French Colonial period.

Information on women and sashes is very scarce. There is one painting I could find with a woman wearing a sash. It is in the book *Eastman Johnson's Lake Superior Indians* by Patricia Condon. Eastman Johnson's painting, which is dated in the 1850s, is of an Ojibwa called "Standing Wind Woman" (Johnson 50). Cradle boards were sometimes wrapped up in a sash, proving that women were as resourceful as men when creating uses for them. There are a few paintings of this in the McKenney-Hall portrait book (Horan 232).

The book *Assomption Sash* by Marius Barbeau has a drawing of three of the finger-woven sashes of a French collection. They are a representation of the type of sash that is of a solid-color body with the beads forming the design and that sometimes has a different colored selvage. In describing them Barbeau said:

They are woven out of sheep's wool; three of them are black wool; several are decorated with French beads; some of their fringes are tinselled with metal pendants and adorned with beads, dyed porcupine quills, and tufts of horsehair [I believe this to be deer hair]; most of them are finger braided, one of them in the diagonal basketweave of the Iroquois; and their designs are akin to those of later Indian and French Canadian sashes—diamonds, zigzags, hour glass, and sawtooth. (22)

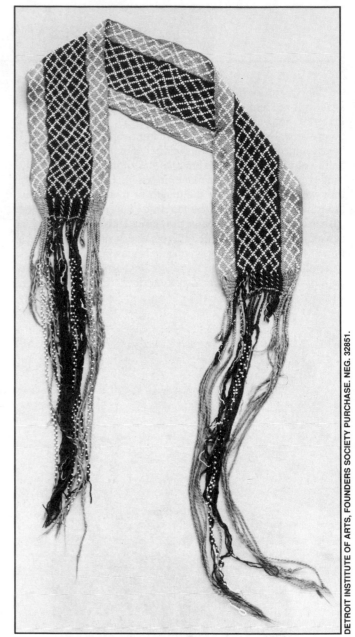

A Potawatomi sash, circa 1850, with a central dark brown band, narrower red stripes at the border and a diaper pattern worked in white beads. The yarns continue for the the long fringed ends, which are partially braided. The sash measures 64 inches long and 4-1/2 inches wide.

DETROIT INSTITUTE OF ARTS, FOUNDERS SOCIETY PURCHASE. NEG. 32851.

This quote is a little confusing because Barbeau does not say how the designs were executed—by the beads or by the weaving. Also, if they weren't finger-braided, then how were they woven? He doesn't mention a loom. These are frustrations you come upon when researching this subject. One way to finger weave and still get the aforementioned designs of diamonds, zigzag and sawtooth is by the technique known as moosehair embroidery. Most of the old sashes pictured in *The Assomption Sash* are moosehair embroidery and were collected before 1780.

The Assomption sash is a type of sash that is unique among all the others. Assomption sashes were produced by French

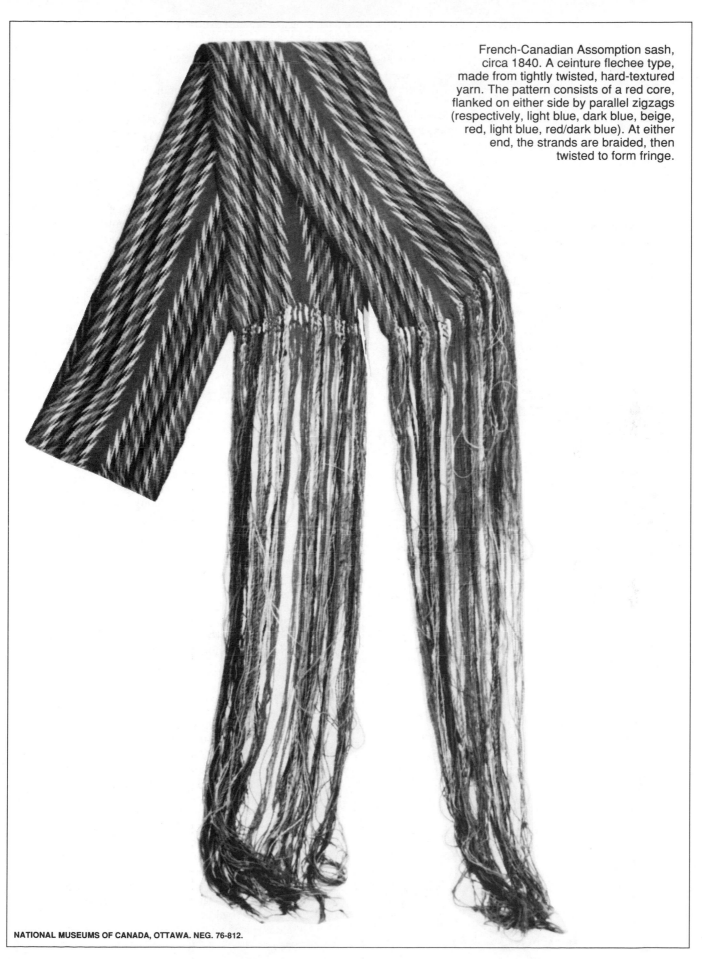

French-Canadian Assomption sash, circa 1840. A ceinture flechee type, made from tightly twisted, hard-textured yarn. The pattern consists of a red core, flanked on either side by parallel zigzags (respectively, light blue, dark blue, beige, red, light blue, red/dark blue). At either end, the strands are braided, then twisted to form fringe.

Canadians living in L'Assomption County, Province of Quebec, for the fur trade. They are dated around 1800 and were long and wide, being woven from a type of yarn produced just to make these sashes. From the book *The Assomption Sash*, we get a description of the wool used:

The wool required for making sashes was of a special type—rough and hard, and dyed in advance. The wool was purchased in skeins arranged in bundles of 10 pounds of each color. The colors were bright, fresh, and fast. After the wool

An Eastern Great Lakes sash, circa 1780, finger woven of fine, hard-textured, olive green wool. Irregularly sized, opaque white glass beads are interwoven (strung on natural-colored cotton thread), forming a net-like pattern down the middle of the sash, flanked on either side by a zigzag line. At the ends, the strands are twisted together and knotted to form two-ply fringe.

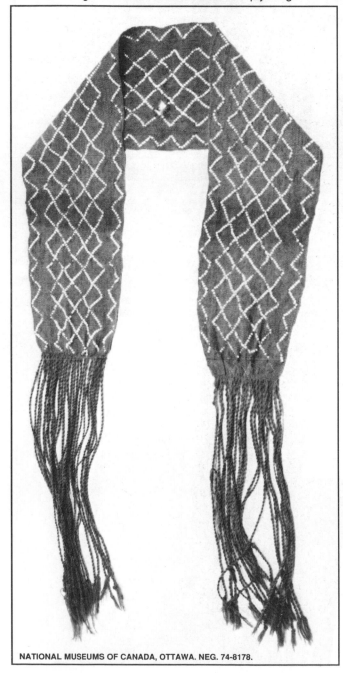

NATIONAL MUSEUMS OF CANADA, OTTAWA. NEG. 74-8178.

was received it was twisted on the spinning wheel at home, and two single threads were spun into one to give more solidity to the strands. (Barbeau 31)

If you ever get to feel an original Assomption, you can tell that they have a texture all their own.

The weaving of the Assomption sash for the fur trade was first done for the Northwest Company and later for the Hudson's Bay Company (Barbeau 3). In time it became a cottage industry with people only doing certain tasks, as explained below:

In the later stages of their home manufacture, for convenience they [Assomption sashes] were produced in standardized form. The workers had to make them by the dozen at the lowest possible price. Middle-men, who controlled the production, hastened it by means of the specialization of the makers; some of them spun the wool hard and into double strands, others warped the double strands into sets, and the weavers, in the winter, worked at home from early dawn until 10 or 11 at night, for less than 30 cents a day, to be paid in goods. The result of standardization and trade abuses ruined the craft and brought about the production of a mechanically woven sash in England for the Hudson's Bay Company. (Barbeau 3)

Some of these sashes were over 15 feet long and around 10 inches wide. These were probably specially woven items, because the trade sashes were not so large. I have been told these very large sashes were used by the voyageurs. Supposedly, they wrapped themselves tightly about the middle with the sash for support when they carried heavy packs during portaging. I don't know if this is true, but it makes a good story. If it is true, wrapping themselves with a sash didn't always work, because some died from strangulated hernias.

Period paintings are a source of information concerning a number of finger-woven items, including bags. However, paintings with finger-woven bags shown prominently are not very numerous. Benjamin West painted two works with Iroquois subjects wearing bags. In the painting *The Death of Wolfe*, the eyes are immediately drawn to the bag on the Iroquois warrior. This is probably the best subject study of what an Iroquois of the 18th century looked like. In the background of the painting, one can see a powder horn strap and bag strap on the Ranger that are both finger-woven. West's painting *General Johnson Saving a Wounded French Officer from the Tomahawk of a North American Indian* again has an Iroquois warrior in all his native glory wearing a finger-woven bag and horn strap. I can't recommend these paintings enough.

Another West painting I have looked to for much information is *Colonel Guy Johnson*. Johnson is wearing a finger-woven sash and a very fine pair of garters, and a bag, the bag strap and a horn strap are just visible on the Iroquois in the background. Two Peter Rindisbacher paintings that are reproduced in *Bo'jou Neejee!* are also worth study (Brasser 195). The interesting thing about these paintings is that the men are wearing the bags around their necks instead of over the shoulder, which brings me to another question I must address. Some finger-woven bags, and the quill-decorated, black leather bags, have straps so short that a person would have to wear the bag around their neck. These paintings are further proof that not all bags were shoulder bags.

An interesting design element seen on some utilitarian or storage bags is small woven panels separated by gaps. These

A late 18th century Miami pouch finger woven of black yarn with white glass beads interwoven in geometric patterns (horizontal zigzag lines on back). On the top front, the warp ends are braided together then caught under a binding of blue printed cotton (which also forms the lining) and red silk. Fringes of skin thong are strung with metal cones and bunches of orange hair. Fragmentary edging of opaque white glass beads remain along the top. Cotton thread and sinew were used in sewing the pouch.

Ottawa shoulder bag,
circa 1820, is woven with wool
yarns and glass beads.

panels surround the mouth of the bag and extend to the beginning of the actual body of the bag. I know of five bags dated to the 18th century that have this type of bag opening. On one of these bags the woven panels surrounding the opening alternate between weaving and a series of four-strand braided warp threads. One carrying bag in the Pitt Rivers Museum collection in Oxford, England, has a top similar to those used on the utilitarian bags that date back to pre-historic times. This

feature is very unusual for carrying bags, because it is usually only seen on the storage bags.

The open panels mentioned above seem to serve no purpose. On the storage bags they could have been used to close the bag with a drawstring thong laced through the openings. But there is no evidence that the carrying bags were ever closed in such a manner. This feature may be just a carry-over from the way all ancient bags were begun when

This wide Ottawa sash, circa 1830, has long, partially braided fringes. It is woven of wool yarn in stripes of varying width in ochre red and navy blue. Each stripe has a zigzag pattern worked in white beads. In the central red stripe, the zigzag lines overlap to form a lattice or interlace effect. The woven portion of the sash measures 55-3/4 inches long and 9-5/8 inches wide.

starting to weave. Another theory, since these are all Algonkian bags, is that it might just be a style they favored, similar to the Algonkian trait of having beaded designs on both sides of the bag.

The lining of a bag could be considered a decorative element. Some bags had trade cloth liners and some patterned material, while other bags had no liners whatsoever. Quilled panels have also been used as a decorative finish for bags, being sewn on after the bag was woven. Another decorative trim used to bind the edges of a finger-woven bag is silk ribbon. The mouth of the bag is the edge most frequently bound, but I have seen the two sides of the bag bound with silk too. The binding is applied after the bag is woven.

In the 18th century they didn't stop at the top of the bag with decoration. The bottom edges of most bags were decorated. One means of doing this was to plait the yarns that hang from the bottom of the weaving. This, I have been told, is all that is necessary to keep the bottom of the bag joined together. The bottom edges were also decorated with brass cones filled with deer hair. The thongs that held the cones were quite frequently quill-wrapped.

There is an interesting bag in the Chicago Field Museum on which I should comment. It is a small belt pouch or "shot" pouch that is finger-woven. The back of the pouch has a red body with a blue selvage, and the front has a red body and a green selvage. The bead patterns differ on either side of the bag, which was made using the oblique weave technique. The fringes on both ends of the bag are quite long and are extensively laced with white beads. There is a hand-sized opening in the middle of the front of the bag. This bag, of course, is worn folded over the sash or belt: It is the only period finger-woven belt pouch I have ever seen.

Garters are what every well-dressed frontiersman needs to keep their leggin' flaps standing out stylishly. There are many examples of garters cited in early writings and shown in paintings. One such painting is the Catlin painting of Red Jacket, the Seneca chief, in *The Covenant Chain*. Something you should notice about the old garters is that they are just long enough to go around the calf of the leg and then tie with the fringe. Also notice the sash in Catlin's painting. I've never seen matching garters and sash, to my knowledge, so go ahead and get wild, have mismatched sash and garters. You'll probably be more authentic if you do. Of interest to some people are the heddle loomed garters. Dates on those are unknown to me, but Indian heddle looms do go back to the 1850s. The Indian-loomed garters are not usually dated in the books I have.

Another use for garters that I have seen is to wrap a pipe stem. Although unusual, I have seen this more than once. A

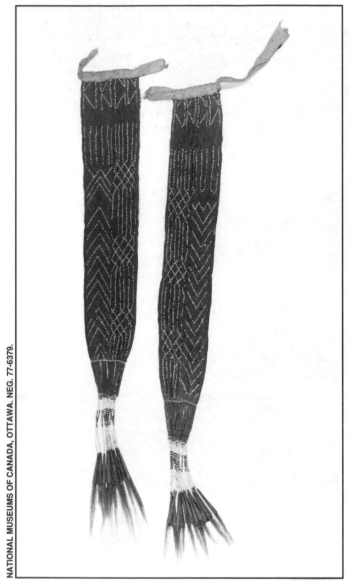

These Ojibwa-type garters, circa 1780, are finger-woven from fine, hard-textured yarn. Small, white glass beads strung on sinew thread are interwoven forming geometric patterns. Colors are olive green and maroon with contrasting edging in the same colors. The quill-wrapped fringe is formed by braided warp threads and finished with tin cones and tassels of red hair. The opposite end of each garter is bound with yellow ribbon.

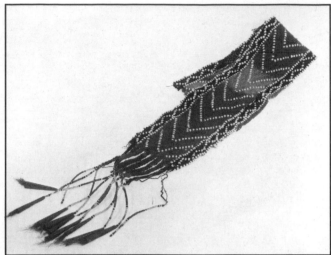

An Eastern Great Lakes garter pendant woven of ochre-red and black wool yarns. Opaque white beads threaded on a separate blue thread are interwoven to form a repeated chevron design down the center and a vertical zigzag motif along each black band. A vertical row of white beads is worked along each edge of the black band.

Bodmer print shows a garter tied at the wrist, and in the book *Akicita* there is a picture of an Osage protective object wrapped with what appears to be a garter (Walker 33). Here's another use for a small garter, all you woodland interpreters with a manly plucked head. Wrap a garter around your scalp lock as James Smith recommends in his book *Scoouwa*. Painful, but effective.

Finger-woven garter pendants are something I have only seen in collections. I cannot recall ever seeing a finger-woven one in a period painting. I have seen the picture of Joseph Brant wearing a type of garter pendant other than finger-woven, and there are some Western and mid-Western Indians wearing garter pendants, but not the long finger-woven ones. Most finger-woven garter pendants have elaborate beaded designs and wrapped quillwork on them. One thing very interesting about the pendants is that there is a break in the bead-work design near the top of most of the old pieces. I assume this is where the pendant folds over the top of the garter. One garter pendant that I recall has an eagle feather attached to it. For such a decorative item not to turn up in paintings or in the old writings is odd. If anyone has more information on this subject, I would be most grateful to hear from you.

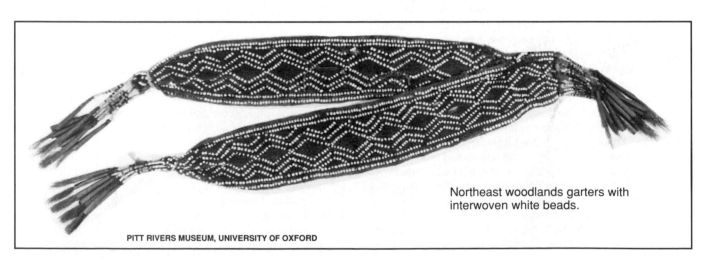

Northeast woodlands garters with interwoven white beads.

MAKING A SASH

The diagonal weave is the simplest form of weaving and the best one to begin to understand how the threads move. Later, you can learn the more difficult techniques. When I first learned to weave, I worked with only a few threads, around 12. This helped me to keep from getting confused about where all the threads were going. You may also want to start with a small number of threads.

You must first choose some type and color of yarn. I like arrange all of the yarn strands in a neat, orderly row, and if you're doing a sash with a lot of colors, it helps you separate and arrange all of the different colors into their proper order. Locate the middle of the yarn and insert the headstick following the method shown in the Figures 1, 2, 3 and 4.

At this time you can twine a piece of yarn just under the headstick. This keeps the yarn compacted when you start to weave, and if you pull the headstick out for any reason, it won't

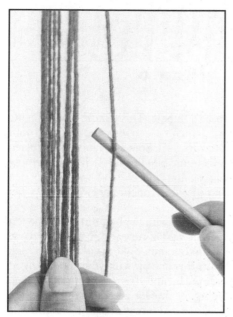

Figure 1

Figure 2

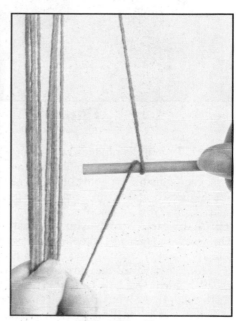

Figure 3

Figure 4

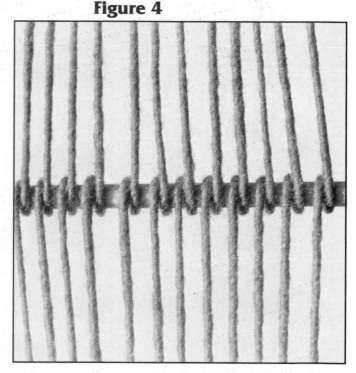

to use 2-ply, hard-textured yarn, because the majority of the old pieces were made of this type of yarn. When I say "hard-textured," I mean yarn that is not spongy like 4-ply yarn. But for practice you can use anything you have around, even, dare I say it, acrylic yarns. Blaaah! The colors you use should be soft, muted shades.

When cutting the length of your threads, you need to add extra length for the material that is used up in the weaving process. Figure up how long you want the piece to be, including the fringe, then add 25 percent more. The next step is to set up the yarn by winding it around two posts that are set the same distance apart as your thread lengths will be. I use the backs of two wooden chairs with upright posts. You could even use some stakes stuck in the ground. Tie one end of the yarn around one of the posts, then start winding the yarn back and forth around both posts. Remember, you need an even number of threads no matter what pattern you are working with. As you wind the yarn around the posts, don't do it tightly, just snug it up. When you have all the threads you need, move one of the chairs toward the other to provide just a little slack in the yarn, so that you can insert the headstick.

I use a piece of 3/8-inch dowel that is eight inches long as a headstick for most of my work. The headstick is used to

Figure 5

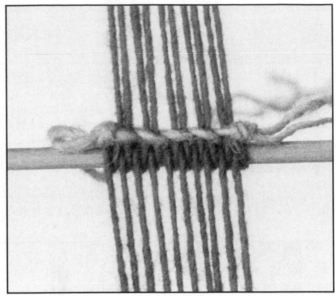

Figure 6

unravel. Twining is produced by wrapping two weft strands around two warp strands while giving the weft strands a half twist each time before going on to the next two warp strands. See Figures 5 and 6. In the pictures that accompany these instructions, you will notice that there is no twining at the top of the piece so that you can easily see the weaving. The weaving is all spread out also in order to show how the threads move.

After I have all the yarn arranged on my headstick, I usually untie the yarn that is tied to the post of the chair. Then cut through all the loops of yarn on that end. I let all of this yarn hang down or lay on the floor while I cut the loops on the other end of the yarn. While I still have the second end in my hands, I fold the yarn back toward the headstick until this half is folded in half. I then fold these yarns in half again until I have this one

side of the threads in a neat bundle. This bundle I tie with one end of a three-foot cord, which I use to hang the prepared yarn from the ceiling so I can work on it. Some weavers like to fasten the loose ends of the yarn in a bundle and tie it to something also. This might help in tension control, but I have never tried that method, preferring just to let them hang. Now you can begin weaving.

Begin the diagonal weave with the first thread on the left side of the headstick (Figure 7). This thread will be the first one pulled through the separated strands. Take the next thread right of the first thread and lift this one up with your index finger. The following thread you put behind your index finger, working all the way across, placing the threads up or down. With all of the threads separated, take that #1 thread and pull it all the way through the opening you just made between the threads (Figure 8). Take this first thread and wrap it around the headstick several times to hold it in place for awhile. Next time when you

Figure 7

Figure 8

Figure 9

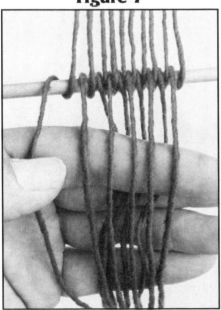

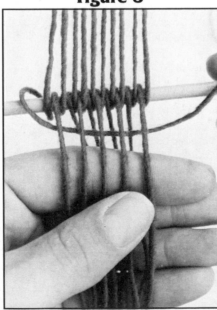

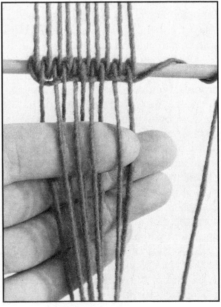

weave from left to right, all the down threads come up and all the up threads go down (Figure 9). This is one way to tell if you have made a mistake, because the threads should always alternate in this manner. Now take the thread that is on the extreme left and repeat the procedure (Figure 10). When you have the second thread pulled all the way through, take the first thread, which is wrapped around the headstick, and pull it down over the second thread that has been pulled through the weave. In this way you place the first thread back into the body of the weave (Figure 11). Secure the second thread to the headstick as you did before. Continue weaving in this fashion.

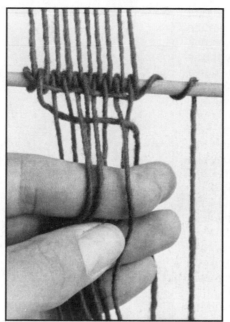

Figure 10

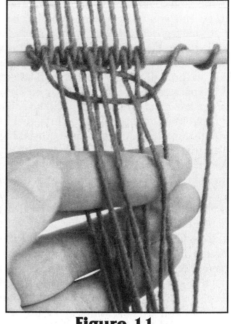

Figure 11

THE CHEVRON WEAVE

The chevron weave is a very simple technique that requires only a few colors to produce a nice colorful design, however you just need two colors to make a chevron sash. One should be lighter than the other in order for the pattern to show up well. With this technique you weave from the middle of the yarn out, so you have to arrange your yarn on the headstick with all of the light color in the middle and half of the dark color on either side. You can increase or decrease the size of the chevrons by increasing or decreasing the number of strands you use.

To begin weaving find the middle of all the threads so that there is an even number of threads on either side. The chevron technique is a little like the diagonal, but this time you take a thread from the opposing side and weave it across. I start with the group of threads on the right side. Take the first thread on the left side of the right-hand group and lift it up on the index finger; the next thread goes down behind the index finger. Continue across like this until you have separated all the threads of the right-hand group. Now take the first thread on the right side of the left-hand group and pull it through the opening you made in the group of threads on the right side (Figure 12). Do you understand so far? Good, let's continue. Wrap this thread around the headstick temporarily. Now separate the threads of the left-hand group, beginning with the the first thread on the right side. (Remember, the very first thread has already been woven so the one that was next to it is now the first thread.) Lift this thread up and the next one down, moving toward the left until you have them all separated. Now take the first thread on the left side of the right-hand group and pull it through the opening you just made in the left-hand group (Figure 13). Wrap the thread around the headstick. You just

Figure 12

Figure 13

Figure 14

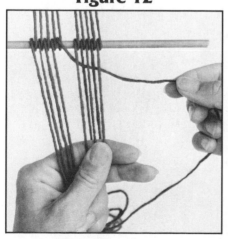

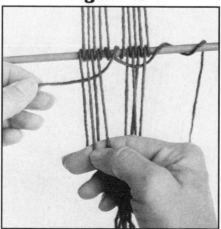

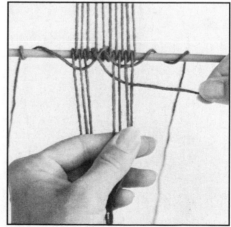

completed your first row, only a couple of thousand to go and you will be done. Now go back to the right-hand group and separate the threads, beginning with the first thread on the left side. This will be a down thread, so lift it up. The next one goes down and so forth all the way across until all the threads are separated. Take the first thread on the right side of the left-hand group, which will be an up thread, and pull this thread to the right through the opening you just made in the right-hand group (Figure 14). Take the thread wrapped around the headstick and return it to the body of the weave by placing this thread over the thread you just pulled through the weave (Figure 15). Take the new thread and wrap it around the headstick. Then go back to the left-hand group. Begin with the first thread on the right side, which will be a down thread. Pick up this thread, down with the next, moving left, until you have them all separated. Now take the first thread on the left side of the right-hand group, an up thread, and pull this thread to the left through the opening you just made through the left-hand group (Figure 16). Take the thread wrapped around the headstick and return it to the body of the weave by placing it behind the thread you just pulled through (Figure 17). Wrap this last thread around the headstick. Continue until weaving is complete. See Figures 18, 19, 20, 21 and 22.

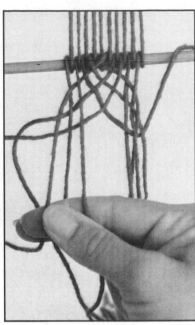

Figure 21

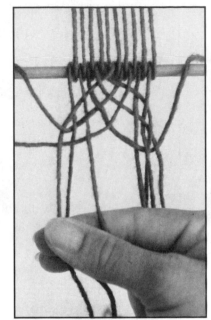

Figure 22

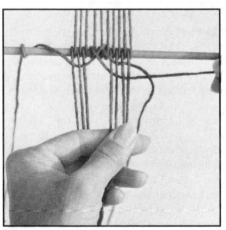

Figure 15

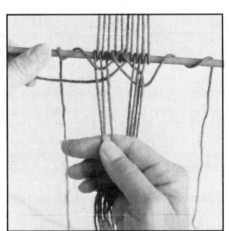

Figure 16

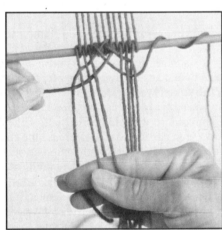

Figure 17

Figure 18

Figure 19

Figure 20

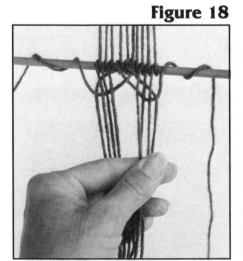

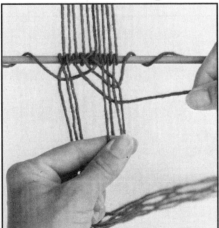

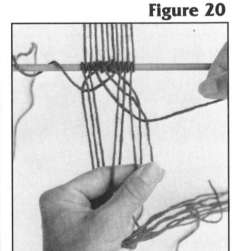

THE OBLIQUE WEAVE

Once you understand how the threads move back and forth and how they return to the body of the weave, the oblique weave is a very easy technique. To begin, figure out the length you need. Don't forget to add the extra 25 percent. Find the center of the whole length and insert the headstick. When I weave garters, I place the headstick just below the fringe and weave from end to end instead of starting in the middle as on a sash. The threads for garters are short enough that you do not have to start in the center. Now, with the threads set up on the headstick, twine across using groups of two threads. Twining is covered elsewhere in this article so I won't explain the procedure at this time. Having the threads grouped in two's helps when you start the first row. When making garters, since I am not beginning in the center, I cut the twining threads long enough so that I can incorporate them into the fringe of the finished piece. You can twist these long threads right into the fringe, hiding them effectively.

To begin the first row of weaving, pick up the two threads on the left side of the weaving. Pass the thread on the right underneath the thread on the left (Figure 23). Hold this thread in your left hand. Now go to the next two threads to the right of the first two you worked with. Again, take the thread on the right side of the pair and pass it under the thread on the left, but this time also pass it over the next thread on the left as well (Figure 24). After you have moved this thread under and over, hold it in your left hand. Continue weaving toward the right, moving the threads on the right side of the groups of two under

and over the threads to the left and then placing the thread you are moving in your left hand (Figures 25 and 26). When you have completed your first row, you will have half the threads in your left hand and half in your right hand (Figure 27). As you look at your first row, notice how there is an upper layer of threads and a lower layer of threads. The idea is to keep bringing the threads in the back up each time you weave a row. This technique weaves from left to right, right to left. At each row the threads merely change position from back to front.

Now that you have the threads in two groups, this is the time to snug up the weave. Just pull the two groups in the direction they are moving. I do this after each row to keep the tension even. Tension is important. It takes a little practice to keep the tension the same all the way through the piece.

This is where things get a little tricky. When the weave starts back toward the right, the first two threads on the bottom layer of threads stay where they are. Since the oblique weave always moves up from behind and over the thread next to it, no matter which direction you are weaving, there is no thread for the first two threads on the right side to cross over. The third thread on the bottom threads can come up and cross over the

Figure 23

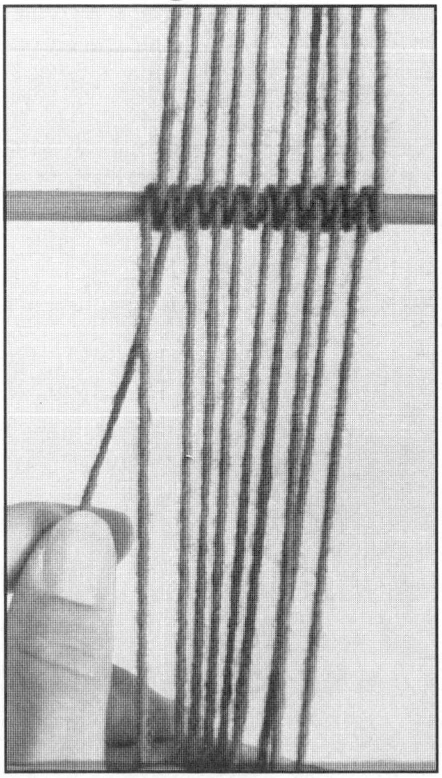

Figure 24

Figure 25

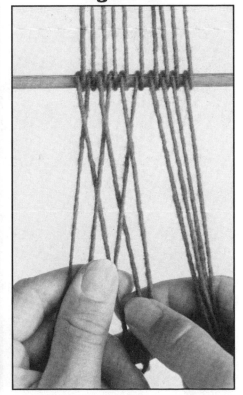

207

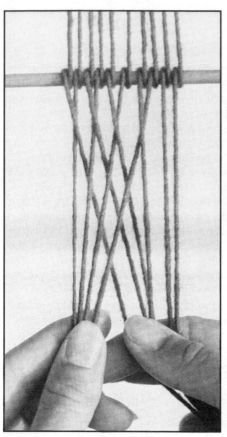

Figure 26

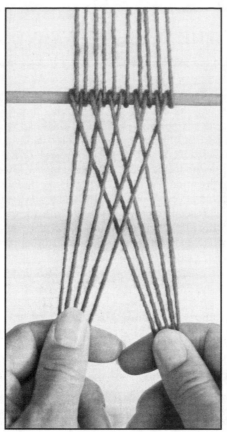

Figure 27

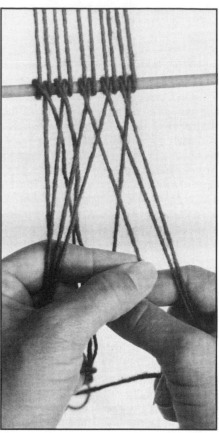

Figure 28

first thread of the top layer. This layer slants toward the left (Figure 28). After you have brought the thread up and hold it in your right hand, continue across until you have all the back threads brought forward and in your left hand (Figure 29). All the threads slanting left should be underneath now and in your left hand, except the last two on the left side of the weave (Figure 30).

As you begin to weave the next row, this time toward the right, you also bring a thread back into the weave. This is easily done by simply bringing the first thread on the left side, a bottom thread slanting left, over the thread just to the right of it, this is an up thread slanting left, and place it in your right hand(Figure 31). This thread that has just been brought back into the weave will be the first thread to be crossed over by the thread being brought up from behind. The second thread in on the lower layer of threads on the right side moves up and

Figure 29

Figure 30

Figure 31

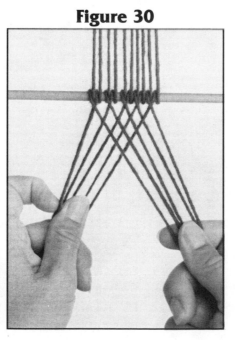

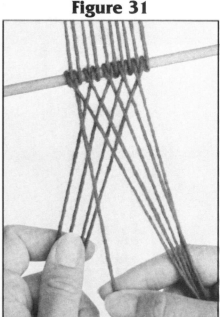

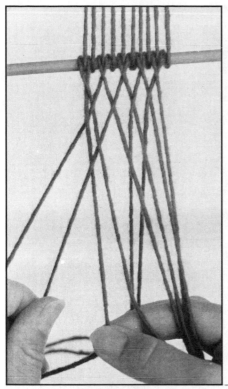

Figure 32

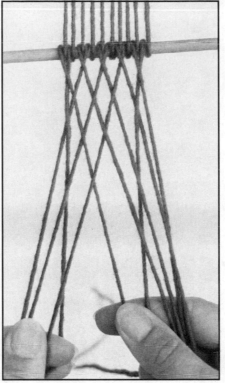

Figure 33

Figure 34

crosses over the first thread of the upper layer, which is slanting toward the right (Figure 32). Weave on across (Figure 33) bringing all the back threads forward until you have all the threads that are slanting left brought up and in your left hand (Figure 34).

Your fourth row of weaving, going back toward the left, will bring all of the back threads slanting right, forward. You must start by bringing the first thread on the right side, an up thread, back into the weave. This time you take the thread and bring it behind the thread just to the left of it. Pass the returning thread over the thread next to it on the left. Place the thread you just brought back into the weave in your left hand (Figure 35). Whenever you return a thread to the weave, the threads on the left side always come forward and return to the weave while the threads on the right side always wrap back around to be woven in (Figure 36). When you have returned this thread, weave across to the left, continuing with the above directions.

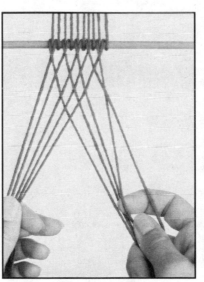

Figure 35

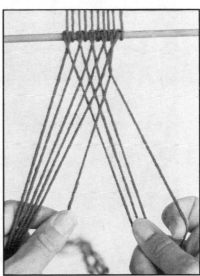

Figure 36

One thing I would like to add about the oblique weave is that the weaving tangles at the bottom quite readily. You have to untangle the threads as needed or when you need a break from weaving. The best way to untangle is to hold on to just one set of threads and pull out one thread at a time. The threads pull out easily then.

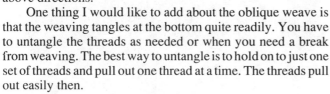

Chippewa garters, circa 1840,
measuring 40 inches long by 3-3/4
inches wide. The woven portion is
13-3/4 inches long.

SELVAGE

Most finger-woven items have a selvage that is a different color from the body of the weave. According to some museum descriptions, some selvages have been sewn on, but that's the hard way. It is easy to weave a selvage onto the piece at the same time you are weaving the body. The procedure I am about to describe is the way I attach the selvage when I am weaving a piece.

When you set up the threads on the headstick, place the threads for the selvage on either side of the main threads. Use an even number of selvage threads on both sides. You can use as little as four strands to a side, for just a hint of color, or you can add enough threads to weave wider bands of color. I like to copy original pieces, so whatever the width is on the original piece is how I weave it.

Simply treat the selvage as part of the whole weaving.

There is no separate weave for the selvage. Pick those threads up along with the rest of the threads when you are weaving to the right. It is when you are weaving to the left that you make the interlocking part of the weave. As you come to the last strand of the selvage it has to be brought back into that part of the weave in order to keep the colors from mixing. So take that thread, the last one on the left side, and bring it forward and back into its own weave. Next to that thread you have the first thread on the right side of the main color. It is about to be turned back into the weave again. So when you bring these two threads together just lock them around each other and they will then be moving back into the weaves of their own colors. The same movement is made on the left side of the piece you are weaving when you come to the last thread of the main color and the first thread of the other selvage.

An 18th century Eastern Great Lakes sash woven with olive green yarn with small white beads. The long warp ends are quill-wrapped and strung with metal cones and red hair. Glass imitation wampum beads are strung between the fringes.

NATIONAL MUSEUMS OF CANADA, OTTAWA. NEG. 74-7297.

211

A Great Lakes heddle loom garter from a private collection. It's made with red, green and blue yarn with white beads.

CONCLUSION

Finger weaving is really amazingly simple, but it takes all these directions, which probably sound a bit confusing. But take heart, the description is harder than the technique of weaving actually is. Read the directions slowly and carefully while studying the photos. Practice, then practice some more. A weaver friend once told me that you should always keep the first piece you make to keep yourself humble later on. She was right. My wife still wears the first sash that I wove. I find it a bit embarrassing and wouldn't mind if she kept it hidden.

As I have already noted, much research remains to be done on this subject. There are really only two books that I know of dealing exclusively with finger weaving, and historical evidence consists of a handful of sentences in personals accounts and journals, in addition to the few fragments that have survived the ravages of time. For now, information on this topic is scarce, but who knows what will be discovered tomorrow?

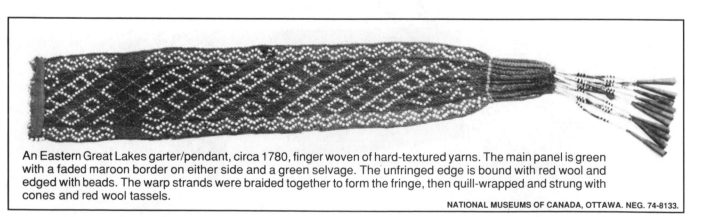

An Eastern Great Lakes garter/pendant, circa 1780, finger woven of hard-textured yarns. The main panel is green with a faded maroon border on either side and a green selvage. The unfringed edge is bound with red wool and edged with beads. The warp strands were braided together to form the fringe, then quill-wrapped and strung with cones and red wool tassels.

APPENDIX A: WORKS CITED

Barbeau, Marius. *Assomption Sash.* Ottawa, Ont.: National Museums of Canada, 1972.

Benson, Adolph B. *Peter Kalm's Travels in North America.* New York: Dover Publications, 1937.

Black, Glen. *The Angel Site: An Archaeological, Historical, and Ethnological Study.* 2 vols. Indianapolis: Indiana Historical Society, 1967.

Brasser, Ted J. *A Basketful of Indian Culture Change.* Paper 22. National Museum of Man. Mercury Series. Canadian Ethnology Service. Ottawa, Ont.: National Museums of Canada, 1975.

—. *Bo'jou, Neejee! Profiles of Canadian Indian Art.* Ottawa, Ont.: National Museum of Man, 1976.

Catlin, George. *Red Jacket.* Gilcrease Institute of American History, Tulsa, OK. Plate 2 in *The Covenant Chain.* By Jaye N. Fredriekson. Ottawa, Ont.: National Museums of Canada, 1980.

Horan, James D. *The McKenney-Hall Portrait Gallery of American Indians.* New York: Bramhall House, 1986.

Johnson, Patricia Condon. *Eastman Johnson's Lake Superior Indians.* Afton, MN: Johnson Publishing, 1983.

Kinietz, W. Vernon. *The Indians of the Western Great Lakes.* Ann Arbor: University of Michigan Press, 1965.

Mason, Ronald J. *Rock Island Historical Indian Archaeology in the Northern Lake Michigan Basin.* Kent, OH: Kent State University Press, 1986.

Smith, James. *Scoouwa: Indian Captivity Narrative.* Columbus: Ohio Historical Society, 1978.

Trigger, Bruce G. *Handbook of North American Indians, Northeast.* Vol. 15. Washington, D.C.: Smithsonian Institution, 1978.

Turner, Alta R. *Fingerweaving Indian Braiding.* New York: Sterling Publishing Co., 1978.

Turner, Geoffrey. *Hair Embroidery in Siberia and North America.* Oxford, England: University of Oxford V.K., Pitt Rivers Museum, 1954.

Verelst, John. Four Iroquois Kings of 1710. Series of untitled prints.

Walker, James. *Akicita.* Los Angeles: Southwest Museum, 1983.

West, Benjamin. *Colonel Guy Johnson.* National Gallery of Art, Washington, D.C.

—. *The Death of Wolfe.* National Gallery of Canada, Ottawa. Illus. 91 of *Thunderbird and Lightning.* By J.C.H. King. London: British Museum Publications, 1982.

—. *General Johnson Saving a Wounded French Officer from the Tomahawk of a North American Indian.* Derby Museum and Art Gallery. Illus. in "The Captive's Return, Bouquet's Victory." By Paul E. Kopperman. *Timeline* April-May (1990): 2-15.

APPENDIX B: WORKS CONSULTED

Beads: Their Use by Upper Great Lakes Indians. Catalog. Grand Rapids, MI: Grand Rapids Public Museum, 1977.

Chandler, Milford G. et al. *Art of the Great Lakes Indians.* Catalog. Flint, MI: Flint Institute of Art, 1973.

Conn, Richard. *Native American Art in the Denver Art Museum.* Denver: Denver Art Museum, 1979.

Densmore, Frances. *Chippewa Customs.* St. Paul: Minnesota Historical Society Press, 1979.

Lyford, C.A. *Iroquois Crafts.* Reprint. Ohsweken, Ont.: Iroqrafts, 1982.

—. *Ojibwa Crafts.* Steven's Point, WI: R. Schneider Publishers, 1982.

Mainfort, Robert C., Jr. *Indian Social Dynamics in the Period of European Contact.* E. Lansing: Michigan State University, 1979.

Orchard, William C. *Beads and Beadwork of the American Indians.* New York: Museum of the American Indian—Heye Foundation, 1975.

Phillips, Dr. Ruth B. *Patterns of Power.* Catalog. Kleinburg, Ont.: McMichael Canadian Collection, 1984.

Scholtz, Sandra. *Prehistoric Plies: A Structural and Comparative Analysis of Cordage, Netting, Basketry, and Fabric from Ozark Bluff Shelters.* Fayetteville: Arkansas Archaeological Survey, 1975.

Whiteford, Andrew Hunter. "Fiber Bags of the Great Lakes Indians." *American Indian Art* 2.3 (1977): 52, 54.

APPENDIX C: RESOURCES

Filature Lemieux Inc.
C.P. 250/125
Rte 108
ST-EPREM, Beauce Sud
Quebec, Canada G0M 1R0
— You may request their sample catalogue. I only use the two-ply yarn. It is the closest to the original that I can find.

If anyone would like to contact me, please write:
Tim Connin
Rt 2, Box 215
Continental OH 45831

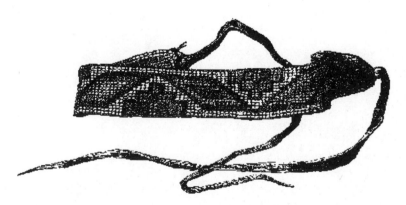

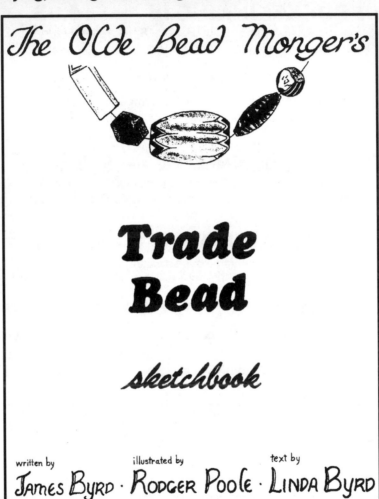

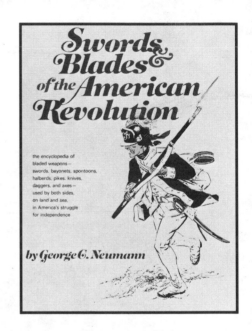